Kingdoms of the Yoruba

ROBERT SMITH

KINGDOMS OF THE YORUBA

METHUEN & CO LTD
11 New Fetter Lane · London EC4

First Published in 1969 by Methuen & Co Ltd
© 1969 Robert Smith
Printed in Great Britain by
Richard Clay (The Chaucer Press) Ltd
Bungay, Suffolk

Distributed in the USA by Barnes & Noble, Inc.

Contents

1. THE YORUBA KINGDOMS AND THEIR NEIGHBOURS

This map is intended to illustrate the political divisions of the Yoruba between the foundation of the Kingdoms and c. 1830. The limits shown for the Kingdoms and groups are extremely tentative. They are mainly based on the 'cultural groups' shown on the map attached to Forde (1951); important exceptions are in the northward extension of the Ẹgba before c. 1830 and the inclusion of the Ifẹ, Ijẹṣa, Ọwọ, and Owu Kingdoms. The Ọyọ Kingdom at its zenith probably extended on the north-east as far as the Niger between Ogudu and the junction of the Mọṣi with the Niger, an area now mainly inhabited by Nupe.

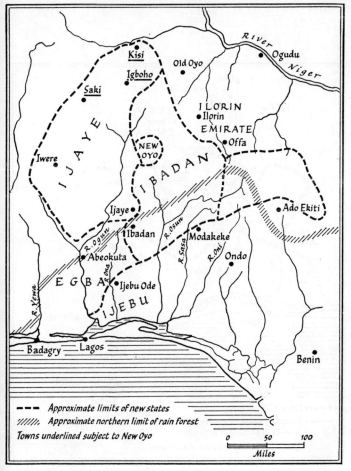

2. THE NEW STATES, *c.* 1836–62

This map is intended to illustrate the rearrangement of the Yoruba
provinces under Alafin Atiba with Ijaye preponderant in the western
Ẹkun and Ibadan in the eastern as shown on the map in Morton-
Williams (1967), p. 47. The eastern extension of Ibadan dates only
from the 1850s. The regrouping of the Ẹgba, both shifting southward
and extending west across the river Ogun, with their new capital at
Abẹokuta, should also be noted.

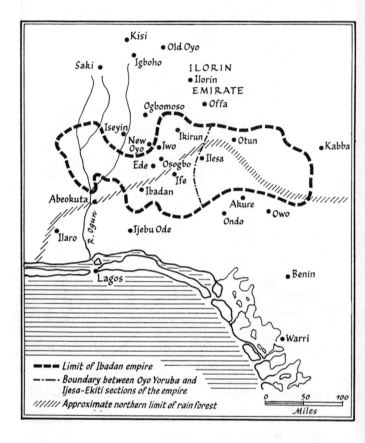

3. IBADAN AND ITS NEIGHBOURS, 1862–86

This map is based on that in Awe (1964), p. 60. It will be seen that from 1862 Ibadan absorbed the northern part of the former Ijaye territory and also Ibarapa in the upper Ogun. On the other hand, towns such as Ṣaki and Iṣeyin in the northern part of the former eastern province of the Ọyọ Yoruba (see map 2), were independent of Ibadan and remained only loosely subject to the Alafin at New Ọyọ.

Preface

The history of tropical Africa, whose sources are largely unwritten even for periods quite near in time to our own and whose study has been undertaken systematically only in late years, bears the marks of its necessarily provisional character. But in fact any history of any area or any people, however rich in primary and secondary material, shares this character. In any study of the past, whether near in time or remote, there are always new ways of looking at the material and new evidence to be adduced. History can never be more than a selection, both deliberate and fortuitous, of the factors in a situation. 'Ultimate history', which would need no addition, correction, or modification, and which to Acton seemed to lie only just beyond the reach of his generation, is an elusive, unattainable – though always attractive – goal.

The past of the Yoruba of West Africa, who form the population of the Western State of Nigeria, must be reconstructed, so far as the period preceding the penetration of their country by Europeans from about the mid-nineteenth century is concerned, almost wholly from tradition, or 'oral evidence' in the cumbersome phrase, a method which is only now achieving respectability among historians. As J. D. Fage pointed out in his inaugural lecture at Birmingham in 1965, 'The sense of history, the need for history can be quite independent of the ability to write'; many African societies in the absence of writing 'developed formal oral records of their past and elaborate methods of maintaining these records for their posterity'. In the case of the Yoruba, the historian who is prepared to use such material is fortunate, since they are a people unusually rich in tradition, expressed and conserved in many ways. Their country is made up of different kingdoms all having specific and complex traditions about their origins and subsequent history, preserved deliberately and ritually by officials who bear almost the character of professional historians. Although these traditions are often of a legendary and miraculous kind, they may be sifted, correlated, and cross-checked as any other evidence until a residuum is obtained which is acceptable as 'truth'. Moreover, such accounts can usually be supplemented in other ways: from ceremonies recalling and re-enacting the past which are performed on public occasions, from place and proper names and titles, from a treasury of proverbial and epigrammatic phrases (called *owe*). All these preserve, although often enigmatically, fragments of the past. Unhappily, as new forms of society impose new ways of thought and new conventions, much of this repository of knowledge is being lost. Within a generation tradition may be so weakened among the Yoruba as to cease to be an important source of new information for the historian.

To supplement tradition and to correct, corroborate, or confirm it, there are few other sources. Barely a dozen unambiguous references to the Yoruba in written material before the nineteenth century are known, and these throw only a fitful light on their circumstances. But while it is unlikely that much new written evidence will be discovered, there is greater hope of obtaining information from archaeology. This is still a rather neglected field in West Africa, but it is probably here that the greatest advances in early Yoruba historical studies can be expected, in conjunction with such newer ancillary studies as comparative linguistics and the analysis of the distribution of blood-groups.

The construction of a coherent narrative of the past, which must precede any attempt at interpretation, provides as great a problem for the historian of the Yoruba as the recovery of his material. It is a platitude that oral tradition must be treated with caution and reserve – as must all evidence – and that precision is needed in the use of terms and the indication of sources. Since a supernatural element frequently intrudes into tradition, especially (but not exclusively) into tradition about earliest times, it is useful to distinguish between 'myth', in which the supernatural plays a large part, and 'legend', which strains credulity less or not at all. A further distinction may be made (and is made in this book) between 'legend', which is tradition related by word of mouth, and 'tradition', which is a wider term and embraces all methods of recording the past – re-enactment ceremonies, for example – which are not ulti-mately based on contemporary written material or on archaeo-logy. Again, tradition is subject to falsification in several well-known ways: for example, to what has been called 'legendary elision' (the suppression of the 'middle ages' in a people's history by assigning all events to either the period of the origin of their society or to recent times) and 'legendary stereotyping' (the compression of a narrative by reducing and stereotyping the names of persons and places), or to the pro-duction of official, often justificatory accounts of the past by means of 'Authorized' and then 'Revised' versions of events. Moreover, among the Yoruba tradition is closely concerned with title to land, and this often leads to the production by different towns or different families of rival 'Authorized Versions' and to competition based on these accounts for precedence and chieftancies. The difficulties which beset the historian working from tradition are indeed many, and they differ at many points from the difficulties which arise in connection with other kinds of evidence. Yet, as Vansina has shown, there is no priority among classes of historical material. All evidence must be subjected to rigorous, even sceptical, examination, and in using tradition the historian must strive to apply the same standards, if not the same criteria, as he applies in the use of other sources.

The Yoruba awareness of their past, expressed in the

abundance of their tradition, has led over the last half-century to an increasing flow of historical publications. Many local histories have been produced, in both Yoruba and English. These are of varying standard, and nearly all lack a critical basis, but in every case they contribute in some degree to the recovery and understanding of the history of the Yoruba in the wider national sense as well as locally. More recently, academically trained Nigerians, and a few expatriate historians, have been producing books, articles, and theses which deal with Yoruba history analytically and according to modern techniques of research and presentation. Most of these latter, however, have concentrated on the last hundred or so years, avoiding thereby heavy dependence on tradition. Both groups are dominated by a figure who stands midway between them: the Reverend Samuel Johnson, a Yoruba and an Anglican priest of Ọyọ, whose *History* of his own people constitutes a masterly narrative based on tradition and related in majestic English prose. Johnson's work lacks the references to sources which would have trebled its value to later historians and is handicapped by his preoccupation with the affairs of Ọyọ and by his religious determinism. Nevertheless, the *History of the Yorubas* is a classic to which resort will always be made. The present writer's first acknowledgement must therefore be to the Reverend Samuel Johnson.

Meanwhile the process of reconstructing the Yoruba past is gaining momentum, even though at present hypotheses predominate over established fact. An attempt, such as this book, to give a general account of the major Yoruba kingdoms, is likely to be overtaken within a very short time by new evidence and reinterpretations. The writer still hopes that his work may serve as a summary of knowledge and current theories and perhaps also provide for those working in this field an indication of points where their efforts are most needed. His thanks are now most sincerely rendered to his many helpers. In particular, he expresses his gratitude to the great number of local rulers (the ọba), their chiefs and officials, and other residents of their towns, who have patiently answered his many and importunate questions about the days of their ancestors. His thanks are due to his colleagues in the Universities of Lagos and Ifẹ for help in various ways; he owes special gratitude to Mr R. C. C. Law, who read his manuscript and made many useful suggestions, generously sharing his deep knowledge of West African written sources. He also benefited greatly from the advice of Mr Festus Adetula. Finally, he acknowledges his debt to the students of Lagos and Ifẹ, many of whom gave their time to interpreting for him their history and customs, as well as their language.

PART I

PART I

I · The Yoruba and their Homeland

The political structure of West Africa in the twentieth century tends to cut across the history both of the peoples living there and of their earliest contacts with the world beyond. This is partly the result of the drawing of frontiers by the European empire-builders of the last century in such a way that in places they divided a people between two or even more states. The extent to which this was done has sometimes been exaggerated. A more important factor is that the countries which have developed from the coastal annexations of the British, French, and Germans are all based upon that 'penetration of the interior' which was a prominent object of European missionaries, traders, and officials alike; thus they group together peoples whose disparate histories, cultures, and languages reflect the different worlds of the Guinea forestlands and the savannah.

Nigeria exemplifies this contrast. Its six northern states (until 1967 the vast Northern Region) consist almost entirely of open countryside, of the type known as savannah (either grassland or woodland), whereas the states to the south are much more thickly wooded, especially within a hundred miles of the coast, where the forest is dense. The contrast is repeated in the social organization and history of these regions. Until the conquest of the whole country by the British at the end of the last century, the north was dominated by the Hausa (or, from early in the same century, Hausa-Fulani) and Bornu emirates, which have their place in the history of the empires of the West Sudan, while to the south-east the Ibo and, farther south again, the Efik, Ibibio, and other people of the Niger Delta preserved a society which was highly fragmented.

The Yoruba in the south-west, and also their neighbours to the east, the Bini or Edo of Benin (now the Mid-West State), make a transition and a link between these extremes. Much of their homeland lies in the forest, while the rest can be described as woodland savannah, and yet states developed here which, although generally on a smaller territorial scale than the states to the north, evolved forms of government which could be adapted to areas far beyond the founding metropolis and to situations involving a form of international relations between themselves and with other peoples. It can also be claimed that the Yoruba and Bini kingdoms were, as Michael Crowder puts it,[1] 'purely African states whose growth was stimulated neither by contact with Islam nor Europe'. They preserved their government, religion, and ways of life in this relative isolation until the Europeans who had been trading on the coast from the fifteenth century onwards changed their role in the nineteenth century and became proselytizers of their religion, their economy, their culture, and finally their political forms.

It is not difficult to explain the rise of states in the West Sudan, where lateral communications across the savannah are relatively easy, as the pilgrimage routes to Mecca show; even the great Sahara was traversed by caravan trails leading to the Barbary ports, and an almost ideal vehicle for the desert had been available since Roman times in the camel. But in the Guinea forest the position was different. Here, climate, disease, and limiting agricultural conditions made life hazardous, while the dense undergrowth hindered communications. The coast was forbidding: the beaches beaten with surf, and beyond them the intricacies of the mangrove swamps. Such conditions would seem to combine to hinder the rise of organized communities on a scale which could be dignified by the term 'state', much less 'empire'. Yet, despite these unfavourable conditions, such states as Abomey, Ashanti, Benin, and the Yoruba kingdoms arose both in the forest depths and on its fringes. Although they seem to have emerged somewhat later and more slowly than the better-known states of the grasslands, their polities and cultures were no less distinguished than those of, for example, Ghana, Mali, Songhay, Hausa or Bornu.

The origins of the Guinea states are likely to have been as varied as their subsequent histories and institutions. The evidence about early times, coming almost entirely from tradition, is unsatisfactory, but a number of factors which must have been of importance can be isolated. The first is the development in the Guinea forest of a type of food production capable of supporting an organized society. This depended upon the presence of suitable crops and of metal tools for their efficient cultivation. The dating of this development for any part of Guinea is still a matter of controversy. Among the most important food crops the common yam (*discorea*), the coco-yam (*colocasia*), plantain, and banana seem to have been introduced from Malaysia about the beginning of the Christian era, while maize and cassava were brought to Africa only in the sixteenth and seventeenth centuries. But several species of yam, as well as the kola tree and the oil-palm, are now known to be indigenous to West Africa, and the theory that the forest and humid zone could not be inhabited to any significant extent until after the introduction from outside the continent of new crops is no longer tenable; it has been claimed, for example, that 'there was already an ancient province of yam culture, extending over the whole forest and woodland zone of Africa', before the coming of the Malaysian plants.[2] On the other hand, the use of iron apparently did not spread into the forest until about A.D. 300–500, so that cultivation and population must have been restricted until well after that time.

The next factor is trade. Here two distinct sets of trade relations and movements must be considered. On the coast there were the European traders, drawn there from the late fifteenth century in search of the reputed gold of Guinea and then of such tropical products as pepper and other spices, but for whom the slave trade came all too soon to predominate. For the most

part, however, contact between these Europeans and the West
Africans was limited, and in any case almost entirely confined
to the coast, the Africans there jealously guarding their control
of the trade with the interior. More important in this connection
than the sea-borne trade was the trade between the forest and
the savannah. The kola nut, indigenous to the Guinea forest,
was in great demand in the Sudan, especially after the spread
of Islam, as it was one of the few stimulants allowed by that
religion. But at first it had been gold for which Guinea was
chiefly famed; reports of this trade stimulated the Moorish conquest of Songhay at the end of the sixteenth century, just as
over a century earlier it had lured the Portuguese explorers ever
farther south in the West Coast voyages. Ivory was produced
from the elephant herds, and there was some trade in slaves,
although this does not seem to have been on any considerable
scale until the nineteenth century. The forest products travelled
across the lagoons, up the river highways and along intricate
tracks through the bush until they reached the Sudan, and not
only the Sudan, since, through the markets of Kano, Timbuktu,
and lesser centres, they were brought across the desert to
Barbary and the Mediterranean. The widespread use of cowries
on the West Coast, which has so far been traced back to the
seventeenth century,[3] is evidence both of the extent to which
communications had developed in Africa – cowries were imported via Egypt from the Indian Ocean – and of the existence
of a form of money economy which was independent of
European contact.

The third factor which seems likely to have affected the rise
of the older Guinea states is the influence of the states of the
West Sudan. In these latter, indigenous concepts of government fused, in proportions which are controversial and must
have varied from place to place, with Islamic concepts. They
may also have been influenced by remoter ideas from the Nile
Valley transmitting, perhaps via Meroe, a distant echo of the
Pharaohs of Ancient Egypt and a knowledge of iron working

which may have been evolved in Meroe itself – though this last speculation is as yet unsupported by archaeological or other evidence. The degree to which the idea of the Sudanic state and its civilization and techniques influenced Africa south of the savannah is a live question for historians, and perhaps the recent tendency has been to exaggerate it.[4] But it is credible that events such as the fall of Ghana (to the Almoravids in 1076), the decline of Mali (in the late fifteenth century), and the fall of Songhay (in 1590) affected societies several hundred miles to the south of their area.

The last factor to be considered here is a more remote one, and more difficult to trace: the influence of the Mediterranean and Near Eastern worlds, an influence which, though tentative, often interrupted, and relayed at third or fourth hand, was of great antiquity. The Moors of North Africa were interested not only in the products of the West Sudan but also in those of Guinea farther to the south, and above all its gold, obtained through the markets of the Sudan but derived from the alluvia of the upper Senegal and Niger valleys. The word 'Guinea' itself almost certainly derives from the Berber word for Negro, as in, for example, the Bab Aguinaou ('Gate of the Negro') in Marrakesh.[5] Until the Moroccan invasion of the Sudan, the caravan trade across the Sahara had a continuous history of at least fifteen hundred years, and thus political, cultural, and economic developments on the Mediterranean coast two thousand miles away were liable eventually to affect the people of Guinea. The Arab conquest of North Africa in the seventh century, for example, is likely to have had repercussions far to the south, and it has even been suggested that either this or perhaps the later movement up the Nile and then westward across North Africa of those turbulent Beduin tribes, the Beni Hillal, and Beni Sulleim may have brought about the move either of the Yoruba people or of a group of conquerors who later became assimilated with them in the present Yoruba homeland. Again, it seems possible that the knowledge of iron-working came to the Yoruba from the Mediterranean area, since the type of furnace used by them is identical with Roman furnaces found in Europe.[6]

The states which arose in the Guinea forest and immediately to its north all seem to have owed something to the preceding factors, though in greatly varying degrees. Not unexpectedly, therefore, they had in common certain characteristics. At the centre, and usually as the outstanding political phenomenon, was a divine king with whose well-being the well-being of the whole people was identified and who either claimed descent from a god or himself personified a god. This institution may account for a second important attribute of many of these states, the prevalence of towns on a scale unusual in Africa, since such conglomerations of people probably took their rise from the settlement of a divine ruler. With this urbanization there developed an emphasis on internal trade. The Guinea state was a commercial emporium; sometimes the king himself had a kind of monopoly over all trading, the article most vigorously dealt in being cloth, whether imported or manufactured at home. Oliver and Fage write:[7] 'It was this universality of trade in cloth and other luxuries [in beads, for example] which, together with the largely urban pattern of settlement, chiefly distinguished the Guinea region from all other parts of Africa south of the "Sudanic" savannah belt, at least during late medieval and early modern times.' Security along the trade-routes, combined with specialization in agriculture and crafts, led to the development of markets on a greater scale than elsewhere in Africa. They contributed also to the last, and best-known, of the characteristics of the Guinea states to be noted here. This was the high degree of skill attained by many of the peoples, and notably the Yoruba, in the plastic arts: wood, stone, and ivory carving, sculpture cast in bronze or brass, terra-cottas, and the rarer mud sculptures and wall paintings. This art of Guinea must in many cases be the product of specialists and is an index of the social and economic conditions prevailing there. Sometimes, too, it provides the historian with more direct evidence, as in the case of the mud reliefs in the palace at Abomey, which depict incidents in the wars between the Dahomeans and the Yoruba in the nineteenth century.

The Yoruba of West Africa are a numerous people with many kings, among whom some twenty or more are rulers over what were formerly distinct and independent states, while the rest, amounting in one list to over 1,000, are subordinate rulers whose territories consisted of single towns and groups of villages.[8] They form the third largest ethnic group in Africa's most populous country, some nine million of them living in the rich forest and farmland of south-western Nigeria; there is also a Yoruba irredenta in Dahomey and Togo, cut off from their brethren by the European frontier makers in the Scramble for Africa at the end of the nineteenth century, while a diaspora, derived partly from their trading operations and partly consisting of Moslems who have failed to return home from the pilgrimage to Mecca, is found over a wide area stretching from the Senegal to the Nile. They are a Negro race whose language belongs to the Kwa group (within the Niger–Congo family of languages) which predominates in West Africa; though it remained unwritten until the 1840s, Yoruba is rich in oral literature, and there are many dialects. Primarily they are a farming people, cultivating their family lands in individual holdings. At the same time they have many ancient towns, so that they appear to be the most urbanized of the people of tropical Africa; today Ibadan, the capital of the Western Region, and Lagos, the Federal capital but Yoruba in its history and the bulk of its population, each have well over half a million inhabitants. Their art and culture are being increasingly studied; the incomparable 'bronzes' of Ifẹ, for example, are no longer seen as isolated and enigmatic phenomena, but are now confidently interpreted as testimony to the greatness of the Yoruba past and to its continuity.

The homeland of the Yoruba – *ilẹ Yoruba* – stretches from the swamps and lagoons of the coast across the rain forests, rising gradually towards the oil-palm bush and woodland savannah and the distant bend of the Niger. For the most part it is a fertile and verdant country, watered by many rivers and streams, and with a landscape which varies from the gloom and mystery of the swamps and high forest to the exhilarating panorama of the northern uplands, where rocky hills stud a park-like scene which recalls the paintings of the Romaı tic School in Europe. It was in the extreme north or this area that was founded the great city and capital of the Ọyọ, while Ile Ifẹ, the traditional cradle of the race and their spiritual centre, lies in the forest over a hundred miles to the south. When in the early years of the last century Old Ọyọ was overthrown by the Hausa–Fulani armies a great migration southwards followed, swelling the towns in the forest and on its edge. Today the boundary of the northern states with the Western State cuts through the northern third of the historic homeland, leaving many Yoruba in the districts of Ilọrin and Kabba.

The Yoruba have undoubtedly occupied this homeland (as big as England) for many centuries. When the Portuguese first arrived on the coast in the fifteenth century their political organization into a number of major and minor states had already been evolved, and may well have been in existence for several hundred years, as an examination of their king-lists and other oral data suggest. For the period preceding the formation of the states almost nothing is known. But the Yoruba seem never to have constituted a single political entity; their very name was confined until less than a century ago to the northern group among them, the Ọyọ (from whose own name it perhaps derives), while the rest were called by the different names of the proliferating kingdoms. Their language, despite its many dialects, provides the main evidence of a common origin and cultural heritage; the name sometimes applied to this language, *anago*, has been used by their neighbours, especially the Daho-

means, to describe the people, while another name, or nickname, was Olukumi ('my friend').

A second pointer to a common origin of the Yoruba kingdoms is the existence over the whole country of a cycle of myths
and legend which purports to describe the creation of the world
and its people and the foundation at Ile Ife, the world's centre,
of the first kingdoms.[9] Into these myths are woven the names of
the heroes whom the Yoruba regard as their founding ancestors.
A commonly found version[10] tells how Olorun, owner of the sky,
let down from heaven a chain by which Oduduwa, father of all
the original Yoruba kings, descended to the primordial ocean
below. Oduduwa threw into the waters a handful of soil, and on
this he placed a cock and a palm nut. The cock scratched at the
earth, which became land, and the nut grew to a tree with sixteen branches, symbolizing the crowned rulers of Oduduwa's
house. The political counterpart to this story relates, on the
other hand, that Oduduwa was a son of Lamurudu, King of
Mecca, who migrated westwards until he came to Ife and settled
there. From Ife his children and grandchildren went forth to
become the founders of kingdoms and royal dynasties in all
parts of Yorubaland.[11] These stories of the creation of man –
the myths – and of the foundation of the Yoruba polity – the
legends – are found in all the kingdoms, and most of the royal
houses trace their descent to Ife. The details vary considerably,
but the traditions remain recognizably the same in basis.
Rarely do they have the coherence of, for example, the myths
of Ancient Greece, but the historian may nevertheless conclude
that in this context incoherence is one of the marks of authenti-
city.

There has been much speculation about the origins and pre-
history of the peoples of West Africa. The growing appreciation
of Negro art stimulated this, and in particular the discovery of
the art of Ife led to numerous, sometimes fantastic, hypotheses
to account for objects whose artistic value was so high (and
which seemed to resemble and equal the classical art of Europe)

that they could not, it was said, have been in any way connected with the present inhabitants.[12] Anthropologists propounded the 'Hamitic theory', according to which the Negro populations of Africa were conquered at some remote period by a 'white people', the Hamites, who brought with them from the north of the continent a superior culture from which derives any cultural and technical achievement of the Negroes of West Africa in the centuries preceding European contact. This theory has been subject in the last few years to devastating criticism[13] and is no longer tenable.

The Yoruba legends relating how their ancestors 'came from the east' are by no means peculiar to them: indeed, they are found among many other West African peoples. These legends are often interpreted to imply an Egyptian origin, and this view, despite the naming of a 'King of Mecca' in one version of their legend of origin, has been enthusiastically propounded by Yoruba historians.[14] This interpretation may seem to some extent supported by the possibility that certain of their techniques, for example, iron-working and the *cire-perdue* (lost wax) method of casting metal objects, and forms of government, in particular the 'Sudanic state' and the divine kingship, may have been diffused from the Nile Valley. But these possibilities are far from justifying the acceptance of the Egyptian theory, while other parts of the argument, especially the supposed resemblance in language between ancient Egyptian and Yoruba, can be dismissed.[15]

The best hope of throwing light upon the earliest times of the Yoruba seems to lie now with archaeology. New techniques, which are already adding to the depth of historical knowledge of West Africa as of other parts of the world, may be important here, and methods of excavation suitable to the physical conditions are being worked out.[16] Yet in this field, too, the difficulties are immense. The characteristic building materials of West Africa, mud and bamboo, are notoriously impermanent, especially in a climate noted for the violence of its rainstorms. Again, little success has yet been obtained in dating such artifacts as the metal and terra-cotta sculptures of the classical period at Ifẹ* or the pottery fragments which abound on sites such as Old Ọyọ.

Finally, there are two other, relatively new, sources from which help may be sought in this problem. The first is serology, or the compiling and interpretation of the distribution of blood groups among the population. So far, however, little useful information is available from this about West Africa.[17] Linguistic data, on the other hand, has already produced interesting, though very general, findings. These are mostly based upon glottochronology, the rebarbitive name given to the analysis of relations between languages, especially their pace of change, which leads to inferences about their respective ages. Christopher Wrigley has deduced from 'the general linguistic configuration of Africa' that the Niger–Congo group of languages, which includes Yoruba, must have separated from one another at a period very much more distant than 1,500 years, his minimum for the differentiation of the Bantu languages, and he concludes that 'unless we posit a large number of separate but parallel migrations into West Africa' the present inhabitants 'must have been living in that region for several thousand years'.[18] It has been tentatively suggested elsewhere, on the basis of comparative word-lists, that Yoruba separated from Edo, Ibo, and Ijo about 5,000 years ago, from Idoma 6,000 years ago, and from Igala 2,000 years ago.

If the broad conclusion from the linguistic evidence is accepted, then the traditions of origin which are preserved by the Yoruba seem to refer to movements over only comparatively short distances or, less probably, to the advent of a small group of alien conquerors who quickly became assimilated with their new subjects. It seems likely that in either case movement was from the grassland, where cultivation was earlier advanced and where there might be some population pressure, into the

* See footnote on p. 31.

forest, and the legend of Oduduwa and the royal progeny of Ifẹ seems to be a distant memory of such a movement.

To speculate beyond this point is hazardous, since new myths are all too easily created. There has, for example, been a tendency in recent writing about African history to attribute the origin of most states to the conquest of the people of one culture by people of another, postulating a sharp distinction between the rulers and the ruled. Stereotyping of this kind usually results in over-simplification and other distortions, for while most states in the world develop under the stimulus of older states, their origins are many and diverse.[19] Meanwhile, new material on the subsequent history of the Yoruba is being uncovered, and as more is established about what may be called their 'Middle Ages', this should in turn shed light on earlier times. But this kind of reconstruction has especial dangers for the historians, whose study permits generalizations but has no laws and whose material is unpredictable humanity; extrapolation unsupported by evidence should usually be left to scientists and mathematicians. Early Yoruba history now waits, not over-hopefully, upon archaeology and its ancillary sciences.

II · The Primacy of Ifẹ

At the heart of the life of all the Yoruba lies Ile Ifẹ. All roads in their religion, history, government, and art seem to lead there. Some contend that the whole people should properly be called 'Ifẹ' rather than 'Yoruba', a name which originally applied to the powerful Ọyọ alone and only in the nineteenth century was given, first apparently by the Christian missionaries, to the subjects of all the kingdoms and to their common language. The traditions of the creation of the world and of the origins of the peoples and their states centre on Ifẹ, the source whence all the major rulers derive the sanctions of their kingship and which, burdened with gods and their shrines and festivals, is the centre of religion.[1]

This primacy of Ifẹ is nearly everywhere admitted among the Yoruba,[2] but it is not easily defined. Until recently historians adhered to the theory, on the authority of Johnson, that there was a kind of Gelasian duality in the Yoruba polity, with the Alafin of Ọyọ as the paramount political ruler and the Ọni of Ifẹ as spiritual head.[3] This conception even affected the application of Lugardian indirect rule to Yorubaland by the British in the first part of this century. But it is open to question on two grounds. First, it is evident that the political ascendancy of Ọyọ for long periods over most of Yorubaland, including possibly Ifẹ itself, never led to the assimilation of the component kingdoms of this empire, which retained their identities, politically and culturally, and reasserted their independence whenever possible. Secondly, it has been claimed that the influence of the Ọni over the Yoruba kingdoms other than his own was not confined to religious matters, but was also exercised

15

politically through ancient constitutional devices.[4] This contention, which would rarely find acceptance beyond Ifẹ itself, is discussed in Chapter VIII below. But an interesting demonstration of the veneration felt for the ruler of Ifẹ took place in 1903, when the British Governor of Lagos invited the Ọni to pronounce upon the claim of an Ijẹbu ọba, the Ẹlẹpẹ of Ẹpẹ, to wear a beaded and fringed crown, a type deriving from Ifẹ. The Ẹlẹpẹ's pretension had been bitterly contested by another Ijẹbu ruler, the Akarigbo of Ṣagamu. The Ọni travelled to Lagos for a meeting with the Governor and the Lagos chiefs and there ruled that only twenty-one of the ọba of Yorubaland were entitled to wear such crowns, and these did not include the Ẹlẹpẹ, who was thereupon fined £100 by the Governor, Sir William MacGregor. This visit in itself marked a breach with tradition, however, since no previous Ọni had been known to leave his palace (*afin*) after his accession except for religious and state ceremonies within the capital, and his journey caused consternation in the land. A contemporary account of this event claims that during the Ọni's absence from the Afin Ifẹ many other Yoruba ọba, including the Alafin, left their palaces and dwelt outside their walls until they were assured of the Ọni's safe return. But no confirmation of this picturesque detail can now be obtained.[5]

Oduduwa, sent from heaven by the Creator Olodumare (called also Ọlọrun, 'Owner of the sky') to establish land upon the surface of the waters, was both first ruler of Ifẹ and ancestor of the royal dynasties in the other principal kingdoms of the Yoruba. This much of the myth is common to most of the country, but thereafter the accounts diverge considerably. The historians of Ifẹ add many details about subsequent events, but agree about these neither among themselves nor with the historians of other kingdoms.[6] Paradoxically, such divergence is in an important sense reassuring, since it shows that an 'Authorized Version' has not yet been established. Moreover, while it is useful to try to identify and then knit together common factors in the differing accounts, it must be remembered that the reconciliation of conflicting tradition, a process which often leads to its rationalization, can provide no more than a hypothesis.

The Ifẹ accounts agree in describing the descent of Oduduwa from heaven upon the Ọra hill with sixteen companions to share in his task of colonizing the earth. From the Oke Ọra the party moved a short distance to settle on the place where the Afin Ifẹ still stands at the centre of the town. But dissension soon broke out between Oduduwa and Obatala, one of the foremost of his followers. To Obatala, as to Oduduwa, both divine and material functions are attributed. On the one hand, it was he to whom Olodumare entrusted the fashioning of men out of clay, into which models the Creator breathed life, and on the other, he is described as one of Oduduwa's subordinate rulers at Ifẹ. In this latter capacity he rebelled against the authority of Oduduwa, who, with the help of Ọbameri (sometimes described as the first among the sixteen and sometimes as Oduduwa's eldest son) drove him from the town. The quarrel was composed, but Obatala retained leadership of the people whom he had met in the surrounding forest. These, known as the Igbo (possibly after a variety of bird[7]), have been held to be the indigenous people whom Oduduwa and his followers had found already dwelling at Ifẹ. After his death Obatala was venerated as 'the great god' (*Orisa-nla*), and his festival is one of the most important events in the Ifẹ year.[8]

Myth now shades into legend, and all versions of the Oduduwa cycle give prominence to the dispersal from Ifẹ at some point in Oduduwa's lifetime of the princes of the royal family, who travelled away from their home in all directions to found new kingdoms and dynasties. This exodus has been ascribed in one account to a drought, a feasible enough occurrence towards the end of a long dry season in Yorubaland. The tradition further suggests that a decision to extend the scope of the Yoruba settlement may have been precipitated by the pressure of a growing population towards the end of a long and successful reign, combined with an impetus similar to that which had led Oduduwa and his original followers to Ifẹ – more probably, as has been suggested earlier, from the savannah lands to the north than direct from heaven to the Ọra hill. The place in Ifẹ at which the dispersal was decided upon is still known as 'the place of conference', Itajero. Here the children of Oduduwa (or, in other accounts, his grandchildren by his son Akanbi) were given crowns and sent away to found kingdoms. Sometimes the number of these princes is given as sixteen, elsewhere as only seven. One of the princes founded a new dynasty in the already established kingdom of Benin,[9] and another (who cannot be traced further) ruled over Popo, an indeterminate area stretching from Badagry along the coast into modern Togo, while the rest became rulers of the major kingdoms of the Yoruba. According to the Ọni's ruling at Lagos in 1903, the number of crowns conferred by Ifẹ amounted to twenty one, some, perhaps the majority, on this occasion and the rest presumably by Oduduwa's successors on the throne. This story of the dispersal is told in all the major kingdoms whose ọba claim descent from Oduduwa, varying widely in its details but always recognizable in its principal elements.

It was apparently at some time after the dispersal that the people of Ifẹ began to suffer from the depredations of the Igbo from the nearby forest. The unearthly appearance of these people filled them with such terror that they were unable to offer any resistance. Thus the town was several times burnt to the ground by the raiders before salvation came through the heroism of Mọrẹmi. This was a local woman who, after sacrific-ing and making promises to the *orisa* (god or godess) of a stream near the town, allowed herself to be taken captive by the Igbo. Because of her beauty she became the favourite of their king, and from him she learnt that the fearful Igbo were simply ordinary humans who disguised themselves for war in all-concealing garments of raffia fibre. Then she succeeded in escaping, and on her return to Ifẹ taught the people to defend themselves against the Igbo by setting fire to their costumes with lighted torches. By these means the Ifẹ were at last able to overcome their enemies. But when Mọrẹmi repaired to the stream to express her gratitude her gifts were all rejected by the orișa until she was brought to offer her only son, Ẹla Olorugbo. The defeat of the Igbo and Mọrẹmi's terrible sacrifice are commemorated at Ifẹ in the annual Edi festival,[10] while the episode has been interpreted both as an encounter between the aboriginal inhabitants of the forest and the newcomers led by Oduduwa and as a clash between rival factions within the town.[11]

Tradition is silent about the death of Oduduwa. His twofold role as emissary of the Creator and as leader of a migration is reflected in the reverence paid to him both as a principal member of the Yoruba pantheon, a god of indeterminate sex who is nearly everywhere worshipped either under this name or as Ọlọfin, and who is widely regarded as a symbol of Yoruba unity, and also as first ọba of Ifẹ, the Ọni or Ọnife. There are differing accounts of his successors in the latter role. Some say that his son Ọbalufon reigned as second Ọni, then his youngest son (or grandson) Ọranyan, who is also remembered as founder of Ọyọ, the most powerful and extensive of the Yoruba kingdoms but who even in Ọyọ tradition is believed to have died and been buried at Ifẹ, and next, as fourth Ọni, Alaiyemore or Ọbalufon II, son of Ọbalufọn I. Other versions describe Obatala as either second, third, or fourth Ọni. At Ọyọ it is related that it was Ọranyan who succeeded Oduduwa and that before he left Ifẹ for Ọyọ he appointed one of his father's former slaves, the son of a woman who had been condemned to death for some crime, to take charge of the royal treasures remaining there. This man, Adimu, became the founder of the present kingship of Ifẹ and ancestor of subsequent Ọni, whose title, according to Johnson, is a contraction of the phrase *ọmọ ọluwọni*, 'the son of a sacrificial victim'.[12] But this is rejected at Ifẹ itself, where

C

the succession of their ọba from Oduduwa the national hero, and thus his seniority among all the ọba of Yorubaland, is naturally preferred.

The names of many subsequent Ọni are recalled at Ifẹ, but there seems to have been no practice there of reciting these names formally at installation ceremonies or other times, and no complete or chronological list has been compiled. The reigning ọba (1967) has been described as the 47th,[13] but this is derided in Ifẹ as far too low a number, and those associated with the court speak of over four hundred Ọni having reigned. There are two royal graveyards in Ifẹ, but these have not been excavated, and they do not shed much light on the present problem; the first, at Lafogido near the Afin, has been much built over, while the second, in the forest outside the walls at Igbo Odi, described as the burial place for those ọba whose reigns were not markedly successful, contains some thirty or forty mounds, some or all of which may be graves of Ọni. An Ifẹ historian, J. A. Ademakinwa, has recorded the names of forty-five Ọni following Alaiyemore, belonging to four different royal compounds (or houses where the families are regarded as of royal descent and eligible in their turn for the succession). He could not indicate the order in which these ọba reigned, and he added that there were five other compounds in the town from which had come Ọni whose names he was unable to supply.[14]

No documentary record of Ifẹ earlier than the mid-nineteenth century is known, nor does it seem likely that any such record was ever made. But it has been suggested that two Portuguese writers of the early fifteenth century refer incidentally to Ifẹ in the course of their descriptions of the contacts between their countrymen and the kingdom of Benin. The earlier is Duarte Pacheco, who in describing the slave trade from the West Coast writes:

To the East of this Kingdom of Beny, 100 leagues inland, there is known to be a country which has at this time a King called Licasaguou. He is said to be lord of many peoples and to possess great power. Near there is another great lord, who has the name 'Hooguanee'. He is considered among the Negroes as the Pope is among us.[15]

The second possible reference occurs in *Da Asia* by De Barros:

Among the many things which the King Dom Joao learnt from the ambassador of the King of Beny, and also from Joao Afonso de Aveiro, of what they had been told by the inhabitants of those regions, was that to the east of the King of Beny at twenty moons' journey – which according to their account, and the slow pace at which they travel, would be about two hundred and fifty of our leagues – there lived the most powerful monarch of those parts whom they called Ogane. Among the pagan princes of the territories of Beny he was held in as great veneration as are the Supreme Pontiffs with us. In accordance with a very ancient custom, the Kings of Beny, on ascending the throne, sent ambassadors to him with rich gifts to inform him that by the decease of their predecessor they had succeeded to the Kingdom of Beny, and to request him to confirm them in the same. . . . All the time this ambassador was at the court of the Ogane he never saw him, but only some silk curtains behind which he was placed, like some sacred object.[16]

In these accounts, 'Licasaguou' has been identified with the Alafin and 'Hooguanee' and 'Ogane' with the Ọni. But difficulty immediately arises from the directions which are given, since both Ọyọ and Ifẹ lie to the north-west, not east, of Benin. The identification of the Ogane with the Ọni has been discussed by A. F. C. Ryder, who concludes that the Ogane is more likely to have been a ruler in the Nupe–Igala area straddling the Niger–Benue confluence than the Ọni of Ifẹ. Ryder has also cast doubts on the widely accepted theory of the derivation of both the dynasty and also the associated lost-wax technique of

brass-casting at Benin from Ifẹ, showing them to be based on
traditions which in Benin can be traced no further than records
made after the British occupation in 1897.[17] Nevertheless, the
description in De Barros of the Pope-like ruler hidden behind
silk curtains and his relationship with the Benin kingship accord
so well with the veneration with which the Ọni is still regarded in
both Yorubaland and Benin and with the traditions as recorded
by the local historians in both places that the debate on these
enigmatic texts is not closed.

Difficulties in establishing a coherent account of the past of
Ifẹ have led to the suggestion that the present town does not
stand upon its original site. This would be far from surprising,
since many, perhaps most, Yoruba towns have traditions of
migration; Ifa verse is said to refer to six different Ifẹ, and it is
known that in the nineteenth century the present Ifẹ was twice
abandoned for short periods. J. O. George wrote at the end of
the last century that 'the old Ile Ifẹ was much farther in the
interior', but he cited no authority or evidence for this, while
Ryder has recently suggested that the ruling dynasty may have
removed to the present site at some time after the sixteenth
century.[18] For some years since the Second World War archaeological investigations have been carried on at Ifẹ, though inter-
mittently and on rather a small scale. The results so far throw
little light on the dating of the town. Willett, who has been responsible for most of this work, cautiously concludes that since
the antiquities discovered there are so many and so varied, the
site must have been occupied for many centuries.[19]*

The present Ifẹ, with its population of some 150,000, is contained within a double circuit of the earthen 'walls' which are
characteristic of Yoruba towns, covering here an area of somewhat over two miles. The outer wall is apparently that built by
Ọni Abeweila between the collapse of Old Ọyọ about 1835 and
his own death in 1849, while an inner and older wall runs at a
radius of about one mile from the centrally placed Afin. It is

* But see the footnote on p. 31

evident that at some time in the past the town occupied a considerably greater extent than the present enclosure, since several of the sacred groves associated with the town lie well beyond the outer walls; moreover, potsherd pavements, which are found in palaces and large compounds in several parts of Yorubaland, have been discovered at distances up to four miles from the Afin in several directions. Pavements have also been uncovered under both town walls, which suggests that the walls were built long after the disappearance of the buildings associated with these particular pavements. Presumably all the buildings of ancient Ifẹ, like most of those of the present day, were constructed by puddling mud on the site, and it is impossible by present archaeological techniques to establish either the dates of surviving walls or even to distinguish confidently between collapsed buildings and the surrounding soil. Willett has written that, 'The "pavement period" is in part, if not entirely, later than the introduction of maize into West Africa at the beginning of the sixteenth century, for pottery decorated with the impressions of maize cobs has been found beneath at least one pavement.'[20] But this is far from conclusive, since no starting or terminal points have been suggested for a pavement period, and indeed the making of pavements in the more important compounds seems never to have entirely died out.[21]

In the absence of other evidence, it seems reasonable to assume, as do the inhabitants of Ifẹ and indeed all Yoruba, that the present town both represents the 'cradle of the Yoruba', as it is so often called – the place where the dynasty of Oduduwa was established and whence it spread over the land – and also that it stands on or very near to its original site. That the town has contracted at some period is clear from its archaeology. Local historians, in particular the present Ọni himself, have referred to traditions of a drawing together of the people after the dispersal of the princes and their followers.[22] But it seems more likely that the contraction indicated by the relation between the existing town walls and the groves and pavements was a consequence of forgotten wars, perhaps arising from the restless ambition of the Ọyọ.

It is not the central position of Ifẹ in the history of the Yoruba which has given the town its wider fame but the incomparable 'bronze' and terra-cotta sculptures, mostly human figures, which have been discovered there during the present century. The art of Ifẹ is now known throughout the world. Attention was first called to it by the German anthropologist Leo Frobenius, who spent some weeks investigating the sacred groves and shrines of Ifẹ in 1910 and 1911. During these visits he was shown the bronze head known from the grove where it had been buried as Olokun, the sea-god of the Yoruba,[23] and collected a number of terra-cotta heads and fragments. He also recorded many of the stone monuments which he saw in various parts of the town. His publication of these unexpected finds caused excitement, and some understandable scepticism, in Europe, and aroused the interest which has led to the many later discoveries. In 1919 the existence in the Afin of the bronze Ọbalufon mask (reputed to represent Ọbalufon II, the third or fourth Ọni) and the large terra-cotta head called Lajuwa (after a palace official said to have attempted to usurp the Ọni's throne) was disclosed to the public, and then in 1938–9 seventeen bronze heads and the upper part of a male figure were found buried in the Wunmonije compound, one of the royal houses of Ifẹ. A number of small bronzes and terra-cottas were next discovered in 1957 during excavations at Ita Yemoo on the eastern side of the town. Since then there have been many other finds, though of nothing so spectacular as those from Wunmonije.[24]

The twenty major figures now known, unlike most African sculpture, are all in a naturalistic style, and are apparently somewhat idealized portraits of individuals; sixteen of them are life-size. Of the heads it has been written that 'they would stand comparison with anything which Ancient Egypt, Classical Greece and Rome, or Renaissance Europe had to offer.'[25] The smaller bronzes, four of which represent full-length standing figures, are of almost equal excellence. Like the larger heads, they were made by the lost-wax method of casting and are in much the same style, though the full-length figures have heads which occupy a quarter of the overall height, a proportion characteristic of African art. To quote Willett again, these 'show a broader range of subject (than the heads) . . . and a humour which was quite unsuspected.'[26] The terra-cottas form a much larger body of work and, since the majority are in the same naturalistic style as the bronzes, make it almost impossible that Ifẹ art should represent the output of one isolated genius (as was once suggested) or even one generation. They consist of fragments of full-length figures and of heads, at least some of which appear to be portraits, and there is even a full-size stool in this material whose making must have required as much skill as did the casting of the bronzes.

In addition there remain in and around Ifẹ a number of stone monuments and other objects which have no discernible stylistic connection with the bronzes and are usually held to be anterior to them. These consist of monoliths, crudely carved figures of humans and animals, and decorated stools, and are found mostly near the centre of the town, especially in the area of the palace, and in the groves and shrines. Since they seem in most cases to occupy their original positions, whatever their purpose, they are classified, unlike the bronzes and terra-cottas, as primary material. The most notable is the eighteen-foot-high granite column known as the Ọpa Ọranyan, or 'staff of Ọranyan', studded with a mysterious pattern of 123 nails. The Ọpa is said to mark the grave of Ọranyan, but no burial pit has been found in the vicinity, and it has been alternatively suggested that it was originally dedicated to Ogun, the god of iron and war.[27] Equally interesting are several elaborate quartz stools, objects which (alone among the stone carvings) provide a link with what Willett has called the 'Classical Period' of Ifẹ, since similar representations are found in bronze and terra-cotta.

For the historian the art and antiquities of Ifẹ raise a number of major questions. Who were the artists? Were they ancestors of the present inhabitants of Ifẹ, or did they belong to quite another people? When and where did this art flourish, and if at Ifẹ itself, did it precede or follow the establishment of the dynasty of Oduduwa? What was the purpose of the sculptors and what kind of society produced and nourished this school of artists? And what is the relationship between this art, the art of the Yoruba in general, and the art of neighbours of the Yoruba in West Africa? Unhappily, to none of these can answers be confidently returned, and the historian must speculate against a background even more puzzling than in the case of the political origins of the Yoruba kingdoms. Apart from the stone monuments and perhaps the so-called Ọbalufon mask and Lajuwa head, all these antiquities have been discovered on secondary sites, that is they seem to have been brought from elsewhere and to have been *in situ* at the place of discovery only for a comparatively short time.[28] Moreover, they seem to have been neither understood nor much valued at Ifẹ before the present century, and to bear no real relationship to the myths and legends associated with the Oduduwa dynasty or Yoruba religion, despite some rather suspect attributions.[29] Again, no recollection exists in Ifẹ today of the intricate lost-wax technique by which all the bronzes were cast, and tradition throws no light upon its introduction nor whence it came. Another mystery lies in the source of the materials used in the bronzes. These are in fact not really bronzes (though it is convenient to continue to call them so), since they contain little tin and are either of brass or, in a few cases, of almost pure copper. But copper is not found in Nigeria, and must have been imported from far afield. Finally, the naturalism characteristic of this art, which is naturalism of the highest order, remote from experiment, distinguishes it sharply from almost all other African sculpture, including that of other Yoruba schools.

These challenging difficulties have led to a wealth of speculation, ranging from the theories of Frobenius, who thought that he had discovered the traces of a Greek colony on the Atlantic coast, to almost equally unlikely suggestions about wandering Roman or Renaissance artists or the ubiquitous Portuguese. But as archaeological investigation and comparative studies continue, more rational interpretations emerge. In the first place, it has been realized that the facial characters of most of the sculptures are undoubtedly negroid, and indeed striking similarities to the modern inhabitants of Ifẹ can sometimes be detected, as well as family resemblances between different groups of the sculptures. The striations, or skin scarifications, which appear prominently on some of the faces, and in the large bronze figure on the abdomen, probably represent tribal marks, though most are in a form not used by the Yoruba within recent times.[30] An important development has been the discovery of a number of terra-cottas in the naturalistic or classical Ifẹ style in association with others which are non-representational and immediately recognizable as 'African'. These finds, at the small village of Abiri near Ifẹ, at Ọbgọn Ọya near the Ọni's palace, and on a farm along the Ondo road, reveal, in Willett's words, that 'beside the naturalistic art of Ifẹ, and almost certainly contemporary with it, there was a freely imaginative style as well'.[31] Moreover, since attention was first drawn to the antiquities of Ifẹ, finds have continued apace, and excavations in and around the town produce a flow of objects. Thus the theories of a non-African origin for the art become ever more unlikely, and in their place it is reasonable to assume that these antiquities were the product of a civilization in Ifẹ itself which was ancestral to the present culture of the Yoruba, and that both the artists and their human subjects were the ancestors of the Ifẹ of the present day.

The isolation of the art is now beginning to break down. As

Yoruba art as a whole is subjected to study, links, both incono-graphical and technical, with classical Ifẹ are observed. Many centres of bronze casting, using the lost-wax method as at Ifẹ, existed, and indeed still exist, in the rest of Yorubaland, and also elsewhere in Nigeria.[32] The nine bronze figures from Tada and Jebba in Nupe country show striking affinities in style and technique with the Ifẹ sculptures – indeed, one of them, the famous seated figure from Tada, has been claimed by Willett as belonging to the Ifẹ corpus.[33] At Benin tradition relates that the art of bronze-casting was brought there from Ifẹ. Denis Williams has, however, pointed out a small but significant technical difference in the preparation of the Benin and Ifẹ bronzes. Moreover, Benin art is stylistically very different from that of Ifẹ, especially in its comparative lack of naturalism, and it has been suggested that it was evolved in other materials than bronze, such as wood, terra-cotta, and ivory.[34] Finally, the revelation in recent years of the Nok art and culture, covering a wide area of north-eastern Nigeria, has seemed to provide both Ifẹ and Benin with a remote ancestry, since the objects found on the Nok sites (mostly terra-cotta figures of humans and animals in varying degrees of semi-naturalism) show stylistic affinities with the sculptures from both places, as well as with other West African art. But these objects have been ascribed by radio-carbon tests to a period between c. 900 B.C. and c. A.D. 200, and thus there is a gap of a whole millennium between the latest date for the Nok culture and the earliest date which has been suggested for the Ifẹ bronzes.

As to the purpose and the subjects of the Ifẹ sculptures, the suggestion has been advanced that the major heads are port-raits of the Ọni and of leading members of his court for use in the ceremonies for the dead which are still held by the Yoruba, and other West African people, at an interval of usually about a year after the hasty burial of the corpse necessary in a tropical climate. Willett has pointed out that in the second funeral cere-monies at Ọwọ, called *ako*, effigies of the dead, with naturalistic

heads mounted on roughly carved bodies, were carried in pro-
cession and subsequently buried. He concludes that the bronze
heads of Ifẹ were used in the same way, the small holes in the
tops of the heads being intended for the attachment of crowns
(rather than for hair, as has also been suggested).[35] Resemblances between the symbols of authority still used by the Ọni and
his chiefs and those depicted on the sculptures increase the like-
lihood that the heads were portraits of rulers and of their
courtiers, probably those required to follow the king to his
grave. This explanation applies equally to the life-size heads
and full-length figures in terra-cotta, but the majority of the
terra-cotta heads and the smaller bronzes must have had a
different purpose. Most probably these latter were produced for
the shrines of the numerous cults of Ifẹ, on whose altars they
were placed, or in commemoration of sacrificial victims, human
and animal, at these shrines.[36]

The ever-growing quantity and variety of the sculptures from
Ifẹ and the evidence of links between the art of Ifẹ and that of
its neighbours make it clear that this was the production of a
whole school of artists working within a tradition. On the basis
of his view that the heads were effigies of the dead, Willett has
advanced alternative theories about the duration of the
classical period. If the nineteen major bronze heads (to which
possibly the half-length figure should be added) are all portraits of Ọni, then, allowing about twenty years for each reign,
they would seem to have been produced over a period of some
300 or 400 years. But if they represent not only the kings but
also members of the court (as seems more likely), then the great
period may have covered only a couple of generations.[37] The
stylistic homogeneity of the major works suggests, indeed, that
they were all produced within one or at most two hundred years,
but African art is in general so conservative that this can only
be tentatively advanced.

The dating of any part of Ifẹ art provides the greatest problem of all. Willett considers that Ifẹ art reached its peak in the

thirteenth or fourteenth century and that the stone and terra-
cotta sculptures, with their greater variety of style, flourished
considerably longer, both before and after the bronze or classical period. The end of bronze casting in Ifẹ may then have been
due to the cessation of supplies of metal from farther north, perhaps because of the spread of Islam in the fifteenth and sixteenth centuries.[38] This theory seems to be based upon the
tradition at Benin that bronze casting was introduced there
from Ifẹ during the reign of Oba Oguola, apparently in the late
fourteenth century. But, as has been seen above, the traditional
connection between Ifẹ and Benin has recently been questioned
so effectively that it can no longer be assumed that the art
and culture of Ifẹ are anterior to those of Benin. Denis Williams
has pointed out that until about the sixteenth century the
Yoruba, like other West African people, were dependent for
their production of iron upon local ore and inefficient local
smelting, which, he claims, led to a 'chronic iron hunger'.[39]
After about 1500, however, the supply of metal was supplemented by imports in increasing quantities of iron and copper
in wedges and 'pieces' and later (from the mid-seventeenth
century) as bars, wire, and manillas, and this in turn led to a
greatly expanded and improved metal industry in the Guinea
forests. It may therefore be that the bronze sculptures of Ifẹ and
Benin were roughly contemporaneous and both products of this
belated metal age. The extinction of the art at Ifẹ might be
explained by the unrecorded factors, whether catastrophe or
decline, which accounted for the contraction of the town at
some time before the building of its present older (and inner)
wall, and which, as suggested above, could have been a consequence of the depredations of the powerful Ọyọ.

As to the society which produced the art of Ifẹ, nothing is
known, since the antiquities include almost no objects of every-
day use. Yet such art presupposes a setting of sophistication.
The inspiration and aesthetic judgement which enabled the
artists to create their sculpture must have been rooted in a

culture of distinction and maturity, which in turn could only have evolved against a background of a sufficient political stability. Modern analogies among the Yoruba suggest that the sculptors were also the craftsmen who cast the bronzes and fired the terra-cottas, but whether or not these functions were performed by the same men, considerable technical knowledge and skill were required. These artists and craftsmen, from the quality of their work, must have been professionals whose activities were only possible in a society where economic life had attained a high degree of organization and differentiation.

There are few facts in this account of the history of Ifẹ. The traditions and the antiquities can be put together to form hypotheses, and though those now current are more acceptable both to the historian and the local patriot than the prejudiced speculations of Frobenius and others at the beginning of this century, they do not at best amount to more than probabilities. The search for new evidence continues in the realization that present theories, like those of Frobenius, may have to be abandoned in the light of discoveries to come. But the primacy of Ifẹ in the life of the Yoruba – their religion, their political system, their culture – is unlikely ever to be contested. Until now, Ifẹ preserves its major mysteries inviolate: its kingship, gods and shrines, its incomparable sculptures, cannot as yet be placed confidently in any coherent pattern. For the Yoruba, all this is seen through the eye of faith. Ifẹ remains the centre of his universe: *Ifẹ ondaiye, ibi oju ti imọ wa*, 'Ifẹ, the creator of the world, whence comes the light.'

NOTE. Since this book went to press, five radio-carbon dates from Ifẹ have been announced by F. Willett (Thurston Shaw, *Radio-carbon Dating in Nigeria*, Ibadan 1968, privately circulated, p. 14): (1) from excavations below potsherd pavements, two dates of the tenth and twelfth centuries respectively; (2) from a layer in which terracottas were excavated, an eleventh century date; (3) from the burial place of the heads of the Oba of Benin (Orun Oba Ado), two dates of the sixth and tenth centuries respectively. Willett writes that these confirm the antiquity of the site, while (2) suggests that the terracotta sculptures associated with Ifẹ were being made before Europeans first visited Benin. Interpretation of this small sample cannot go further.

III · The Rise of Ọyọ

In the remote north-eastern corner of the Western State of
Nigeria are the remains of a great city: Ọyọ ile ('home Ọyọ'),
now usually called Old Ọyọ to distinguish it from its successor
town some ninety miles to the south, and known to the Hausa
and Nupe and to its first European visitors as Katunga. Here
was the capital of the kingdom and empire of the Ọyọ, ruled by
the Alafin, said to descend from Ọranyan, the youngest son (or,
in another account, the grandson) of Oduduwa. The Alafin's
title describes him simply as Lord of the Palace, but his
authority was that of king (*ọba*) of the Ọyọ people, and he
was also 'Lord of the World and of Life' (*Alaiyeluwa*),
'Owner of the Land' (*Onilẹ*), and 'Companion of the Gods'
(*Ekeji Oriṣa*).

The site of Ọyọ ile is on the edge of the Yoruba highlands,
which here slope towards the River Niger; from this area
streams flow north to the River Mọsi and south to the Ogun.
This is a gently undulating country covered with low savannah
woodland, diversified by frequent rocky hills and outcrops and
by the giant baobab (the characteristic tree of the West Sudan,
and perhaps deliberately planted here for its supposed benign
influences). Some fifteen to twenty square miles were enclosed
by the earthen walls encircling the town, which may still be
traced, while the remains of compound walls, numerous grind-
ing holes in the rocks (for the crushing of maize, cassava, and
yams), and the abundance of pottery fragments on the surface
testify to the large population which lived here before the
abandonment of the town in the first part of the last century.
Today the site is deserted and thickly overgrown; lying twenty

miles from a motorable road and ten miles from the nearest village, it is rarely visited.[1]

Tradition relates that Ọyọ was founded by Ọranyan as part of the great dispersal of princes from Ifẹ. The account given by Johnson, the Ọyọ historian, differs from that of Ifẹ since it claims that on Oduduwa's death Ọranyan succeeded to the throne of Ifẹ and was entitled Alafin there. The dispersal was occasioned by a military expedition against 'Mecca', an explanation which more probably reflects a fanning-out over the land of a dominant race of conquerors such as happened in England after the Norman Conquest. The story continues that the royal brothers quarrelled and that Ọranyan with his followers made his way through Nupe country into the land of the Borgu, or Ibariba as the Yoruba call them. Here Ọranyan consulted the king about where he should settle and was then guided by a serpent, on which the king had fixed a charm, to a hill called Ajaka, where the serpent halted. Still following the instructions which he had received from the king, Ọranyan built his town here, calling it Ọyọ, meaning the 'slippery place' where his horse had slid and stumbled on the hillside.

After establishing the settlement at Ọyọ, Ọranyan next removed to Oko (whose site has not been identified), where he remained for several years. But at the end of his life he is believed to have returned to Ifẹ, where he died and was buried. Meanwhile his elder son, Ajaka, ruled at Ọyọ as his father's regent and successor until eventually he ceded the throne to his more vigorous brother, Ṣango. The new ọba's first act was to refuse tribute which the ruler of Owu had demanded from Ajaka. After routing the army which the Olowu had sent against him, Ṣango proceeded to remove the government from Oko to Ọyọ, recovering the latter town by a trick from Egboro, the Ọlọyọ-koro, a prince who ruled over a people living at Ọyọ before the arrival of Ọranyan and his followers from Ifẹ.

Ṣango was equally reputed as a warrior and a magician. But the exercise of his magical powers was to have a tragic result, for one day when demonstrating to his courtiers his power to call down lightning, he accidentally destroyed his palace and whole household. After this disaster, either in despair or in order to escape the hostility of his people, he hanged himself on an *ayan* tree. The gentler Ajaka then resumed his reign, while Ṣango entered the Yoruba pantheon as god of thunder and lightning.

Johnson writes that with the next reign, that of Aganju, Ajaka's son, the period of the 'historical kings' begins, after that of the legendary first three rulers. Although Crowder comments here that 'we are still very much in the land of legend',[2] Johnson's distinction is useful, since from this point there is a decline in the miraculous content of the traditional accounts. The picture is still shadowy, but certain features can be discerned. It seems clear that the Alafin's kingdom was only one among a number of Yoruba states which were already in existence and had sprung like Ọyọ from the womb of Ifẹ, and that it was by no means the most important. It is significant that Ọranyan, Ọyọ's founder, is described as the youngest either of Oduduwa's sons or grandsons and that Ajaka was compelled to pay tribute to the ruler of Owu (a town about 125 miles to the south and only about twenty miles from Ifẹ itself). The very site of Ọyọ on the extreme edge of Yoruba country suggests that its founder was forced by his junior status to settle farthest from the base at Ifẹ. This site, moreover, was dangerously near to two difficult neighbouring people: to the north and west, across the River Mọsi – which provided an effective barrier only in the wet season – lived the Borgu, renowned as warriors, and across the Niger, some thirty to forty miles to the north-east, were the Nupe, who controlled the river crossing at Jebba island. But this situation proved to have advantages. The town lay under a range of low, rocky hills which ran from north to south down the western walls and formed an extended acropolis. It was strategically placed athwart the tracks which led from the southern forests and across the nearby Niger towards the markets of the West Sudan. Most important, it lay within the savannah, where lateral communications were far easier than in the dense forests to the south and where horses could range comparatively freely and also be maintained, and occasionally bred and reared, without succumbing to the tsetse fly as in the south. Thus the Oyo were enabled to raise a cavalry force as an important, probably predominant, element in their army. There is an apparent reference to the Oyo cavalry by a Dutch writer of the late seventeenth century, Bosman, who describes the army of an unnamed inland power which had overrun the kingdom of Ardra (or Allada) as 'all Horsed' and adds that 'This Nation strikes Terror into all the circumjacent *Negroes*'.[3] Finally, the traditions indicate that Oyo maintained close relations – which might frequently become hostile – with its northerly non-Yoruba neighbours, the Hausa, Nupe, and Borgu, the first of whom, at least, were in turn in touch with the distant Arab and Berber across the Sahara. This must have been as much a stimulus as a danger; both trade and warfare would serve to bring the political, military, and technical ideas of the Sudan and even beyond to the Oyo and through them to the other Yoruba.

Thus the state of Oyo came to be firmly established as a power in northern Yorubaland, at a period which can be provisionally and tentatively assigned to the fourteenth century.[4] The names of two early Alafin (if the title was used then), Aganju and Oluaso, are recalled as long-lived and strong rulers. Between their reigns came that of Kori, who is believed to have established a subordinate king at Ede, on the frontiers of the growing Oyo influence and nearly 100 miles to the south. The duty of this ruler, entitled the Timi, was to protect the kingdom against the neighbouring Ijesa, or, in another tradition, against the Nupe.

Under Onigbogi, Oluaso's son, a time of troubles began.[5] There was discontent both in the capital and in the subordinate towns. While the army was dealing with rebellion by one of these towns, Oyo itself was attacked by Nupe from across the

D

Niger. Onigbogi was forced to flee from his capital, making his way north-west into the country of the Borgu, a people who, like the Yoruba, were divided among a number of kingdoms. Here he might expect to find friends and allies; not only was his wife, the Iyalagbon (mother of the Aręmo or eldest prince), a woman of Borgu but also the senior of the Borgu rulers, the King of Bussa (farther up the Niger), claimed a common ancestry with the Alafin, since according to the tradition of his country both descended from Kisra – that elusive hero who figures in Nigerian legend as an ancestor also of the Hausa and who, like Oduduwa, entered West Africa 'from the east'.

Relations between Onigbogi and his Borgu host – who was more likely to have been the ruler of Nikki than of Bussa[6] – were apparently cordial, for Onigbogi was allowed to settle with his followers at a place called Gbere, apparently a few miles north of the Mọṣi, the river which formed the boundary between the Borgu and the Ọyọ.[7] Here Onigbogi died, to be succeeded by his eldest son Ofinran. But now relations between the exiled Ọyọ and the Borgu began to deteriorate, and eventually Ofinran decided to return to his own land. According to a story preserved by the Bada of Ṣaki,[8] he was opposed in this by the Borgu, and the escape had to be accomplished by a ruse, a Nupe man in Ofinran's party carving models of archers which were placed in the bush to cover the withdrawal of the Ọyọ.

From Gbere the Alafin travelled some fifty miles to the south into his own country, halting eventually at Kuṣu on the banks of the Okin stream. Here the Court remained for some years, during which, it is said, the Ifa and Egungun mysteries were introduced among them. At last Ofinran was ready to set out again for the old capital, but he died before he could leave, being succeeded by his son the Aręmo Egunoju. His *oriki*, or praise words, describe him as one 'not fearing a fight' (*Ofinran ko kọ'ja*). The new Alafin now left Kuṣu, but before he turned in the direction of Ọyọ ile he settled for some years in the town of Ṣaki. Eventually, after disagreements with the Ṣaki people, he set out towards Ọyọ. But about half-way along his path he came to a hilly place where two streams flowed together; here, propitious omens suggested that a halt should be made and a town established. Thus it came about that a new capital, called Ọyọ Igboho, was founded, destined to be occupied by Egunoju for the rest of his reign and by three of his successors.

Igboho offered security to the Court after its long wanderings and its natural defences were presumably soon strengthened (it became famous for its triple walls), so that the Ọyọ were enabled to resist the continued menace from the Nupe and now also from the Borgu, dangers which, it may be assumed, made hazardous the reoccupation of the ruined and more exposed former capital. Egunoju's reign was followed by that of Ọrọmpọtọ, who, according to tradition in Igboho (though not in New Ọyọ), was a woman ruler (*ọba obinrin*), but who in any case is remembered as having formed a large army whose rearguard alone consisted of 1,000 horsemen and 1,000 foot-soldiers.

Ọrọmpọtọ was succeeded by Ajiboyede, called also Ṣopasan, whose stern character is recalled by his *oriki*: '. . . the world complained to God, and God gave them ọba Ṣopasan who flogged many of them to death.' During this reign the Nupe sent yet another expedition against the Ọyọ, which penetrated as far as Igboho itself. The counter-attacks of the Eṣọ, the Alafin's Noble Guard of seventy leading warriors, had failed to halt the enemy when the tide of battle was turned by a curious episode. In order to protect the Alafin, a warrior named Ajanlapa exchanged clothes with him and drew on himself the concentrated fire of the Nupe bowmen. His dead body, transfixed by their arrows, remained upright, his teeth set as in a grin. The Nupe, supposing themselves to be opposed by a supernatural being, fled in terror from the field, leaving their king a prisoner of the Ọyọ. Ajanlapa's son was later honoured with the right of intimate attendance on the Alafin and of deputizing for him on certain public occasions. This office, whose holder was called the *Osi 'efa* ('the deputy on the left hand'), has continued at Ọyọ to this day.

The last of the Igboho Alafin was Abipa, said to have been born to one of Egunoju's queens as the royal party was approaching Igboho from Ṣaki (his name is a contraction of *a bi si ipa* – 'one born on the wayside'). The menace from the Nupe had now been contained, and Abipa determined to carry out the return to Ọyọ ile. His leading nobles, unwilling to abandon their farms and houses at Igboho, tried to frustrate his decision by a trick. Hearing that the Alafin had decided to send an advance party to reconnoitre the site of the old city, each dispatched there one of those unfortunates called *enia oriṣa*, 'people of the gods': the Baṣọrun sent a hunchback, the Asipa a leper, the Alapini an albino, the Ṣamu a man with a projecting jaw, and the Akiniku a cripple. When the royal messengers arrived at the site of the former palace, where they were to offer sacrifices, these odd creatures roamed all night over the nearby Ajaka hill with torches in their hands, hooting and shrieking *'ko si aiye, ko si aiye'* ('no room, no room'). The terrified messengers hastened back to tell the Alafin of their adventure, but Abipa soon learnt what had happened and sent six hunters to round up the bogus phantoms. From this episode he received the attributive name by which he is often referred to in Ọyọ, *Ọba m'ọrọ*, 'the king who caught ghosts', and Old Ọyọ itself is often called Ọyọ ọrọ, 'Ọyọ of the ghosts'. The story is still re-enacted during annual festivals at Ọyọ and on the installation of a new Alafin (and in recent years has provided a plot for one of Duro Ladipọ's folk operas).

Ọyọ ile was re-occupied, it seems, only towards the end of Abipa's reign, a halt being made for some time at an intermediate place known as Kogbaye ('not room enough'), perhaps while the former capital was being repaired or rebuilt. When at last the royal party re-entered Ọyọ, sacrifices were offered by the palace priests, and the Alafin gained further honour with his people by handing over for this purpose a son newly born to one of his wives. His oriki refers to him as '. . . the royal catcher of ghosts who sacrificed his son for the peace of the world' (. . . ọba mọrọ ti o fi 'ọmọ re tun'lẹ nitori ki aiye le roju). The return was marred, however, by a quarrel with the Ijẹṣa, who had been absent from the delegations sent from other parts of Yorubaland to congratulate the Alafin. Subsequently the Ọyọ army set out to punish the Ijẹṣa, but was forced to retreat with the loss of many warriors.

Meanwhile, after the departure of the Alafin, Igboho continued to be a place of importance, and in the early nineteenth century it was still accounted by Lander, the Cornish traveller, as 'the second town in the kingdom'.[9] Despite the stormy events of that century, the town survived, and today the Alafin's representatives still rule there, the remains of its three lines of massive earthen ramparts can be seen, and the graves of four of the five Alafin who died in exile (Ofinran, Egunoju, Ọrọmpọtọ, and Ajiboyede) are tended by an official established there for the purpose.

The exile of the Alafin from Ọyọ has been described at some length partly in order to illustrate the nature and wealth of oral material which is available, and the extent to which Johnson's account, based on material gathered mainly at New Ọyọ, can still be supplemented, even for such relatively distant periods, from additional sources, and partly because the recovery in the fortunes of Ọyọ which occurred during the sojourn at Igboho seems to have marked the beginning of the rise of Ọyọ to its predominant position. Under a series of resolute and capable rulers, this northern Yoruba state was rescued from near collapse and the foundations for future advance were laid. The introduction (at Kuṣu) of new forms of religion, Ifa and Egungun, which survive among the Yoruba to this day, must have had a tonic effect upon the morale of the Alafin's subjects. A military reform carried out by Onigbogi, by which half the Eṣo were required always to be available for the defence of the capital, and the enlargement of the army, with emphasis on the cavalry, which is suggested by the account of Orompoto's re-organization, made the Oyo strong enough to face and repel the attacks of their Borgu and Nupe neighbours. Again, the history of the royal succession suggests that some constitutional advance may have resulted from the difficulties which the kingdom underwent during the exile, since, after Orompoto (a doubtful example in any case) and with the exception of Ayibi, no regencies or accessions to the throne of minors were recorded in Oyo. It seems likely that either at Igboho or in the hundred years after the return to Oyo ile the principle was established by which the most suitable of the princes stemming from Oluaso became candidates for the succession on the Alafin's death, to be chosen by the Council known as the Oyo Mesi, thus superseding the system of primogeniture which had apparently been followed previously. (The first Alafin to whom Johnson refers as having been 'elected' was Ayibi, and in his case, though he was too young to rule, the electors wished to do honour to his dead father, whose own father, the hated Alafin Jayin, had been suspected of murdering him.)

Finally, the Alafin at Igboho were favoured, as are all successful men in the end, by good fortune. This was especially so in their external relations. While the fall of Oyo ile was in large measure due to the dynamism and power of the Nupe (who may have been welded into one kingdom at about this time), the recovery of Oyo at Igboho seems equally to reflect a slackening of Nupe aggressiveness. Thus, having met the challenge of adversity (to use Toynbeean language), the Oyo were enabled first to hold out against the onslaught of their enemies, then to return to their former capital, and lastly to establish their own empire from the Niger bend, and perhaps beyond, to the coast south of Dahomey.

The return of the Oyo to their old capital, now strengthened against the Nupe and Borgu, was followed by an expansion of their kingdom. In the first place they asserted, or perhaps re-asserted, their authority over the country to the south of the capital, extending roughly to where the present New Ọyọ lies on the edge of the forest. Here in the Ọyọ kingdom, or 'Yoruba Proper' as it was called in the last century, are still found many old towns, such as Ṣaki, Iseyin, Igbetti, Kiṣi, and Ilọrin, all owing allegiance to the Alafin but ruled by their own ọba. Until the Moslem 'holy war' against the Ọyọ by the Fulani in the nineteenth century, this northern part of Yorubaland seems to have been more prosperous and populous, and certainly contained many more towns and villages, than today.

The Ọyọ next began to extend their influence over the other Yoruba kingdoms. It is difficult to determine the extent to which they were successful in this, and tradition is silent about the process of expansion. The strong Owu kingdom became their vassal state in the south, while Ẹdẹ protected them on the south-east. But they were now entering a region where the forests detracted from the effectiveness of their cavalry, and Johnson's only reference to Ọyọ's wars against her sister-states of the Ifẹ tradition is his account of how the army, unaccustomed to fighting in the bush, was defeated by the Ijẹṣa in the reign of Alafin Ọbalokun (just as they had been under his predecessor Abipa). It seems likely that the Ọyọ never succeeded in controlling either the Ijẹbu or the southern Ekiti; the hills and forests of the latter would have constituted an especially formidable obstacle, and it has been suggested that this area was regarded in Ọyọ as a reservoir where captives could be taken for the slave trade, which came to play a large part in their economy from the latter part of the seventeenth century. This was also an area where expansion was checked by the powerful Edo kingdom of Benin. The traditions of the latter relate that war occurred between Ọyọ and Benin in the time of the warrior Oba Ehengbuda, who is believed to have reigned in the last quarter of the sixteenth century. At the end of this war the armies of the Oba and the Alafin are said to have planted trees at Ọtun in the savannah of northern Ekiti to demarcate the frontier between their kingdoms.[10] Though it is impossible to substantiate the claim that Ifẹ and Ijẹṣa were brought within the 'empire' of Ọyọ (either as semi-independent provinces or merely as tributaries), there is no doubt that the extensive countries of the Ẹgba and the Ẹgbado were subject to Ọyọ, and it was through the latter's territory that ran Ọyọ's vital south-western trade-routes to the coast.

The growth of Ọyọ was by no means confined to Yorubaland (and it is unlikely that any distinction was made or felt between Yoruba and non-Yoruba before the nineteenth century). To the east and north of the capital respectively, parts of the territories of their old enemies and neighbours, the Nupe (called 'Tapa' by them) and the Borgu ('Ibariba'), were conquered by the Alafin's armies, a development which probably preceded the extension of the power of Ọyọ to the south and south-west. These non-Yoruba areas, as far as the Niger on the north-east, probably, remained tributary to Ọyọ until quite late in the eighteenth century. That the Alafin had confidence in the loyalty of his northern subjects is shown by the appointment of Nupe as his representatives in the client kingdom of Ijana in south-western Yorubaland[11] and by the Borgu origin of the ruling families of several towns in Yoruba Proper, notably Ṣaki, Kiṣi, and Ogbomọṣọ.

But it was in the economically important south-west that Ọyọ's expansion was most marked. In the reign of the warrior king Ajagbo (probably about the middle of the seventeenth century), 'Iweme in the Popo country' (the small state of Weme on the Nokwe coastal lagoon) was destroyed by the Alafin's army,[12] which implies that the Ọyọ had already brought under control the intervening territories of Ketu, Ẹgba, and Ẹgbado. Then in 1698 they overran the kingdom of Allada, some twenty-five miles inland, apparently a repetition of a previous attack in 1680–2.[13] During the first half of the eighteenth century, a period which has been described as Ọyọ's 'golden age of imperial conquest', the Ọyọ succeeded in imposing their authority over the emergent Fon kingdom of Dahomey (sometimes known after its capital as 'Abomey'), farther inland from Allada, and the coastal area which was the home of the Ewe and Adja people (who, it has been claimed, are related to the Yoruba and originally migrated from their country[14]). Between 1726 and 1730 the Ọyọ army undertook four expeditions against Dahomey, the first being a consequence of an invasion in 1724 of Allada, now tributary to Ọyọ, by Agaja, the Dahomean king, and the subsequent ones being occasioned by Agaja's invasion in 1727 of Whydah, which, with Weme and Allada, sent messengers to Ọyọ imploring the Alafin's help. In 1730 the Ọyọ reached an important agreement with the Dahomeans under which the latter were to pay an annual tribute to the Alafin and to respect the independence of the surrounding states.[15] These expeditions took place during the reign at Ọyọ of Ojigi, one of the most successful Alafin and a ruler who could rely on the support of such prominent men among his chiefs as Baṣọrun Yau Yamba and Gbọnka (general) Latoyo. After Ojigi's death about 1735 the Dahomeans broke the agreement of 1730, and the Ọyọ army was twice dispatched against them, until in 1748 Tegbesu, Agaja's successor, agreed to a re-imposition of the 1730 terms, said to include an annual payment of forty men, forty women, forty guns, and 400 loads of cowries and corals. This tribute was paid each November to Ọyọ representatives at Kana (or Calamina), a few miles southwest of Abomey. In addition, Ọyọ 'ambassadors' were sent to Abomey, where they could keep the Alafin informed of events in the Dahomey kingdom.[16]

Johnson records that the glories of Ojigi's reign were consummated by a military expedition which encircled the Alafin's domain, first going north (through the Nupe province) to the Niger, proceeding south along the west bank until the coast was reached, then west to the country of the Popo, and returning north-eastwards to the capital. This demonstrated, Johnson writes, the 'sovereignty' of Ọyọ over a vast area which, he adds, even included Benin.[17] The account seems exaggerated. As suggested above, it is unlikely that the authority of Ọyọ was ever a continuing reality in south-eastern Yorubaland, and it is even more unlikely that Benin was subject to Ọyọ, though there was debatable territory between them. Nevertheless, the tradition of this great sweep through the land by the Alafin's army indicates that at this time Ọyọ power was felt from the coast to the Niger bend, and that the empire in this reign stood at the zenith of its power and its greatest territorial extent.

At the centre of this formidable state of Guinea was its divine king, the Alafin. Ọyọ history is mainly recollected according to the Alafin, in whose reign occurred memorable events. This, although a convenient and natural method for the *arọken* (the court drummers and official historians) to follow, does not imply that the Alafin was always a dominant figure nor that he wielded autocratic power; he was in fact subject, like all Yoruba ọba, to elaborate restraints embedded in the custom (which can justifiably be called the constitution) of the kingdom. He had to submit his decisions in the first place to his council of seven notabilities, the Ọyọ Mesi, whose principal officer was the chief known as the Basọrun. In turn, the Ọyọ Mesi were checked by the council of the Ogboni, a society which, in its worship of the earth, embodied both religious and political sanctions. An Alafin of strong and resolute character could initiate and carry through a policy, obtaining the support and perhaps sometimes overruling the opposition of his counsellors. But not all Alafin were of this calibre, and the constitutional restraints on them were always stringent. The Ọyọ Mesi were even entitled to pronounce a sentence of rejection on an Alafin, upon whose receipt (it was sometimes tactfully conveyed by a symbolic gift of parrots' eggs), the king was bound to commit suicide. The first recorded rejection and suicide seems to be that

of Alafin Ayibi.[18] Another rule, apparently established during
the reign of Ojigi, provided that the Arẹmọ, the Alafin's eldest
son, should take poison on his father's death, the intention
being doubtless to protect the ọba and his officers against the
possible ambitions of a prince who was usually associated with
his father in the Government.[19]

The system of government of the capital was repeated on a
smaller scale in the provincial towns of the kingdom, and
paralleled also in the subject kingdoms. There are many
indications that these latter were allowed by Ǫyǫ to retain a
large measure of independence, although regular tribute had
to be paid and the Alafin sometimes assumed the right to
nominate a new ruler, and his confirmation of one was required.
Ǫyǫ authority was expressed in a form of indirect rule by the
stationing all over the empire of resident political representatives known as *ajẹlẹ – asoju oba*, 'the eyes of the king' – who
in turn were supervised by the *ilari*, the royal messengers from
Ǫyǫ. But in some places client kingdoms or towns were founded,
as was the case at Ẹdẹ or among the Ẹgbado on the road to the
sea.

The military strength of the Ǫyǫ goes far to explain their predominance over their neighbours. Another factor underlying
the growth of Ǫyǫ's power, and also its expansion south-
westwards, was the capital's position as a commercial centre.
Ǫyǫ ile was so situated that it linked together the trade of the
coast, where from the late fifteenth century European traders
had been active, with that of the cities of the West Sudan. Most
important, the Ǫyǫ had become by the late seventeenth century
exporters on a large scale of slaves for the Atlantic trade. In
return they received iron, salt, cutlasses, and such luxuries as
cloth and mirrors; rather oddly, firearms do not seem to have
featured among their imports (except for the tribute from the
Dahomeans) until the early nineteenth century.

The earliest route for Ǫyǫ's south-western trade seems to
have led through the territories of Ketu, then round the Kumi

swamps to Allada, and thence to the port of Whydah (or Ouidah), a distance of over 200 miles.[20] The route ran through country where a break in the forest belt must have enabled the Ọyọ cavalry to give protection to the caravans almost as far as the coast. But the rise of Dahomey towards the end of the seventeenth century threatened this access to the sea, while in the same century the westward expansion of Benin, which had already set up a number of subject towns on or near to the coast, including Lagos and Ado, posed a similar threat. Probably as a result, the trade route was shifted to the east and passed through the vassal kingdom of Ifọnyin and its two off-shoots, Ihumbọ and Ikọlaje, which were founded by the Ọyọ on Ketu territory about 1700.[21] For greater security, however, the route was later moved still farther to the east, leading to the development of Badagry and Porto Novo (Ajaṣẹ), both of which were tributary to Ọyọ, as the principal outlets for Ọyọ trade. This easternmost route – the 'Ẹgbado trade corridor' – was protected by a series of towns, notably Ilaro, Ijanna, and Jiga, which, Morton-Williams considers, were probably founded by Ọyọ during the long reign of Alafin Abiọdun (about 1770–89).[22]

Ọyọ's northern trade was almost certainly of greater anti-quity than its connections with the coast. Probably the main routes were two: one towards the Niger at Bussa, where there was a ford, and the other to the Niger crossing at Jebba island on the edge of Nupe country. The most important items sent northwards seem to have been kola nuts from the forests to the south-west, peppers grown near the coast, cloth, and marine or European salt. Possibly slaves were sent from or through Ọyọ to the northern markets, but there are no indications of such a trade on a large scale. In return, many different items were imported, deriving either from the West Sudan itself or from the trans-Saharan trade, in particular horses, natron, swords, and knives, leather, beads, unwrought silk, and in early times probably Saharan salt (Johnson records that salt was first introduced into Ọyọ during the reign of Ọbalokun, the first

Alafin after the return from Igboho, but he does not indicate its provenance).[23] The Ọyọ probably purchased slaves as well as horses from the Nupe, since in the late eighteenth century they were supplying Hausa slaves to Porto Novo.[24]

Ọyọ's great age of conquest covered the reigns of Ojigi and his second and third successors, Amuniwaiye and Oniṣile. It was followed by 'the age of Gaha' – to use Akinjogbin's terminology – which lasted from 1754 to 1774. The beginning of the reign of Labisi saw the advent to power of Gaha, a son of the former Baṣọrun Yamba, who succeeded to his father's office and then subjected both the Crown and Government of Ọyọ to his personal rule. Johnson summarizes his career thus: 'He lived to a good old age, and wielded his power ruthlessly. He was noted for having raised five kings to the throne, of whom he murdered four, and was himself murdered by the fifth.'[25]

The ascendancy of Gaha and the violent deaths of the four Alafin have reasonably been interpreted as symptoms of the approaching decline of Ọyọ. But Akinjogbin argues that the primary significance of the Baṣọrun's career was that it reflected a dilemma which now confronted the government of Ọyọ: whether to continue on the path of territorial expansion or whether to consolidate and concentrate on the economic opportunities which had been opened up, especially the ever-increasing trade in slaves through Badagry and Porto Novo.[26] He claims that it was the Alafin who were anxious to preserve peace and expand trade, while the Baṣọrun stood for a forward military policy. In the event neither policy could be carried out consistently. Although Gaha succeeded in imposing his will in internal matters, he could make no major war, since under the constitution only the Alafin could give the order for a military expedition (although on one occasion Gaha did insist on war being waged against the Ẹlẹhin-Odo, the Ifọnyin vassal king whose display of wealth when on a visit to Alafin Agboluaje at

Ọyọ had angered him). Akinjogbin concludes: 'The only possible achievement was to maintain a *status quo* and this Gaha
did, to his eternal credit . . . he kept the boundaries of the Empire
intact and completely inviolate.' Perhaps, however, he did more
than that, since a trader's report of 1764 suggests that an Ọyọ
army stationed – or at any rate, operating – as far west as
Atakpame had in that year defeated an Ashanti army there.[27]
That the power of the Ọyọ continued to impress their neighbours is confirmed by what Robert Norris heard of them in
Dahomey: 'The Dahomans may possibly exaggerate,' he wrote,
'but the Eyeos are certainly a very populous, warlike and
powerful nation.'[28]

During the reign of Majẹogbe Gaha's power was at its zenith.
According to Johnson, he had stationed his sons as his agents in
every part of the kingdom, and it was to them instead of to the
Alafin that tribute was paid. Meanwhile Majẹogbe, who was
living in constant fear for his life, attempted to rid himself of
the Bashọrun by magic (or poison?) and had so far succeeded that
Gaha was disabled in both his legs. But Gaha resorted to still
more powerful magic by which he finally encompassed the
Alafin's death, an event which apparently occurred in about
1770.[29] By now the Bashọrun's physical powers were waning,
and Abiọdun, the new Alafin, was content to bide his time until
in 1774 he felt strong enough to challenge him. He negotiated
through an intermediary with the Kakamfo Ọyabi (commander
of the frontier army), who at this time was stationed at Ajashẹ,[30]
and who agreed to lead his troops to Ọyọ to support the Alafin.
There ensued a short, sharp struggle inside the capital between
the Kakamfo's men and Gaha's family and supporters. After a
desperate resistance the Bashọrun's compound was entered and
put to fire, and Gaha himself was taken captive. His end was
violent. Johnson writes that he was ceremonially burnt, but
another account is that his body was cut in pieces and distributed over the empire.[31]

Akinjogbin maintains that the overthrow of Gaha was 'no

more than the usual power tussle in the capital' and did not imply any weakening in the empire. Indeed, Abiọdun's success greatly strengthened his personal authority. Yet the career of Gaha, with its defiance of the hallowed institutions of the kingdom, must in the long run have diminished the prestige of the Alafinate and set an example of disloyalty in high places to future generations.

Abiọdun now proved himself a strong and capable ruler, and his reign is still remembered as an age of peace and prosperity before the storm. The kingdom of Dahomey, for example, was so firmly under the sway of Ọyọ that the Alafin was apparently able to use its army (perhaps to the detriment of his own forces) to carry out his policies in the south-west. In 1784 a strong Dahomean army, joined by contingents from the western Yoruba and supported by Lagos, attacked Badagry; according to Dalzel, 'The operations of the Dahoman army were directed by the Eyeo messengers, who had conducted them hither; and nothing of importance was undertaken without their concurrence.'[32] In 1786, again apparently at the suggestion of Ọyọ, the Dahomeans took Weme, but when they proposed to follow this up by an attack on Ardra and Porto Novo the Alafin forebade the enterprise: 'Ardrah was Eyeo's calabash out of which nobody should be permitted to eat but himself.'[33]

Yet it is evident that during Abiọdun's reign the army, on which the power and wealth of the kingdom depended, declined in effectiveness. The reasons for this are not clear. Akinjogbin surmises that the very nature of the Alafin's victory over Gaha involved a diminution in the influence of the military leaders and thus, he implies, an eventual lowering of the efficiency of the army.[34] This is not wholly convincing, especially as it was the co-operation of the army and its general which had enabled the Alafin to triumph in this crisis. Possibly the sense of security which he felt after ridding the kingdom of its overmighty Baṣọrun led Abiọdun to neglect his military forces, or possibly the inactivity of the first peaceful years of the reign after 1774 diminished the capacity of the Ọyọ for waging war. Whatever the explanation, the Ọyọ army was heavily defeated by the Borgu in 1783, six years before Abiọdun's death in (probably) 1789, and in 1791, during the reign of his successor, the unfortunate Awọlẹ, the Nupe inflicted a similar blow on the kingdom.[35]

By the end of the century the influence o f the Ọyọ to the north and east of their capital, across the Mọsi and to the Niger, had been overthrown, despite the fact that this was an area within which their cavalry operated under favourable physical conditions. It even seems (if credence can be given to a contemporary report in Dahomey[36]) that in the late eighteenth century the Nupe were exacting tribute from the Ọyọ and that the Ọyọ expedition of 1791, so far from being an attempt to reassert ascendancy over the Nupe, was designed to end their own subjection. Still more serious, at about this time the Ẹgba of the southern forest rose in revolt against the Ọyọ ajẹlẹ stationed in their towns and gained their independence, an event which seems to have taken place about 1796. This had two dire consequences for the Ọyọ: first, it endangered their important trade route to the coast, and secondly, it set an example of rebellion to the other Yoruba states under their control. Thus the eighteenth century saw both the apotheosis of the empire of Ọyọ and the first stages of what was to be a swift decline.

IV · Kingdoms of the East:
Ijẹṣa, Ekiti, Ọwọ, and Ondo

Ile Ifẹ, the historic centre of the Yoruba, lies in a level land of
tall and dense forest, a closed landscape befitting its many
mysteries. But east from Ifẹ the scene changes as the wooded
hills of Ilẹṣa are reached and then the rocky summits of Ekiti.
Here, in an Arcadian country where gods and goddesses abound
in the rivers and on the hilltops, kingdoms proliferate. They
range in size from Ijẹṣa, Ondo, and Ọwọ, each occupying something like the area of an English county, to the miniature states
of Ekiti.

Ijẹṣa

The Ijẹṣa have sometimes been grouped by writers about the
Yoruba with the Ifẹ,[1] but their political and cultural traditions,
history, and dialect all emphasize their separateness. Their
kingship is held to derive from Ifẹ, and their ruler, the Ọwa,
wears a beaded crown. Ilẹṣa, his capital, is the centre of a district of some forty square miles, the heart of the former kingdom, which stretches from Ifẹ and Oṣogbo on the west to Ekiti
on the east; it is bounded on the north by the little-known
Igbomina kingdom of Ila under its ruler, the Ọrangun, and on
the south by Ondo, ruled by the Oṣemawe. Writing about the
origin of the Ijẹṣa, Johnson suggests that their name is a contraction from *ijẹ oriṣa*, 'the food of the gods', and refers to that
part of the people already living in the area before the arrival
of the founder of the present kingship from Ifẹ, and who were

looked upon by their neighbours as potential sacrificial victims – hence their name – and slaves.[2] He adds that until the abolition of human sacrifice by the British at the end of the last century, the Ijẹṣa continued to be preferred, especially by the Ifẹ, to other victims.

Ajaka (alternatively Ajibogun), the founder of the Ijẹṣa kingdom, is described in local tradition as a son of Oduduwa by the sister of one of his wives.[3] The legend relates that as Oduduwa grew old his eyes dimmed, so that at last he was advised by an Ifa priest to send for sea-water to bathe them. But the princes held back from making the long and hazardous journey to the coast, until finally Ajaka, youngest or (from the circumstances of his birth) lowest-ranking among them, offered to perform this service. After many adventures and the passage of years, Ajaka returned to his father's court at Ifẹ. When he entered the market-place the people there, astonished to see him after so long an absence, called out *O wa!* ('So you are back') – from which the title of Ilẹṣa's ọba, the Ọwa, derives; he replied *Mo b'okun* ('I have the sea-water') – and was thereafter called Obokun. Then he gave the water to Oduduwa, who (the story contains no more surprises) regained his sight.

During Obokun's long absence Oduduwa's two eldest sons had died, and the other princes, taking with them their inheritance from their father, had left Ifẹ to found their own kingdoms. The only reward for Obokun was a sword, *ida ajaṣẹ*, 'the sword of victory'. With this he angrily pursued his brothers, seized from them a share of the family treasure, and returned to Ifẹ. As he entered the Court he mistook his father, whose face was hidden by the beaded fringe of his crown, for one of his brothers and raised his sword against him. Slicing off the fringe of the crown, he realized, just in time, his dreadful error. Soon after this he left Ifẹ to found his own kingdom and was given by his father a crown which was like that of his brothers' except in one particular, that it had no fringe at the front, a peculiarity still preserved in the crowns worn by the Ọwa Obokun of

Ijẹṣa. The event is described in an Ijẹṣa song:

The ebon rider	*Okunrin dudu ori ẹṣin,*
The lord who was given beads for propitiating the earth,	*Oluwa Okile gb'okun,*
	Ajaka onida arara,
Ajaka, master of the sharp sword,	*O b'okun ja,*
He fought the sea,	*O bokun jo r'ele.*
He danced home with the sea.	

Armed with his sword, Obokun led his followers to a place known as Igbadaye,[4] where they settled. It is said that he alone of Oduduwa's sons returned to Ifẹ (no great journey for him) to attend the ceremonies which followed his father's death. He himself died at Igbadaye, and his son, Ọwa Oke Okile, resumed the migration, leaving in charge of Obokun's grave a follower whose descendants still rule there with the title of Agbadaye. The next settlement was at Ilọwa ('the Ọwa's town'), and then in the next reign the Ọwa and his people removed yet again to Ilemure, renamed Ibokun, where the Ọwa displaced the Ita, a king whom he found already installed there. During their sojourn in Ibokun the Ọwa brought under his control the town of Ilare, whose ruler, the Alare, claimed (like the Ọwa and even the Ita) to have received a crown from Ifẹ. Then from Ibokun the next Ọwa, Ọwari, removed to Ilaje, four miles distant, called after his death Ipole Ijẹṣa. Finally, in the fifth reign, that of Ọwa Oge, the town of Ileṣa was chosen as capital. Tradition relates that it was already famous for the water-pots made by its women, a circumstance from which its name may derive: *ile iṣa*, 'the town of water-pots', though it may also mean 'town of the gods'. It was already ruled by a king, the Onila (the 'king of the okro planters', who had built the town), who now became deputy to the Ọwa and whose successor, the Ọbala, still ranks second in Ileṣa. According to Johnson, the town was rebuilt, and in this the Ijẹṣa called on the help of a prince from the Alafin's family so that it could be laid out on the same plan as that of Ọyọ ile.

A list has been preserved of the names of thirty-eight predecessors to the present ọba; it is alleged that in addition the names of nine Ọwa have been lost, five of these having died before their coronation.[5] Of those named, five are said to have been women, but there has been no female ruler since Yeyeori, the eighteenth Ọwa. Little is recalled about the history of the Ijẹsa in early times. A derisory epithet sometimes applied to them, 'children of sticks' (ọmọ igi), is explained by the myth that Obokun, the first Ọwa, found himself short of subjects and by magic converted bundles of sticks into human beings – which may reflect the thinness of the population in these forests at the period. Johnson adds unkindly that the epithet may instead be accounted for by the nature of the Ijẹsa, who are 'as proverbially deficient in wit as they are remarkably distinguished for brute strength'.[6] At all events, the Ijẹsa, as ọmọ Obokun, were famous warriors, and in their heyday (which may have preceded the rise of the Ọyọ empire but more probably came during Ọyọ's decline at the end of the eighteenth century) their kingdom evidently occupied a considerably greater extent than the present boundaries of Ijẹsaland, since Ijẹsa communities are found in the Ọsun area to the north-west (usually accounted a part of Ọyọ), and to the east among the Ekiti, Akoko, and Ọwọ.

Over many of the places conquered or settled by his warriors, it was the Ọwa's custom to place as ruler one of his sons. Descendants of these princes are known in the kingdom by the title of Lọja. There are now seventeen Lọja among the minor rulers of Ijẹsaland, and every new Ọwa was required to have served as a Lọja in the provinces before becoming eligible for the throne.[7]

At some time, probably in the seventeenth century, a group of Ijẹsa founded the now-important town of Oṣogbo on the River Ọsun, some twenty miles to the north-west of Ilesa. This may have been intended, as Johnson suggests, as an outpost against the Ọyọ and an answer to the establishment by them of the warrior Timi as ruler at nearby Ẹdẹ.[8] Apart from this, there are no indications in Ijẹsa tradition about relations with their powerful Ọyọ neighbours. Nothing is heard, for example, of the stationing in the kingdom of the Alafin's ajẹlẹ nor of the visits with presents which, Johnson alleges,[9] were made annually by the Ọwa to the Alafin. This is not surprising, since tradition tends to suppress the disagreeable – though on the part of the Ọyọ, Johnson does record the defeat of an expedition sent by Alafin Ọbalokun into Ijẹsa country, 'the Ọyọs being then un-accustomed to bush fighting'.[10] On balance, the claim by Ọyọ to have achieved political hegemony over eastern Yorubaland seems likely to allude to no more than the occasional exaction of tribute.

Ọyọ was not the Ijẹsa's only powerful and ambitious neigh-bour. To the east lay the kingdom of Benin, and though the Ekiti provided a buffer between them, Benin seems at times to have exercised some influence at Ilesa. It is related that the seventh Ọwa, Atakunmasa, spent a number of years in exile in Benin. During his absence the throne was occupied by two women rulers, also styled Ọwa. Kẹnyo's version of the legend is that the purpose of the ọba's sojourn in Benin was to 'to study effective medicine . . . in order that his wives might begin to bring forth male children'. The Benin account is that after an already long reign the Ọwa's restless subjects wanted a change of ruler, and so sent Atakunmasa into exile; the Oba of Benin eventually summoned their elders and persuaded them to allow the Ọwa to return.[11]

Ekiti

The Ekiti and Ọwọ form the marches of the Yoruba with the Igbira, Kukuruku, and Edo or Bini of the Benin kingdom. There are many recollections of incursions here by the Benin army, and it seems that at times parts of the area were subject to the rule of Benin. At least one of the Ekiti dynasties, that of

Ikẹrrẹ, was established by Benin, and in some towns there are groups who, though they are now Yoruba-speaking, trace their descent from Bini settlers there – for example, the Ado living in the Igiso, Eyinke, and Oritogun wards of Akure. Little is recorded about relations between the Ọyọ and the people of this area, and Ekiti traditions are silent on the subject. As suggested in the last chapter,[12] Ekiti may have been looked upon by the Ọyọ as too difficult and rugged a terrain to control politically, and convenient therefore to be left for slave-raiding. The establishment of the Ọyọ–Benin frontier at Ọtun does, however, imply that the northern part of Ekiti was regarded as within the sphere of Ọyọ.

The name 'Ekiti' denotes a country of hills, and it is perhaps this physical feature which, more than any other factor, accounts for its division into a number of small kingdoms or city states, all centring on towns which are in the traditional definition *ilu alade*, 'towns with crowned ọba'. There has long been uncertainty as to which towns can properly be considered as belonging to Ekiti. Usually sixteen ọba are named, and from 1900 a sort of federal assembly of these rulers has met; this, the Pelu-pelu (from *pe olu*, 'to call the lords together') was based on the military league of the late nineteenth century known as the Ekiti Parapọ. All authorities seem to agree that the four leading rulers are: the Ore or Owore of Ọtun, the Ajero of Ijero, the Elẹwi or Ẹwi of Ado, and the Ẹlẹkọle of Ikọle. About the others there is less agreement, but the rulers of the following sixteen towns have been included in different lists: Efọn Alaye, Ogotun Iddo, Aiyede, Igbara Odo, Ọyẹ, Omuwo, Ire, Isẹ, Itaji, Ikẹrrẹ, Isan, Emure, Aramọkọ, Oke-Messi, and Akurẹ.[13] Most of these claim to derive their crowns and dynasties from Ifẹ.

Between the four leading *ilu alade* there has been controversy about precedence. When the Pelu-pelu first met in 1900 the presidency was given to the Ore of Ọtun, but after the administrative separation of Ọtun from the other Ekiti towns leadership passed to the Ẹwi of Ado-Ekiti, who represented the Ekiti ọba at the conference of Yoruba rulers held at Ibadan in 1939. The Ẹwi claimed, indeed, that his being placed third in rank at the 1900 convention was a mistake, arising in part from his deference to the Ẹlẹkọle (placed second) as his senior by age. But more probably Ado had lost prestige with the other Ekiti through having held aloof from the Parapọ and not having taken part in the Kiriji war fought by the Parapọ at the end of the last century.

The history and legends of Ado have been recorded by a local historian, the Rev. A. Oguntuyi. The legend of origin which he recounts follows a familiar pattern. The ancestor of the present ruler of Ado was one of Oduduwa's sixteen sons, known from his talent as an orator as *Ẹwi*, 'the speaker'. He left Ifẹ at the time of the dispersal of princes in the company of the prince who was destined to found a new dynasty at Benin. For a time these two settled side by side at Benin, but eventually they quarrelled, and Ẹwi with his followers returned westwards. The party halted in various places, and at length Ẹwi died, to be succeeded by an unrecorded number of rulers, now called 'Ẹwi' after him. Finally, they came to the site of Ado, where they made their home among the hills. The Ẹwi at this time was named Awamaro ('the restless one'), and the present ọba, his descendant, is enumerated from him as the twenty-first, though Fr. Oguntuyi thinks that a number of names of additional Ẹwi have been forgotten.[14]

As in many other places, Ado tradition records that the emigrants from Ifẹ found on their arrival that there was already an organized settlement of people living there who, it seems, spoke either the same language as themselves or one similar enough to be understood without difficulty. In this case the earlier settlers were known as the Ilẹsun and their ruler as the Ẹlẹsun. They received the newcomers kindly, but a subsequent struggle for power led to their overthrow and to the execution of the Ẹlẹsun. At the grave in the Erekesan market where Awamaro buried the Ẹlẹsun's head, all subsequent Ẹwi have carried out propitiatory ceremonies as part of their installation rites.

Oguntuyi suggests that the settlement by Awamaro at Ado was made at the end of the fourteenth or early in the fifteenth century. His precise dating for all subsequent reigns seems to have been calculated from the number of years traditionally ascribed to each reign. It can hardly be more than an approximation, but by no means a far-fetched one. During the first three or four centuries of Ado history two themes predominated. The first was the gradual expansion of the Ẹwi's rule over the surrounding district, so that today, in addition to Ado, the Ẹwi rules over seventeen subordinate towns, of which Igede is the largest. The second major theme consisted in a series of defensive wars which Ado fought with Benin. It was the expansion of Ado which apparently brought about the intervention in the area of Benin, since Ikẹrrẹ, a town some ten miles to the south of Ado which had formerly been subject to the Ẹlẹsin, invited the Oba of Benin to send his troops there. According to Oguntuyi, this occurred during the reigns at Ado of Ata, the first ọba after Awamaro whose name is recalled, and at Benin of Ewuare, and if this association with Ewuare is correct it can be ascribed to the middle or second half of the fifteenth century.[15] During the ensuing war Ekiti was overrun by the Bini, while the ruler of Ikẹrrẹ, the Olukẹrrẹ, was himself replaced by a Bini whose title was the Ogoga.[16] The Ẹwi survived, but the Bini seem to have acquired a form of suzerainty over Ado, probably expressed by the payment of tribute. Thenceforth Ikẹrrẹ under its Benin dynasty was to be a rival and a threat to Ado.

A second war between Ado and Benin took place during the reign of Ẹwi Ọbakunrin. It was again occasioned by an appeal for help to Benin by the Ikẹrrẹ, who were protesting against the Ado's attempts to enlarge the area under their control. The Ado say that in this Olupọnnọkusupọnnọ ('let everyone die in front of his own house') war, the Bini for the first time had firearms, but they merely discharged them into the air to cause terror – perhaps the most effective use of the primitive muskets which these must have been. Once again Ado submitted to Benin and affirmed its loyalty.

Another town in this region whose history is bound up with Benin is Akurẹ.[17] Although it has not always been accounted an Ekiti town, lying on the southern edge of the area, its ruler, the Deji, sat among the Ekiti ọba in the local administrative council formed in this century, occupying fifth place, until a re-organization in 1946. Accounts of the origin of the town are contradictory. S. O. Arifalo has pointed out that the people in two sections of the town, the Isikan and the Isolo, have traditions which are distinct from those of the majority of the inhabitants, and that the former claim to be the original owners of the land. Both these groups seem to represent earlier settlers on the site of Akurẹ. As to the present kingship, Arifalo has examined six different accounts.[18] The official version, not unexpectedly, traces the origin of the kingship to Ifẹ, describing how the first ọba, Asodeboyede, received the crown from Oduduwa, his grandfather. The original title of these Akurẹ kings was Ajapada, said to mean 'one who kills a rat with a rattle', derived from an endurance test which Oduduwa forced his grandson to undergo before he left Ifẹ and which is still commemorated at Akurẹ in the annual Ifunta festival when the ọba withdraws into an inner part of the afin for seven days. The majority of accounts agree that the present title of Deji arises from an episode which links the dynasty with that of Ilẹṣa. As related above, Ọwa Atakunmasa, seventh ruler of the Ijẹṣa, journeyed to Benin, where he spent some years in exile. On his way he passed through Akurẹ, and later a son was born there, either to one of the Ọwa's wives or (the story has, of course, fissiparated) to one of his daughters given in marriage to the Ajapada. When the Ọwa returned, again passing through Akurẹ, he saw this child, named Ogunja, and joyfully placed him on his knee, conferring on him a crown and the additional name of Olufadeji. When Ogunja came to the throne of Akurẹ he preferred to use the shortened form of his new name, 'Deji', as his title, and it is thus that his successors are usually known to this day.[19]

The presence in Akurẹ of a sizeable population of Bini origin, known as the Ado-Akurẹ, living in the Igiso, Eyinke, and Oritagun quarters of the town and subject to a chief known as the Olotu-Ekiran,[20] is evidence of the close relations which have existed between the two kingdoms. Akurẹ was the main base for Benin's trade in this area and, indeed, was apparently regarded at times as being within the western frontiers of that kingdom. The Ado-Akurẹ may have constituted a kind of colony like those established by Benin in the south-west, and the name 'Ado' is probably here the Yoruba form of Edo, an alternative name for the Bini. Egharevba, the Benin historian, refers to an attack by the Bini on 'rebellious Akurẹ' during the reign at Benin of Oba Ewuare. During this war the town was surrounded and all resistance eventually crushed. The ruler, whom Egharevba calls the Alakurẹ Orito – a name which does not occur in the list of forty-two rulers compiled by Arifalo – was allowed to remain as nominal head of the town, but Benin's authority was maintained by the posting there of a resident official, the Odionwere (equivalent to an Ọyọ ajẹlẹ).[21] About a century later, in the reign at Benin of Oba Ehengbuda, Akurẹ was again 'rebellious', and the Benin army under the Iyase, returning from a campaign in Yorubaland, passed through it in order to make a show of strength.[22] By the early nineteenth century Akurẹ seems to have regained its independence, but the murder there of an ambassador announcing the accession of a new Oba at Benin was followed in or about 1818 by a re-conquest in which the Deji was taken captive and executed.[23] It is nearly superfluous to add that none of these events have been admitted to Akurẹ tradition as it is related today.

One of the smallest of the independent towns in Ekiti is Ire, some fourteen miles to the north-east of Ado. It is of interest as the centre of the worship of Ogun, god of both war and iron

in the Yoruba pantheon. According to the ruler, the Onire, the
town was founded by Ogundahunsi, son of Ogun, who himself
was a son of Oduduwa – or so they say at Ire, though not at
Ifẹ. On return from a long campaign, Ogun lost his temper with
his son and killed him. Overwhelmed by remorse, he sank into
the earth at the place in Ire where his shrine now stands. The
Onire claims descent from Ogun and recites a list of rulers,
ending with himself as twenty-ninth.[24]

Another small kingdom deserving mention is Idanre, south of
Akurẹ and east of Ondo. Its old town lies under the peak of
Mount Orosun – the highest point in Western Nigeria at 3,098
feet – and until a few years ago could only be reached by rope
ladder up a vertical rock face. The ruler here, the Ọwa, claims
the usual Ifẹ ancestry, but his kingship and government are on
the Benin pattern.[25]

Smaller even than these last two states are the independent
villages of the Akoko to the east of Ekiti. In this area, writes
Forde, 'No right or authority beyond that of the village is recognized and each village or quarter of a village has its own
particular tract of land, the boundaries of which are jealously
guarded.'[26] This form of social organization is in marked contrast to the system of kingship obtaining generally among the
Yoruba and probably results from the uncertainty of life in a
marcher country and from the intermingling here of Yoruba,
Kukuruku, and Bini customs.

Ọwọ

The kingdom of Ọwọ lay athwart the approaches of Benin to
southern Yorubaland. Its role could appropriately be described
as that of a palatinate were it not that the Yoruba, despite
their common language and claims to a common ancestry and
culture, neither acted nor regarded themselves as a nation before the present century. The major units were the kingdoms,
and among these Ọwọ, although lying in an exposed position
between the more powerful Ọyọ and Benin states, was one of

the largest, its territory stretching from the Kabba country in the north (bordering the Nupe) and Akoko in the north-east to Okeluse, some 100 miles to the south. The importance of the kingdom is reflected in its afin, which, containing over one hundred courtyards, is among the largest in Yorubaland. Every town and village in the kingdom was obliged to contribute to the maintenance of this vast building.[27]

Owo's historian, Chief Asara,[28] has arranged his account under the reigns of twenty-nine rulers, the Olowo. The first was Ojugbelu, alternatively called Arere and Omolaghaiye, one of Oduduwa's sixteen sons; his pleasant manner earned him from his father yet another name, Owo, 'respectful', and this came to be applied to his followers and their descendants. According to Asara, Ojugbelu was absent from Ife on a hunting trip when the dispersal of princes took place and was obliged to hasten after his brothers and force them by his sword to give up a share of their father's treasure – a story recalling that of the Owa of Ijesa. He then parted from them and, after a halt at Uji, settled with his followers at Upafa in the south of the present kingdom. Thence, under his son, the Owo removed first to Oke-Imade and then, seeking a good supply of water, to Igbo Ogwata, now called Okiti Asegbo, near the centre of the present Owo town. There was already dwelling here a group of people led by a ruler called the Elefene. For a time the Owo were content to live alongside them, but in a later reign they were driven away. Asara, presumably working from tradition about the length of reign of each Olowo, has assigned a date at the beginning of the eleventh century to the foundation of the kingdom by Ojugbelu.

Asara, whose history (like many local histories) has a strong 'authorized' flavour, maintains that 'from the first dynasty, Owo was never conquered nor defeated by any kingdom'. This does not accord with several references to Owo in Egharevba's history of Benin. The first occurs in the reign of Ewuare, whose army is said to have captured Owo after a severe battle, but

Egharevba admits that the Benin general, Iken, was attacked and killed before he could leave the city, having sent on his soldiers in advance.[29] A few reigns later, under Oba Ozolua at Benin, Ọwọ was again attacked by a Benin army, this time submitting without a fight.[30] Egharevba and Aṣara agree, however, that Ọṣọgboye, heir to Ọlọwọ Ọmaro, was sent as a young prince to Benin for his education at the Oba's court and enrolled as a page to the Oba (*emada*, literally 'sword-bearer').[31] When Ọmaro died, Ọṣọgboye seems to have returned to Ọwọ to claim the throne without first obtaining the Oba's permission to leave the palace, and when messengers were sent to him from Benin he feigned illness. As soon as his coronation had been performed, Ọṣọgboye set about fortifying the town against an attack from Benin, causing a ditch to be dug (and presumably also a wall). The *History of Ọwọ* implies that an attack was made and repulsed, but Egharevba confines himself to saying that the Oba now 'confirmed' the Ọlọwọ's appointment and bade him continue the payment of tribute. What seems to emerge from these conflicting accounts is that the Ọwọ were able to maintain virtual independence for their capital and surrounding district, but that from time to time tribute had to be paid to Benin and probably also that the southern parts of the Ọwọ kingdom were subjected to control by the Bini in order to maintain access to the coast on the south-west (although, as will be seen in Chapter VI, a route by waterway leading to and across the lagoon was also used).

Like many Yoruba towns, Ọwọ was a centre of brass casting and of sculpture in wood and ivory. Here again the influence of Benin is evident, and Ọwọ art has been described as 'intermediate between the Yoruba and Benin styles'.[32]

Ondo

South-west from Ọwọ live the numerous people known as the Ondo, 'the settlers'. Ondo, the capital and principal town, is situated in the north-west of their extensive but somewhat amorphous kingdom in a countryside much broken up by the same system of hills as that which covers Ekiti and much of Ọwọ, and which has served as a protection against the Ọyọ and the Bini; from the latter Ondo must also have been shielded to some extent by Ọwọ. But the eastern and southern parts of the kingdom were much affected by Benin influence and settlers, and the southern region, which stretches to the intricate system of creeks and lagoons on the western edge of the Niger Delta, has been peopled by other non-Yoruba, especially the Ijọ. The Yoruba themselves are essentially an inland race, and those now in the creeks and near the coast are almost certainly late settlers there. The Mahin, living by the lagoon and coastal beach of that name, and ruled by the Amapetu, seem to have no lengthy tradition of occupation of their area, while the community of the Holy Apostles of Aiyetoro was established as a sort of phalanstery or kibbuz on a desolate and remote part of the coast, unclaimed by any of the nearby peoples, only in 1947.

There are three main accounts of the foundation of the Ondo kingship. Egharevba claims that it was founded by migrants from Benin in the time there of Oba Ozolua;[33] Johnson writes that it was founded from Ọyọ by a wife of Alafin Ajaka with her twin children, the king having sent them away from Ọyọ instead of complying with the custom of putting twins to death;[34] finally, there is a tradition preserved in Ondo itself which is similar to Johnson's account but substitutes Ifẹ for Ọyọ and is in more specific terms, and, moreover, is re-enacted annually at the ọba's festival there.[35] According to the Ondo account, it was one of the wives of Oduduwa who gave birth to the twins, a circumstance which was regarded at Ifẹ with such horror that the mother with the two babies was driven into the forest. One twin was a boy, and it was he who founded Ẹpẹ, about ten miles to the north-west of Ondo. The other was a girl, Pupupu, who became founder of Ondo and whose son Airo was the second ruler there and the builder of the town walls. The present ọba, entitled the Oṣemawe, claims to be the forty-seventh to reign over the kingdom.[36] The origin of the dynasty is reflected in the importance given to women in the government of Ondo. There is, for example, a council of women chiefs which has access to the council of males, and the Oṣemawe's installation is carried out by the leading woman chief, the Lisa Labun. But although Ondo, for reasons which are unrecorded, has far surpassed Ẹpẹ, now a mere village within the kingdom, the seniority of the ruler of Ẹpẹ, the Jegun, is acknowledged. As elsewhere, traces of settlers preceding the establishment of the present dynasty are found. Here they are the Idoko, a people who still form a separate group in Ondo with their own gods and who do not participate in the Ondo festivals.

V · Kingdoms of the West: Ketu, Ṣabe, and Dassa

The western kingdoms of the Yoruba lie for the most part beyond the frontiers of Nigeria in the neighbouring state of Dahomey – the latter a French creation in the same sense that Nigeria was created by the British, and taking its name from the Fon kingdom in the south-east of the country which had Abomey as its capital. There are nearly 200,000 Yoruba speakers in modern Dahomey, where they form about 9 per cent of the population, living in their towns and villages in the centre and south of the country, and they even extend into Togo still farther to the west. By the French administrators they were called Nago or Nagot, a word probably deriving from an opprobrious nickname given them by the Fon.[1]

Like other Yoruba, those of the west formed themselves into kingdoms. The two most important of these, Ketu and Ṣabe in central Dahomey, trace their origins to the dispersal of princes from Ifẹ, while a third, Dassa, seems to be of less antiquity. To the west of these former states, and spilling over the Togo frontier, are the groups of Yoruba speakers known as Itṣa or Ṣa; it has been suggested that at a remote period they migrated westwards from the neighbourhood of Ileṣa, but there seems little basis for this beyond a superficial resemblance in the names.[2] A separate small group, which extends to the vicinity of Atakpame in Togo, is known as the Ifẹ and claims to have migrated direct from Ile Ifẹ. To the south of Ketu a group which seems to be Yoruba in language and religion is the Ahori or Holli, living in the marshes north of Pobe. On the coastal lagoon Porto Novo, the capital of modern Dahomey, seems to have been originally a Yoruba town and is known to the Yoruba as Ajaṣẹ (which could mean 'conquered by the Adja').[3] In the hinterland of Porto Novo and stretching north to Pobe a number of once-independent towns and districts preserve traditions of migration from various parts of Yorubaland.[4] Finally, the Fon themselves are usually held to descend from a fusion of Adja conquerors with indigenous Yoruba living on the Abomey plateau.

Apart from that of Ketu, the histories of all these Yoruba are exceptionally complex and confused. Their kingdoms and chieftancies, situated precariously among other peoples and separated from each other by alien territories, were neither sufficiently large nor well organized to contain the external dangers which beset them in the eighteenth and nineteenth centuries. In the south the Gun and the Fon attacked, infiltrated, and overran their homelands; farther inland their enemies included the Fon again, the Borgu, then the Fulani of Ilọrin, and even their kinsmen from Ọyọ and Ẹgba – the latter, indeed, were known to the Ṣa as 'the sons of war' (ọmọjagun). The impression which emerges is that these were the advance guard of a migration which finally petered out, leaving them in an exposed position far from the centres of Yoruba life and sources of strength.

Ketu

An account of the westward migration from Ile Ifẹ which resulted in the foundation of Ketu and Ṣabe was recorded by the Yoruba missionary, and later Bishop, S. A. Crowther, in Ketu in 1853 and was used by Parrinder in his *Story of Ketu*.[5] Under the leadership of Ṣopasan,[6] a grandson of Oduduwa, the migrants crossed the Ogun river and then split into three groups: the first, under Ṣopasan and his nephew Owe, moved westwards and eventually founded Ketu; the second travelled first to the north-west and then was forced south again, founding

F

the kingdom of Ṣabe, while the third, according to this account, turned north up the Ogun and eventually founded the kingdom of Ọyọ. The first party settled on the hill known as Oke Ọyan, apparently in the vicinity of Ṣaki (the River Ọyan is a tributary of the Ogun), and later moved to Aro, where Ṣopasan died and was succeeded as leader by Owe.[7]

In the reign of the seventh ọba, Ede, another migration took place, and this, like the original one from Ifẹ, also split into three parties: one founded a village called Idofa after the hunter who was its leader, the second settled in Ibarapa country at Igbo Ọra, and the third, apparently the principal one, under Ede and guided by the hunter Alalumon, settled on the present site of Ketu, building their town around an iroko tree (whose alleged fragments can still be seen). Tradition recounts that Ede was accompanied from Aro by 120 families, the founders of the present wards of Ketu town. The history of the journey from Aro to Ketu is re-enacted during the installation ceremonies of every ruler, the Alaketu. One principal event which is recalled is the borrowing of fire by Alalumon on the first night at Ketu from Ya Panka, an old woman who was found living a few miles to the south. Apart from this episode, there are other indications that the Ketu encountered people already in occupation of parts of their new homeland; Parrinder considers that these cannot have been Yoruba,[8] but there is not sufficient evidence for an assertion either way.

The traditions of Ketu have been unusually well preserved and recorded. The list of Alaketu, which numbers forty-nine (including the present ọba, who was installed in 1963), is one to which considerable weight can be attached, since it was the special duty of a herald, the Baba Elegun Oyede, to recite the names and parentages of all preceding Alaketu during the coronation ceremonies. Moreover, approximate dates of reasonable reliability can be assigned to reigns from the eighteenth century onwards, partly (as in the case of Ọyọ) by cross-reference to the history of Dahomey as recorded by European writers.

Today the most striking feature of Ketu, now a remote and neglected town, is its fortifications, comprising a circuit of massive earthen walls, still in some places over twelve feet in height and nearly as broad, outer ditches to a depth of some eight or nine feet and twenty feet wide, planted with thorns, and above all the great Idena ('Sentry') Gate, a fortress in itself with inner and outer covered gateways and a central courtyard, certainly the most impressive example of Yoruba military architecture in existence.[9] Ketu historians attribute the building of these fortifications to Ṣa, the fourteenth Alaketu, and add that the ọba himself supervised the work, which was accomplished by the townspeople with the aid of two giants living near by. The Idena Gate is said to stand upon the place where Ede first entered the site of his new capital and where later a hunchbacked weaver, one of those already living on the spot when the immigrants from Ifẹ arrived, was killed as a propitiatory sacrifice – a circumstance from which the town and kingdom are said to derive their name (a proverb in the form of a riddle: *Ke 'tu ike? Ke fo ilu?*: 'Who can straighten a hunchback's hump? Who can break our town?'). Ṣa's successor, Alaketu Epo, completed the fortifications, and it is claimed that to give strength to the walls the clay was mixed with palm oil instead of water.

The extent of the kingdom can only be tentatively described. On the east it included Mẹko, some twenty miles distant from Ketu (and now within Nigeria). This had been founded as a farm from Ketu and gradually grew into a town whose wards retained the names of the different areas of Ketu whence the inhabitants had come. During the reign of Ande, the thirty-ninth Alaketu (*c.* 1760–80), a dispute arose over the Balẹ of Mẹko's claim to wear a crown and to rank as an ọba, but even down to the present time the subordination of Mẹko to Ketu is acknowledged by its inclusion in the ceremonial intineration of his kingdom by a new Alaketu, though he now has to cross a modern international frontier in performing this. To the west the kingdom was probably bounded by the River Weme (Ouéme), while on the north the Okpara seems to have separated Ketu from Ṣabe territory. Southward from the Ketu kingdom were the marshlands of the wild Ahori, who seem never to have achieved any notable degree of political organization.

For the first centuries of its existence – perhaps for some 400 years if the suggestions about chronology in Chapters I and VII are near the truth – the history of Ketu seems to have been uneventful. It may be that the passage of time has simply erased all record of triumph and disaster. On the other hand, it is equally likely, and somewhat more probable, that in this early period, when the Guinea forest and its hinterland were much denser[10] and more lightly inhabited than in modern times, a city state or small kingdom would be able to protect itself and to expand without much fear of disturbance or even much contact with outsiders. But if this happy isolation lasted up to the seventeenth century, conditions changed considerably in the following century. Ketu found itself in the path of the encroaching Ọyọ, a related state, but none the less an aggressive neighbour, and for a period, probably of a hundred years or more, it seems to have been subject or tributary to the Alafin, though doubtless regarded as a distant and unimportant vassal when shorn of those areas where Ọyọ had erected its satellites to guard the route to the coast. Two of Ọyọ's subordinate rulers, whose territories had apparently been previously a part of Ketu, the Ẹlẹhin Odo of Ifọnyin and the Onikọ of Ikọlaje, are remembered as having been accustomed to travel in company with the Alaketu to pay their annual tribute of thatching grass to the Alafin.

But Ọyọ was not the only, nor in latter days the most dangerous, menace to the peace of Ketu. On the west the kingdom found itself confronted by the powerful Fon state of Dahomey.[11] From the reign of Agaja in the early eighteenth century, the Dahomeans had been intent upon controlling territory along

the coast. As has been seen in Chapter III, they came into
conflict in this region with the Ọyọ, a conflict which resulted in
the imposition of tribute on Abomey by Ọyọ. But Dahomey
showed great powers of recovery, and the peace settlements of
1730 were followed by a rebuilding and consolidation of
strength which enabled the kingdom to retain its hold on the
slave port of Whydah and the coast as far east as Badagry. It
was also extending to the north-west, and after a war with the
Ashanti agreed upon a new frontier with that state. In 1789 the
Dahomeans invaded Ketu for the first time. According to
Dalzel, they crushed all resistance and carried off many captives, but Ketu tradition claims that they confined themselves
to pillaging the nearby village of Iwoye and abstained from an
attack on Ketu itself. Whatever the truth about this first
encounter, Ketu was destined, like much of western Yorubaland, to suffer dreadfully at the hands of the Dahomeans in the
next century.

Ṣabe

Ketu tradition describes how the westward migration of the
Yoruba from Ifẹ split into three groups after crossing the River
Ogun. The second of these, under the 'youngest prince' in the
Ketu version, moved north-west and settled at Kilibo, 'the
forest of lions', whence they were forced southwards again to
the hills of Ṣabe, where they established their capital.[12] A rather
different version of what is nevertheless recognizably the same
legend was gathered at Ṣabe by Fr Moulero, who relates that
Saloube, the leader of the Ṣabe migration, was the senior of the
princes, and that his group, after separating from the others at
Oke Ọyan, moved north into Borgu, where Saloube died. Here
his followers founded the town of Parakou. Only under their
third leader, Adjongou, and after an intermediate settlement at
Tchaourou, did they come to Kilibo, where they remained for
the duration of nine reigns. Finally, under pressure from their

Borgu neighbours they retreated southwards into the Ṣabe hills. Here they encountered a people called the Ojodou, whom they defeated after a series of battles, some of whose sites are still remembered and one of which lasted five days.[13]

Fr Moulero has recorded the names of twenty-one rulers of the Ṣabe, from the exodus from Ifẹ until 1848. These include only five rulers at Ṣabe itself, and the list seems, therefore, to be incomplete, especially when it is compared with that for Ketu, which at forty-two for what professes to be the same period is twice the length of that of Ṣabe.

As regards its physical boundaries, the kingdom of Ṣabe can be described as occupying the confluence of the Rivers Weme and Okpara and as extending north to Tchaourou. Today, however, this area is by no means inhabited solely or continuously by the Ṣabe, and in recent years groups of Mahi and Dassa have been settling there. This may imply that the kingdom was never populous, or it may reflect the external troubles which beset it, especially in the last century, when after withstanding for several hundred years the menace of powerful neighbours to the north, Borgu and Ọyọ, it was attacked by newer powers, the Fulani of Ilọrin, the Fon of Abomey, and even their distant Yoruba neighbours from Abẹokuta and Ijaye.

Dassa

About thirty miles south-west of Ṣabe and forty miles north-west from Ketu is the town known in French-speaking Dahomey as Dassa-Zoumé, capital of the former kingdom of the Dassa or perhaps more accurately, Idassa. A list of twenty-six rulers has been compiled for this kingdom,[14] beginning with Jagou Ọlọfin, the founder of the dynasty, who according to tradition came from Ẹgbaland. A peculiar feature of the kingship is that it passes from a ruler to all his children in turn, including apparently women, and then to the eldest son of the first king of the preceding generation (excluding the children of the female rulers). The twenty-six rulers in the list – which includes two women – are arranged in nine generations, and from this it has been calculated, on the basis of allowing thirty years to each generation, that the kingdom was founded about 1700.

Little is known about the history of the Dassa. There is some recollection among them of pressure from Ọyọ, under a leader called in their tradition Adjinakou, a name which does not occur in the list of Alafin but may refer to an Ọyọ general. During the first part of the nineteenth century the Dassa found themselves harassed, like the Ketu and the Ṣabe, by the Dahomeans under their powerful warrior king Ghezo, and they withdrew for greater safety to their hill-tops. Here they founded the present town of Dassa-Zoumé as a strong place.

VI · Kingdoms of the South: Ijẹbu, Ẹgba, Ẹgbado, and Lagos

It has already been suggested that the Yoruba, as their traditions indicate, are in origin an inland people who had moved
south from the savannah into the ever-deepening forest but had
not until comparatively recent times settled near the coast.
Among their major towns, only Lagos, founded apparently
some centuries after the other kingdoms and not attaining
importance until the eighteenth century, lies near the sea; Ile
Ifẹ is some eighty miles inland, and Ọyọ ile, on the savannah
edge, was 200 miles from the sea. Snelgrave was told of the
Ọyọ that, 'For as their national *Fetiche* was the sea, they were
prohibited by their Priests from ever seeing it, under no less a
Penalty than Death.'[1] So fas as is known, the Yoruba did not
venture on the open sea until modern times, and it plays little
part in their oral literature.

Nevertheless, the inhabitants of the southern kingdoms,
Ijẹbu, Ẹgba, and Ẹgbado, must have been aware of the great
and mysterious ocean which washed the boundaries of their
land. The fishermen on the lagoon knew that these placid waters
were separated by only a narrow strip of land from the tumultu-
ous Atlantic waves. Among their gods, they numbered Olokun,
owner of the sea, and Olokunsu his wife, goddess of the bar
which runs eastward from the entrance to the Lagos lagoon to
the Niger Delta. The health-giving properties of salt water
were known, according to the Ijẹsa legend, at the far-off court
of Ifẹ. Then, towards the end of the fifteenth century
outsiders began to appear, coming from the sea. With their
arrival, at first few in number, new developments in religion,

trade, and government began, very gradually, to disclose themselves.

Ijẹbu

> Twelve or thirteen leagues upstream from Lagos [wrote the Portuguese Duarte Pacheco Pereira in the first years of the sixteenth century] there is a large town called Geebuu, surrounded by a very large ditch. The river of this country is called in our days Agusale, and the trade which one can conduct here is the trade in slaves, who are sold for brass bracelets, at a rate of twelve to fifteen bracelets for a slave, and in elephants' tusks.[2]

This seems to be the first clear mention in writing of any of the Yoruba kingdoms – 'Geebu' must be Ijẹbu and the River Agusale either the Oṣun, which flows into the Lagos lagoon in Ijẹbu country, or (less probably) the Ogun, which enters the lagoon to the north of Lagos. It is significant that this early account should refer to the commerce of the kingdom for the Ijẹbu, though hard-working farmers, are still better-known today as traders and middlemen, energetic and enterprising. Although the Portuguese never took the interest in Ijẹbu which they showed in Benin – probably because their reports of the trade in the Lagos lagoon were less encouraging than for other parts of West Africa and also because of the difficulty of access – *Ciudad do Jubu* continued to be marked on their maps in the sixteenth and seventeenth centuries, and there is a belief in Ijẹbu Ode that Portuguese traders once lived in the town. Captain John Adams, 300 years after Pacheco, writes of the same trade in slaves being conducted there and also mentions the export of 'Jaboo cloth'.[3] In one sense, however, it was inappropriate that the Ijẹbu should have thus come to the attention of the Europeans before other parts of the country, since their reputation has long been one of hostility to strangers – meaning not only foreigners but all non-Ijẹbu – as well as intense local patriotism. *Ijẹbu-Ode ajeji ko wọ: bi ajeji ba wo larọ, wọn a fi sẹbo lalẹ* – 'Ijẹbu-Ode, a town forbidden to strangers; if a stranger entered it in the morning, he was sure to be made a sacrifice in the evening.'

The Ijẹbu kingdom was a large one, probably next in size to Ọyọ. At its greatest extent it stretched south-westward to the confines of Lagos and eastward across the River Ṣaṣa to the Oni; on the west it bordered the country of the Egba, on the north the Ọyọ, on the north-east the Ifẹ, and on the east the Ondo. Most of this area of some 2,000 or 3,000 square miles is covered by rain-forest, still dense in places, but nevertheless it is a fertile land (though the soil has often proved rather too light for the spread of the cocoa tree). The southern edge of the kingdom lay along the coastal lagoon whose waters were fished by the inhabitants of the villages on the shore, while the farther side of the lagoon was a remote and sparsely inhabited land of swamps, creeks, and sandy wastes, bordered by the empty beaches beaten by the Atlantic.

The capital of the kingdom and seat of the senior ruler, the Awujalẹ, was the centrally placed town of Ijẹbu Ode. But although the culture of the Ijẹbu is homogeneous and all speak the same dialect, their political organization has always been fragmented. The Awujalẹ was recognized as first among their numerous ọba rather than as king of all Ijẹbu. After the Ode the next largest group was the Rẹmo, their capital now being Ṣagamu, the seat not only of the Akarigbo, the leading Rẹmo oba, but also of three other crowned ọba (the Ẹwusi, the Ẹlẹpẹ, and the Amunisan) and the heads of the other former towns (there were in all thirteen) which concentrated here for greater security in 1872. Other towns in the kingdom with crowned oba were Idowa, Iwoye, Ijẹbu Igbo, Ọwu-Ikija, and Ijẹbu Ifẹ, ruled respectively by the Dagburewe, the Ebumawe, the Orimolusi, the Olowu, and the Ajalọrun.

Accounts of the foundation of the Ijẹbu kingdom describe three separate migrations into the area. The first was led by

Olu-Iwa, who settled at Iwode, now a part of Ijẹbu Ode town. His two companions, Ajẹbu and Olode, marked out the boundaries of the new land and town respectively, and the name 'Ijẹbu Ode' is said to derive from the combination of their names (though an alternative explanation is that *ijẹbu* means 'food of the deep' and refers to the supposed descent of the people from victims sacrificed by an Oba of Benin to the sea, while *ode* is used both in Yorubaland and elsewhere, for example among the Itschekri, to mean 'town'). Then a second group arrived, led by Arisu, and settled in the district known as Ijasi. The third migration was the most important, since it was led from Ifẹ by Ogborogan, afterwards called Ọbanta and recognized as founder of the kingdom and first Awujalẹ.

The legend of Ọbanta relates that he was a son of Oduduwa by a daughter of Olu-Iwa. After the dispersal of princes from Ile Ifẹ he travelled first east to Imẹsi and then south through Ondo before turning towards Ijẹbu. During this journey he was involved in many adventures, some of which are recalled in the elaborate ceremonial journey undertaken by a new Awujalẹ before his installation,[4] and gained numerous adherents to his party. At Igbo he defeated the local ruler in a wrestling match, and from this derived his title, 'one who understands the art of wrestling on land'. (Johnson gives a different explanation, saying that an ilari was sent from Ọyọ during the reign of Alafin Jayin to adjudicate in a land dispute between Isẹyin and Owu Ipole; this ilari later became ruler of Ijẹbu, and the title of Awujalẹ derived from his name Agbeja-ilẹ, 'an arbiter in a quarrel over land'.[5]) On entering Ijẹbu Ode Ogborogan was at once acclaimed by the inhabitants, who called out *ọba wa nita*, 'the king is outside': hence the name 'Ọbanta' by which this founding hero is widely known. There now ensued a dispersal of princes rather like that from Itajero, Ọbanta sending his followers, among whom was Akarigbo, son of the Olu of Igbo, to rule over different parts of the land.

It will be noticed that, like most of the Yoruba legends of

origin, the account of Ọbanta refers to a people already in occupation of the land before the arrival of the party from Ifẹ. Here these included both Ọbanta's predecessors at Ijẹbu Ode in the first two migrations and also those whom Ọbanta met during his journey, especially the Olu Igbo, ancestor of the Akarigbo, and the Oloko of Idoko, who may have ruled a kingdom once more powerful than Ijẹbu.[6] It has also been suggested that the cult of Agẹmọ, the supreme deity of the Ijẹbu (to whom the other Yoruba gods seem to have been considered subordinate) and worshipped all over their country, originated not with Ọbanta, as is held by the orthodox, but in an earlier society.[7]

Ọbanta's descendants reigned after him on the Ijẹbu throne. As with most Yoruba monarchs, the Awujalẹ's power was strictly circumscribed by his chiefs and councils; 'The Awujalẹ did nothing for himself, though everything was done in his name.'[8] According to Ijẹbu custom, only a man born to a reigning ọba – one of those called *abidagba* – might succeed to the throne, and the candidates were chosen in rotation from four branches of the royal house. But in 1960 these rules were set aside in favour of the present ọba, the fifty-second Awujalẹ, a grandson but not a son of a previous ruler.

Tradition relates that during the reign of the thirteenth Awujalẹ there was a split in the succession to the kingdom. This ruler fell ill, and after nominating his brother as regent left the capital to seek a cure in the small town of Idowa, a few miles to the south-west. When he had recovered he found himself prevented by his brother from resuming his rule. Eventually the brothers agreed that the former Awujalẹ should remain as an ọba at Idowa and should take a share of the kingdom's regalia. The present ruler of Idowa, the Dagburewe, claims descent from this Awujalẹ and is guardian of a fine collection of antique crowns and effigies (*okute*) of his royal ancestors.[9]

A testimony to the greatness of Ijẹbu's past, and probably also to the pre-eminence of Ijẹbu Ode among the other divisions of the kingdom, is the survival of much of the course of

the vast earthwork known as the Eredo. This mud-built ram-
part (which may justifiably be identified with Pacheco's 'very
large ditch')[10] has a circuit of some eighty miles and appears to
enclose an area of some 400 square miles around the town of
Ijẹbu Ode. It is still in places twenty feet high, with an outer
ditch of twenty to twenty-five feet in depth. Legend describes
it as the creation of Sungbo, a wealthy but childless woman who
caused it to be built as a memorial to herself. But it has been
suggested more prosaically that it may have been constructed in
two phases, the eastern section being intended for the defence of
the Idoko kingdom, which possibly preceded Ijẹbu as the power
in this area, and the western section being a later fortification
for Ọbanta's capital. There does not seem as yet much evidence
to support this hypothesis, nor can the intention of the builders
be confidently determined. The function of the Eredo in mark-
ing the limits of the Awujale's immediate area of authority –
his *Hausmacht*, so to speak – was probably as significant as its
use as a fortification, though doubtless these two roles were, as
so often elsewhere, complementary. Meanwhile the Eredo
awaits archaeological investigation, and especially a detailed
survey of its course.

Tradition in Ijẹbu throws little light on the external relations
of the kingdom. There are tenuous reports of contact with the
Portuguese, but nothing to support or contest the claims of
first the Ọyọ and then the Bini to have subjected them by arms.
In the case of Ọyọ there is a tradition there[11] that Alafin Ajagbo
(probably reigning in the seventeenth century) entered Ijẹbu
Ode with his army and installed his candidate Fasọjoye as
Awujale. That there was a war about this time with Ọyọ is confirmed at Ijẹbu Ode, although Fasọjoye's name is not recollected there as an Awujalẹ. Johnson, describing the circuit of
Yorubaland by the army of Alafin Ojigi in the early eighteenth
century, implies that the expedition passed through Ijẹbu territory on its return to Ọyọ via the Popo country, and in his
account of the extent of the Ọyọ kingdom under Agbolaje later

in the century he includes Ijẹbu within the boundaries.[12] But an Ọyọ cavalry force would have encountered tremendous difficulty in penetrating the rain-forest, and for the Ọyọ to have retained political or military control here for any length of time seems almost impossible. With regard to Egharevba's assertion that Ijẹbu was conquered by the Bini in the reign of Oba Ozolua and ruled by them 'for some years',[13] Ijẹbu tradition is similarly silent. Yet Dapper, in his *Description de l'Afrique* of 1686, writes that the king of 'Jaboe', by which Ijẹbu must be meant, was one of the Oba of Benin's vassals.[14] There is no doubt that at some time before 1700 Benin had extended its influence along the coast to the west of Ijẹbu and had erected a tributary state at Lagos. This suggests that the Bini controlled at least the southern parts of Ijẹbu territory linking them to Lagos and the coast beyond. But it seems probable that they depended for their communications mainly on the waterways, passing through the creeks around Mahin and across the lagoon, quicker and more convenient than the land route and less provocative to the Ijẹbu. Finally, from the early eighteenth century onwards, the Dahomeans to the west were a growing menace to Yoruba security, despite the checks administered to them by the Ọyọ. Snelgrave mentions what may have been an attack on Ijẹbu by a Dahomean army in or about 1731.[15] But nothing else is known of this war, and even if it took place it seems unlikely that the Dahomeans obtained any major results from an ambitious push so far to the east of their kingdom.

Meanwhile the Ijẹbu continued both to keep away strangers from their towns and to play their profitable role of traders and middlemen, principally supplying slaves to the Atlantic trade in competition with the Ọyọ and importing European cloth and miscellaneous goods. According to Clapperton, Ijẹbu merchants used to travel into Nupe before the outbreak of the civil wars there, and in 1826 their cloth was still being sold as far north as 'Koolfu' (Kolfo).[16] Apart from their ports of Ejinrin and Ẹpẹ at the north-east corner of the lagoon, the Rẹmo town of Ikorodu at the north-west corner developed a famous market, and in the nineteenth century the Ijẹbu were able to control the important trade in firearms between Lagos and the interior through this market. Their commercial ability has never deserted them, and today their country still looks more prosperous than other parts of Yorubaland, with its many 'storey houses' and the Brazilian-style mansions which were built at the end of the last century.

Ẹgba

Since about 1830 the Ẹgba have been concentrated in their great metropolis of Abẹokuta, the town 'under the rock', and in the surrounding district on both sides of the River Ogun. Until the collapse of the Ọyọ and the outbreak of the civil wars in the early part of the last century, however, the Ẹgba state – or the 'Ẹgba forest' as it is more distinctively called – extended considerably farther to the north-east than the present area of Ẹgbaland, and included the sites of Ibadan, Ijaye, and other towns which were subsequently occupied by refugees from the Ọyọ kingdom. Ajiṣafẹ[17] describes old Ẹgbaland as stretching 'from the river Ọba on the north to Ebute-Mẹtta on the south, and from Oṣun River on the east to Ipokia with Yewa River on the west'. Thus its frontiers marched with the Ifẹ and Ijẹṣa kingdoms on the east, Ijẹbu to the south and south-east, Ẹgbado on the south-west, Ketu on the west, and Ọyọ to the north. Much of this area is covered by the rain forest; the name 'Ẹgba' is itself said to be a contraction from ẹgbalugbo, 'the wanderers towards the forest'.

Like the Ijẹbu, the Ẹgba were ruled as a federation rather than centrally, and its towns, said by Ajiṣafẹ to be 'not less than three hundred in number', were grouped into three provinces.[18] The largest and most northerly province was that of Ẹgba Agura (or Gbagura), said to consist of 144 towns, of which seventy-two owed allegiance to the Agura in his capital

at Iddo and seventy-two to the Onigun of Ilugun; later the
Agura became predominant over most of the area except
Ilugun, which then adhered to the province of Oke Ọna. This
second province, Egba Oke Ọna, was so called from its situ-
ation to the south-west of the River Ọna in the vicinity of the
Ijẹbu Rẹmo. The principal ọba was the Ọṣile (or Oloko) of Oko.
The third province, which occupied the south-west of the
Egba forest, was that of Ẹgba Alake. This was originally called
Ẹgba Agbeyin and subject to the Ojoko of Kesi, who was later
displaced as leading ọba by the Alake, whose capital was at
Ake, but who was chosen by king-makers from the five sister
towns (ọmọ iya) of Ijeun, Kemta, Iporo, Itoku, and Ake. Among
the provincial heads the Alake came to be accepted as senior,
followed by the Osile, the Agura, and the Onigun. The different
towns within the provinces also had their ọba, but in the whole
kingdom only the Alake, the Oṣile, and the Agura wore beaded
crowns. All the major rulers now live with their peoples in their
several sections of the town of Abẹokuta, where they were
joined by a fourth crowned oba, the Olowu and his followers
from the ruined town of Owu, and later still by Ọyọ refugees
from Ijaye. The sites of many of the original towns have long
been abandoned, their ruins being now barely discernible in the
bush or in other cases obliterated and forgotten, but a few, such
as Ilugun and Iddo, are again prosperous villages.

The organization of the Ẹgba suggests that their entry into
the forest took place in three or four migrations, each associated
with one of the provinces. Biobaku considers that the first to
arrive were the Gbagura, settling in the north, then the Oke-
Ọna, followed by the Agbeyin, who went farthest to the south;
the arrival of the Alake with his followers represented 'probably a fourth and certainly the last major wave of migration
into the Ẹgba Forest'.[19] Johnson maintains that the Ẹgba
rulers mostly descend from the Ẹsọ, the warriors of Ọyọ, and
cites in connection with this the absence of a distinct royal
family and the consequent eligibility of any Ẹgba, whatever his

birth, to be chosen as ọba.[20] Although some towns, for example, Ilugun, are indeed said to have been founded from Ọyọ, Ẹgba traditions for the most part look to Ifẹ for the origins of their towns. It is in particular maintained that Ajalake, the first Alake, was a son (or grandson) of Oduduwa, who after the dispersal of the Ifẹ princes travelled and for a time settled with the Alaketu – a tradition which receives some support at Ketu.[21] The tradition continues that Ọmọnide ('child of brass '– the most precious metal then known), mother (or grandmother) of the founding princes, had a special love for the Alake which led her to settle with him in the Ẹgba forest. After her death every new Alafin sent presents to the Alake because of Ọmọnide's burial in his town. The prestige accruing to the Alake from his legendary membership of the house of Oduduwa may account for his success in replacing the Ojoko of Kesi as the leading southern ọba of the Egba, though it seems equally possible that the tradition was the result rather than the cause of his ascendancy. The Ẹgba account explains his rise in more material terms, since according to this, the Alake overcame the Ojoko by first breaking his monopoly in the supply to the other Ẹgba of corn, which only the Kesi knew how to grow; his capital at Ijoko was then destroyed and its ruler killed.

There seems no doubt that the Ẹgba were subjected to the empire of Ọyọ at some period, since, in addition to both Ẹgba and Ọyọ traditions about this, a considerable assimilation of culture and governmental practice seems to have taken place; this can be observed especially in the case of the northern Ẹgba, the Gbagura. How and when the Ẹgba came to accept Ọyọ domination is not known, but it seems likely that this occurred during the century following the return of the Alafin from Igboho to Ọyọ ile; Biobaku suggests that the situation evolved peaceably, the Ẹgba having (he asserts) no military organization capable of defending their land and so being prepared to pay tribute to Ọyọ in return for protection.[22] But this Ọyọ overlordship came to be increasingly resented. The Alafin placed his

G

ajẹlẹ in the Ẹgba towns to represent him and to collect annual tribute, and the presence and exactions of these officials, who had become 'the lords of even the kings',[23] eventually provoked a national rising.

The liberator and hero of the Ẹgba was Lisabi, born at Itoku and living in Igbein, both in the Alake's province. He is remembered as a man of gigantic stature, and his career shows that he was a great organizer and leader. At first he worked in secret, grouping his followers into the Ẹgbẹ Aro, a society of farmers pledged to help each other in their work. This society gradually extended over the whole of Ẹgbaland and at the same time changed its character, becoming an underground army, the Ẹgbẹ Olorogun. When the time was ripe, Lisabi gave the signal for a general rising by killing the ajẹlẹ in his own town of Igbein, and from here the movement spread through the Ẹgbẹ to all the other towns of the land. Tradition claims that over 600 of the Ọyọ ajẹlẹ were massacred in this rising. The Alafin replied by sending a large army, made up of Ọyọ, Ibarapa, and Ẹgbado troops, against the rebels. This army crossed the Ogun at Mọkọloki and advanced towards Igbein. Lisabi now showed his qualities as a general. Having ordered the town to be evacuated, he concealed his followers in the nearby Melego ravine and then, as the Ọyọ searched the deserted town, fell upon them, routing them and gaining at one stroke independence for his people.

It is uncertain at what point in the decline of Ọyọ this revolt of the Ẹgba occurred. Circumstances suggest that it may have been at some time during the long reign of Alafin Abiọdun; Biobaku places it during the disturbance at Ọyọ which resulted in the downfall of Baṣọrun Gaha, and Akinjogbin considers that it was in those latter years of Abiọdun which also saw the unsuccessful Ọyọ campaigns against the Borgu (1783) and Nupe (1791).[24] But tradition in the Ọyọ kingdom, as recorded by the Bada of Ṣaki, places the revolt during the short regency of Baṣọrun Aṣamu at Ọyọ, after the suicide of Alafin Awolẹ, and therefore in or about 1796 or 1797.[25] This would accord with what is known of the general military and political decline which had set in at Ọyọ by the end of the eighteenth century and also with developments among the Ẹgba under Lisabi and up to the opening of the long wars of the nineteenth century in Yorubaland.

Lisabi's role was not confined to winning independence for the Ẹgba. Biobaku describes him as the Lycurgus who gave his people laws. He was yet more than that. He taught them the art of defending themselves by arms and fortifications, so that they were able to throw back the raids of their fierce neigh-bours, the Dahomeans. He also encouraged the Ẹgba to take advantage of the changed political conditions of the country by engaging in trade on a wider scale than before, especially in sending kola from their forests to the markets in the north. He boasted that he had fought for the Ẹgba so that they should wear the best kinds of cloth, *alari* and *sekini*, and his country-men still look on him as father of their nation and on them-selves as his children, *ọmọ Lisabi*.

The circumstances of Lisabi's end are mysterious. He is said to have died in the forest, perhaps murdered by a group of jealous chiefs, though another account is that he was killed during a Dahomean raid. It seems that towards the end of his life he lost his popularity with the Ẹgba, despite the benefits which he had brought them. Biobaku suggests that they did not understand his anxiety about the defence of their land and resented the conscription into his militia of men whose labour was needed on the farms.[26]

After the removal of Lisabi's influence and example, political conditions among the Ẹgba deteriorated and local differences re-emerged. Tradition recollects four outbreaks of civil war pre-ceding the wider conflagration of the Owu war.[27] The first arose from a quarrel between the people of Igbein and Itoku, both towns subject to the Alake, over the petty offences of a former slave, now a wealthy trader, Ogedepagbo. The second grew out of a competition for office between rival chiefs in Ilugun, which drew in other towns as mediators and then participants. The third came about when Alake Okikilu raised an army in Ẹgbado under the warrior Agbaje (who gave his name to this war) in order to attack a group of towns in his province whose Court was depriving him of the revenue which he expected from his own jurisdiction. The last was a bitterly fought contest between the Ijeun and Itoku against the Ọba people; this again concerned towns within Ake, apparently the most disturbed and unruly of the Ẹgba provinces.

Thus the stage was set for the Owu war of the early nineteenth century, which was to bring in its wake the direst and most far-reaching consequences for all the Yoruba. Among these consequences was the destruction of the town and kingdom of Owu and the eventual removal of its ruler and people to Abẹokuta, the new metropolis of all the Ẹgba, where they have since then occupied the south-west part of the town.

The Owu did not originally belong to the Ẹgba. Their kingdom lay to the east of the Ẹgba forest across the River Oṣun, with Ifẹ to the north-east and Ijẹbu on the south. Little is remembered about the history of Owu, but the impressive fortifications of the capital, Owu town, consisting of massive earthen walls still some twenty feet high, suggest that here was a formidable power. Johnson describes the Owu as a martial race and adds: 'Hardihood, stubbornness, immorality and haughtiness are marked traits in their character'; to illustrate the equal fierceness of their women he quotes a proverb: 'a child is born at Owu and you ask (whether) male or female: which will be a proper child?' (*abi omo l'Owu, o ni akọ tabi abo ni, ewo ni yio se ọmọ nibe?*)[28] Nevertheless, like their Ẹgba neighbours, the Owu were subject to the Ọyọ, and indeed were proud to act as the Alafin's warriors in the south. 'From the days of Ṣango,' claims Johnson, 'they (had) been very loyal to the Alafin of Ọyọ.' This loyalty in latter days was to lead to their downfall.

Ẹgbado

To the west of Ẹgbaland live the Ẹgbado, their name contracted from *ẹgbaluwẹ*, 'the wanderers towards the river' – probably an allusion to the River Yewa, which runs through their
land to the lagoon at Badagry. They seem never to have constituted a state or federation as did the other major Yoruba
peoples. The traditions of origin of their towns are disparate,
referring to Ifẹ, Ọyọ, Ketu, and Benin, and the population
includes communities of Anago, Gun, Awori, and Ahori (the
last being the people called 'Holli' across the frontier).

The oldest of the Ẹgbado communities are probably the Ilobi
and Erinja, who have traditions of migration from Ifẹ via
Ketu;[29] the Ilobi, indeed, claim that their ancestor, Onidokun
Leke, was a member of Oduduwa's house. Later arrivals in the
area were the Ado and the Ipokia, both tracing their origin to
Benin, though the people of Ipokia have been joined by emigrants from Ọyọ. Other Ẹgbado towns, such as Igan, Egua,
and Aiyetoro, seem to have been founded by Anago groups
moving – or possibly, returning – eastward from Dahomey. But
the most important of the Ẹgbado towns are those founded
directly or indirectly by Ọyọ. There are two main groups of
these, and in each case the settlements were apparently made
by the Ọyọ in order to protect their communications with the
coast.[30] The first group consists of the former kingdom of
Ifọnyin (sometimes called Nago), ruled by the Ẹlẹhin Odo ('the
king behind the river'), and its daughter kingdoms of Ihumbọ
and Ikọlaje, to whose rulers the Ẹlẹhin Odo, with the Alafin's
permission, granted crowns. (Ifọnyin lies across the present
frontier in Dahomey.) They seem to have been founded about
1700, at the time when Ọyọ became aware of the threat to her
route to the coast from the westward expansion of Benin and
the growing power and ambition of the Fon of Dahomey. The
second group was founded probably late in the eighteenth
century by Alafin Abiọdun when the Ọyọ trade route was

moved farther to the east; it includes the two leading towns of
Ilaro and Ijana, established in an area which, perhaps as a result
of slave-raiding, was only lightly populated. Ilaro was ruled by
its ọba, the Olu, who was crowned by the Alafin; according to
Johnson, each Olu ruled for a period of only three years and
then retired to Ọyọ ile with ten of his wives. Ijana was subject
to an official known as the Onisarẹ, who was chosen from among
the Alafin's ilari, the titled slaves; Johnson writes that he was
always a Nupe, but the Onisarẹ whom Lander met in 1830 was
described as a Hausa.[31] Ilaro became the principal town of
Ẹgbadoland, while nearby Ijana took second place. Formerly
their rulers held a ceremonial meeting once a year, sitting back-
to-back on a hilltop boundary between their kingdoms – since
kings should never meet each other – and the Onisarẹ had the
alarming honour of being one of the Ọyọ *abọbaku* – those required to take their own lives on learning of the Alafin's death.

These satellite kingdoms of Ọyọ in Ẹgbado country seem to
have fulfilled well their purpose of protecting the road to the
coast up to and even some years beyond the outbreak of the
general wars of the nineteenth century. They had their own
troops and remained, as Johnson writes, 'very loyal subjects of
the Alafin'.[32] Many travellers passed through the towns between Ọyọ and the coast, and though the tolls which they were
required to pay (in cowries) on entering and leaving had to be
transmitted to the Alafin, their patronage of the local markets
was profitable and the Ẹgbado grew wealthy. When Clapperton
and Lander, the first Europeans to give a first-hand account of
Yorubaland, travelled up this route at the end of 1825 they
were impressed by the order, peace, and prosperity which they
saw around them. But four years later, as the Landers noted,
conditions had deteriorated.

Two towns lying in the mainly Awori area to the south of the
Ẹgba and Ẹgbado countries (and sometimes included in one or
the other) must be mentioned. The first is Ọtta, ruled by a
crowned ọba, the Ọlọta, who claims to derive his title from Ifẹ,

and now a wealthy centre of cocoa production and trade. The second is the former port and slaving centre of Badagry, which is situated, like other West African ports, not directly on the coast but on the coastal lagoon; from the west it is protected by the Yewa estuary and on other sides by swamp and forest. Although surrounded by Awori villages, the town seems to have been founded in the 1730s by Egun (or Popo) refugees driven eastwards by the Fon. As it became important as an outlet for the trade of Qyǫ and for the commerce of the Ęgbado, its population grew, other Popo refugees and Awori from the surrounding district being attracted there, as well as Spanish, Portuguese, French, Dutch, and English slave traders who established their baracoons along the shore. The leading chief, the Akran, was normally a member of the Jęgba ward of the town which traced its descent from Whydah (Ouidah, Hueda), the Popo port some fifty miles to the west,[33] but he had little authority over the other wards. The town seems to have constituted a semi-independent city-state; in the eighteenth century it was apparently tributary to Qyǫ, which controlled the hinterland down to Ipokia in the south, while by 1830, according to the Landers, it had become tributary to Lagos.

Lagos

The interaction of geography and history, of trade and politics, of the outside world and of local affairs: all this is illustrated in the past of Lagos. This is the first of Nigeria's ports and also the terminus of the railway which, far more than the River Niger, has linked together the disparate regions. Today Lagos is the Federal capital, a crowded, cosmopolitan city of half a million inhabitants. Its names reflect its past: to the Yoruba it is Eko, deriving probably from the farm (*oko*) of the earliest settlers, though alternatively – or additionally – it may be the Bini word (*eko*) for a war-camp; to other Nigerians and to the rest of the world it is Lagos, contracted from the Portuguese Lago de

Curamo (the name Kuramo survives for an inlet of the great lagoon near by), while there are traces of yet another, probably later but now almost forgotten name, Onim or Aunis, apparently also used by the Portuguese.[34]

Here at Lagos occurs the first permanent break in the miles of beach and dune of the outer coast-line to the east of the Volta estuary. The bar which had to be crossed in order to gain access to the harbour was one of notorious difficulty and danger, and so shallow and of so narrow a tidal range that until the completion of the breakwaters in 1916 entrance was denied to ships of over twelve feet draught. But once across the bar and in the calm waters of the lagoon, there opened up a vast system of inland waterways connecting Lagos by canoe (and today by motor-launch) with Porto Novo and beyond on the west and with the creeks 100 miles to the east. This Rio de Laguo, or entrance into the lagoon, was noted by the earliest Portuguese visitors to the West African coast. Pacheco writes of it in his *Esmeraldo de Situ Orbis*:

> There is no trade in this country nor anything from which one can make a profit. All this region of the river Lagua, of which we spoke above, as far as the river Primeiro, and beyond for a distance of a 100 leagues, is all broken up inland by numerous other rivers in such a way that the whole consists of numerous islands. It is very unhealthy and is very hot throughout the year, on account of the proximity of the sun. The middle of the winter occurs here during the months of August and September when it rains heavily. The Negroes of this country are idolaters and circumcised, without having any law, and without knowing the reason for their circumcision.[35]

But even if Pacheco's rather superficial account of Lagos is correct in its estimate of trade at the end of the fifteenth century, three centuries later the position had entirely changed. Captain John Adams, describing conditions at the end of the eighteenth century, wrote that 'An active traffic in slaves' was carried on at Lagos, a town 'built on a bank or island, which appears to have been raised from Cradoo lake, by the eddies, after the sea and periodical rains had broken down the boundary which separated it from the ocean'. He continues:

> It has always been the policy of the Lagos people, like those of Bonny, to be themselves the traders and not brokers. They therefore go in their canoes to Ardrah and Badagry, and to the towns situated at the NE extremity of Cradoo lake, where they purchase slaves, Jaboo cloth, and such articles as are required for domestic consumption.[36]

A Portuguese report of 1807 ascribes the growth of the slave trade at Lagos to warfare between Dahomey and Porto Novo which had interrupted supply to ports farther west.[37] By the 1830s the slave trade here was booming, and until the British occupation in 1851 Lagos remained its main centre on this part of the coast.

The early traditions of Lagos[38] ascribe the peopling of this sandy waste near the edge of the ocean to a small-scale migration of Awori Yoruba, who had first settled under the leadership of a hunter named Ogunfunminire about twelve miles up the river Ogun at Iṣẹri, a village which though still mainly inhabited by Awori is now at the southern limit of Ẹgbaland. Ogunfunminire is said to have been a member of the royal house of Ifẹ, but his settlement of hunters and fishermen seems to represent the farthest and latest extension of one of those movements which peopled the Awori region. From Iṣẹri the settlers spread to Ebute Mẹtta (the name means 'three landing places') on the lagoon, but the uncertainties of life on the mainland (perhaps due already to the ambitions of Benin in this area) led them to seek greater safety across the channel on the small island now called Iddo, whence they spread farther to the adjacent larger island – some five by one and a half miles – which is Lagos and which lies by the entrance into the lagoon from the sea. The islanders were at first subject to a ruler known as the

Ọlọfin, on whose death the land was divided among the ten eldest of his thirty-two sons, these ten chiefs being the ancestors of the Idẹjo, 'owners of the land', better known today as the White Cap Chiefs of Lagos. The senior of these, Aromire, had his farm at Isalẹ Eko (meaning 'under' or in modern use, 'downtown' Lagos). The present afin of Lagos is situated on this site and is called Iga Idunganran, 'the pepper palace', a recollection in the Lagos–Awori dialect of the pepper bushes on Aromire's farm.

A series of attacks had now been launched against Lagos by the armies of Benin. At first these were repulsed under the leadership of the Ọlọfin. After the Ọlọfin's death, however, the Bini succeeded in establishing themselves on Iddo island under Aṣẹru, one of their warriors. The impression given by Lagos tradition is that this was achieved by peaceful infiltration rather than by conquest; perhaps the Lagosians, seeing themselves outflanked by the advance of the Bini along the coast to their west, lost hope of being able to prolong their resistance. According to Egharevba,[39] Oba Orhogba of Benin, campaigning in person, made a war-camp on Lagos island which he used as a base for extending his control over the area. Some time later the Oba appointed a ruler for Lagos to represent the interest of Benin and to forward tribute there. The man chosen is named in both Lagos and Benin tradition as Aṣipa. The Lagos account is that the Bini warrior Aṣẹru died while campaigning on the mainland near by and that Aṣipa, an Iṣẹri chief and (like Ogunfunminire and the Ọlọfin before him) of the Ifẹ royalty, carried his body home to Benin, thereby gaining such favour with the Oba that he was sent back to Lagos as its king. Egharevba describes Aṣipa ('Esikpa' in his account, but the name is clearly the same) as a grandson of the Oba of Benin, and adds that after his death his remains and those of his successors were taken for burial to Benin, a claim which is confirmed in Lagos tradition. Aṣipa founded a new dynasty which continued to rule Lagos, using the title either of Ologun (con-

tracted from Oloriogun, 'warrior') or of Eleko, and the present
Ọba of Lagos – the modern use of the general word for king as
the title is reminiscent of Benin – is his twentieth successor and
descendant on the throne. The dynasty's dependence on Benin
was emphasized by the appointment of another chief, the Eletu
Odibo – still one of the Akarigbere, or kingmakers, of Lagos –
who alone had the right to crown the ọba and who in early
times probably maintained close connection with Benin. Meanwhile, the senior descendant of the Ọlọfin, the Ọlọtọ, maintained
a nominal independence as ruler of the northern corner of Iddo
island and as first among the Idẹjọ.

   The period usually assigned to the assertion of Benin's
authority over Lagos is the sixteenth century, and Hodgkin
associates it with the use by the Bini of firearms obtained from
their European trade.[40] This may be too early a dating. Newbury distinguishes between the coming of Benin emissaries and
settlers 'towards the end of the sixteenth century' and the
appointment of Aṣipa as the first Ologun 'at the turn of the
seventeenth century'.[41] But Bini tradition firmly allots Aṣipa's
appointment to the reign at Benin of Oba Orhogba, which
Bradbury agrees with Egharevba in placing in the latter part
of the sixteenth century.[42] It certainly seems more probable
that the dynasty was established at the beginning of Benin's
ascendancy rather than a century or more later. Here, however,
the king-list of Lagos presents a difficulty. Adele, who died in or
about 1836 (after being deposed and later restored), appears as
only the sixth ọba. Thus if Egharevba and Bradbury were right,
and if the list were complete, the average length of reign would
be between thirty-three and forty years, which is too long to be
credible. But it is possible, even likely, that the names of some
ọba have been forgotten, particularly of those early ones whose
bodies were taken to Benin for burial. The problem remains,
and until new evidence is forthcoming no more definite conclusion can be reached than that Benin had established its
ascendancy in Lagos and had founded a dynasty there at some

period before 1700,[43] and that the first, and perhaps also the second, of these developments may have taken place as early as the last part of the sixteenth century.

Communications between Benin and Lagos must have been maintained either through the southern territory of Ijẹbu or, more probably, by waterway. Mahin, giving access to the lagoon at its eastern end, had been conquered by Benin at about the same time that Lagos was brought under control, and tradition records that Oba Ehengbuda met his death while on his way by canoe to visit Lagos.[44] Meanwhile Lagos was becoming prominent in the slave trade. It is said to have been Ọba Akinṣemoyin, fourth ruler at Lagos after Aṣipa, who invited Portuguese slave-dealers to his town, and that in his reign his Portuguese friends presented him with tiles for roofing his palace, the Iga. As Lagos grew richer, the annual tribute rendered to Benin presumably increased and became an important source of revenue for the latter kingdom. This tribute was paid until about 1830, and Egharevba writes that an official was sent to claim it as late as 1845 during the civil war at Lagos between Akintoye and Kosọkọ, the two rival claimants to the throne.[45] Their wealth may well have encouraged the rulers to assert their independence, and according to Dalzel, 'The powerful King of Lagos' took part with the Dahomeans in an attack on Badagry in 1784, an operation from which Benin could hardly have derived benefit.

A few years before the establishment of British influence in Lagos in 1851, there was estimated to be a population of some 25,000–30,000 in the town,[46] occupying the western half of the island, Isalẹ Eko. In addition to Lagos and Iddo, the mainland at Ebute Mẹtta was accounted part of the kingdom, as was also an undefined stretch of coast-line between Badagry and Lekki with its mainly Ijẹbu population. The stage was set for the transformation of this miniature but thriving trading state into a centre of administration and communications and the capital of a large and populous modern nation.

PART II

PART II

VII · The Traditions Reviewed

The acceptance of oral tradition as a form of evidence commits the historian to an attempt to answer questions which neither concern nor would greatly interest the guardians of tradition itself – the rulers and their officials, the drummers, the praise singers, the local patriots. These questions arise from the historian's need to establish a coherent narrative which, however isolated the people concerned, must at some point link up with events elsewhere, and then to interpret that narrative according to his usual criteria. In a reconstruction of the past of the Yoruba, which up to about the middle of the nineteenth century must be largely from their traditions, and before 1700 almost wholly so, many such questions present themselves, and for every question a host of difficulties. A prospect of detailed work, kingdom by kingdom, opens up, but at this stage the questions may be resolved into two broad groups, each of fundamental importance. The first concerns the interpretation of the traditional accounts of the origins of the Yoruba polity, and the second the fixing of the main developments and events in early Yoruba history into, first, a chronological sequence and then into a temporal framework which can be related to, or at least put alongside, the history of other peoples.

In the traditions of origin which are summarized in the preceding chapters of this book, discrepancies and contradictions abound, and even when supernatural elements are left out of account, credibility is constantly strained. In this the guardians of tradition find no difficulty; their duty, and often their passion, is to maintain orthodoxy. The historian must approach tradition otherwise, treating it always with reverence but never with credulity. Yet, despite scepticism, as these legends from many different kingdoms and towns are examined, compared, and then assessed as a whole, one factor stands out, adding substance and weight to their acceptance as historical evidence: the resemblances between these different accounts of origin, especially between those of the major kingdoms, all harking back to Ile Ifẹ and to the hero-figures of Oduduwa and his progeny. The repetition of the story becomes tedious, but such repetition creates its own confidence. Against this pattern local differences and difficulties, irritating as they are to the tidy-minded, contribute to the growing conviction that the legends do in their way show how the different kingdoms and kingships originated, since they make it clear that so far as the central narrative is concerned no 'Authorized Version' has evolved.

This body of legend, then, suggests, perhaps as strongly as such evidence can, that there came to Ile Ifẹ a leader and a group of people who established there a political authority of an enduring kind, that there was a subsequent emigration from Ifẹ of the founders, with their followers, of a number of king-doms, and that there continued to be reference back to Ifẹ as the centre of authority and legitimacy by the scattered 'child-ren of Oduduwa', including both those who had formed and those in process of forming new states and towns. The two first questions which arise from these assumptions ask whence came this dominant group, the house of Oduduwa as they may be called, and then who were the people whom they found already living in the land.

Numerous answers have been proposed to both these,[1] and the subject is still an open and a controversial one. But two points are relevant, equally to each question, and may point to a single answer. The first is that, as noted in Chapter I, linguis-tic evidence seems to show that by the time they began to form the states with which this book is concerned, the Yoruba had occupied more or less their present habitat for several hundred or even thousands of years. Secondly, the traditions relate that as the emigrants from Ifẹ spread over the land they almost everywhere encountered earlier settlers ('the aborigines', as they are sometimes termed)[2] who were often hostile (not unreasonably, since they had a prior claim to the land) but who apparently neither were unfamiliar nor spoke an unknown tongue. It appears likely, therefore, that the Oduduwa cycle describes not a conquest from outside but a process of state-formation from within a people in which the leaders belonged to a dominant but probably not alien lineage.[3]

Another problem concerns the legend of the dispersal of Ọranyan and the other founding princes. Is it feasible that such an emigration in all directions took place at one time, as tradition alleges, or at any rate within the lifetime of the leader who had established his throne at Ifẹ? Here, again, the persistence over a wide area of a narrative in which the essential elements remain recognizably the same argues that an actual event is represented and its memory preserved, and that indeed there was a concerted movement of the younger generation of a vigorous line, a movement which continued a process begun a generation (or perhaps two generations) before at Ifẹ. There is nothing inherently unlikely in this. An analogy with the Normans, as regards their settlements in France, in England, or in Southern Italy, is not far-fetched. In any case there seems no ground for preferring the suggestion of a recent writer that the legend of Oduduwa represents a migration to Ifẹ by a people coming from the Benue valley, while that of Ọranyan refers to a conquest of Ifẹ and its dependencies by a different people, arriving apparently centuries later, from the Middle Niger.[4] It is difficult to find anything in tradition or any substantial evidence from secondary sources (such as differences in dialect or social organization) to support any part of such speculation – that there were two migrations, that they were widely separated in time, that they were made up of differing peoples, that they came from different directions and from a great distance. Nor does there seem any justification for

H

regarding the names of Oduduwa, Ọranyan, and other heroes as representing not individuals but groups of persons.[5] Every movement has its leaders, and it is their names which are usually recollected.

Yet if the broad outline of the legend of a dispersal of princes from Ifẹ is accepted as a possible explanation of the foundation of a number of the Yoruba states, this cannot explain the origin of all the kingdoms, even though most of them claim to derive their crowns from Ifẹ. The criteria necessary to satisfy a claim to have originated from the early and deliberate sending forth of the founders – from Itajero, as the Ifẹ account has it – seem to be, first, a specific tradition to that effect, especially if the kingdom's own tradition is supported by a similar tradition at Ifẹ or in other kingdoms; secondly, a king-list of sufficient length, that is, with about thirty-five names or more, and last, a recognized position of seniority among the other kingdoms of Ifẹ origin. Such criteria would seem to be satisfied most nearly in the cases of Ọyọ, Ijẹbu Ode, Ketu, Ondo, and Ijẹsa, and also for the second dynasty of the Edo kingdom of Benin, while the claims of Ṣabe, Ake, Akurẹ, Ado Ekiti, and Ọwọ, though less strongly supported by tradition, cannot be set aside. This is not to deny, however, that other rulers obtained their crowns from Ifẹ, since, whatever the origin of the Ọni's own kingship – and the Ọyọ legend about Adimu seems somewhat suspect – Ifẹ remained the source of legitimacy to which aspiring rulers would look for the sanctioning of their kingship. Biobaku suggests how this might have happened: 'The Yoruba dotted the tropical forest belt with towns and hamlets. A bold hunter usually led the way and when a suitable site was struck, he founded a town. He might go back to Ile-Ifẹ for the symbol of authority, which was a beaded crown.'[6]

As to what gave these founders of the first states their power to attain leadership and to accomplish a political revolution of enduring importance among the Yoruba, tradition is silent. They may have been associated with some technical innovation, for example, yam cultivation or iron-working or a new weapon – perhaps the bow – or they may have learnt through external contact and unusual receptivity those ideas of strong government and divine kingship which have been termed the 'Sudanic state'. More prosaically, they may have been successful traders, men of wealth and initiative, who came to dominate a race of poor farmers. The possibilities are many, and there are no clear pointers. The simplest explanation seems the most likely: that a family arose (like the house of Hauteville) in which at least two or three generations were exceptionally gifted by nature as warriors and as politicians, and whose ambition made them leaders of their fellow men and founders of states.

Turning to the problem of chronology, the difficulties are at first sight somewhat less, since much has been asserted about the dating of reigns. A closer examination proves disconcerting. The early written references to the Yoruba by European travellers are meagre, and with regard to dating are particularly unhelpful; this is the position up to the end of the seventeenth century, and it is not until the nineteenth century that satisfactory accounts begin to appear. The traditions are related in an almost timeless vacuum. Occasionally indications are given about the lapse of time, usually concerning the length of a reign, but these are inherently unreliable. There are no dates and no recognizable references to datable events elsewhere.

Archaeology has so far thrown little light upon this primary problem for the historian. As seen in Chapter II, excavations at Ile Ifẹ have produced no significant datable evidence.* The investigations at Ọyọ ile in 1956–7 yielded at their earliest levels pottery impressed with maize cobs, an American plant which could hardly have reached Africa before 1500, which at first suggests that the city was founded not earlier than the sixteenth century. But this conclusion would be unwarranted, since only a very small part of the vast space within the town walls was excavated during the short period – two months – which the

* But see the footnote to p. 31.

small expedition spent there; moreover, there is a possibility
that the present site is not that of the earliest foundation.[7]

Thus, until new evidence is uncovered, resort can only be had
again to tradition, bearing in mind that from this source no
more can be hoped than a tentative approximation to a time-
scale. In this situation it is the king-lists which promise the best
means of establishing a chronology. Unfortunately only about
a dozen among the many lists which tradition must still preserve have been recorded – and time runs short as tradition is
submerged by modern preoccupations. But in a few kingdoms it
seems that the lists have been comprehensively and con-
scientiously kept and may be treated with some confidence. In
other towns, however, the information available is confined to
the statement that the reigning ọba follows a known number of
predecessors.

In some cases where king-lists were available, historians have
drawn on traditional accounts of the lengths of the different
reigns and then worked backwards to provide a chronology,
including a date of origin. This was done by Chief Ojo, the Bada
of Ṣaki, in his histories of Ọyọ (in which, for example, he assigns
892 as the year of Ọranyan's death) and Ṣaki, by Fr Oguntuyi
in his history of Ado Ekiti (he claims that the second Ẹwi
reigned precisely from 1444 to 1471), and by Chief Aṣara for
Ọwọ (where the first Ọlọwọ is described as having reigned 'c.
1019'). These writers may have been influenced in this respect
by Chief Egharevba's famous *Short History of Benin*, first published in 1934, in which dates are given for all the oba of the
kingdom from Ọranyan, whose coming is said to have been
'about A.D. 1170'; this list was compiled with the help of the
Esekhurhe, or priest of the royal ancestors.[8] The method seems
likely to be reasonably accurate for reigns within about the last
hundred years, but for earlier periods it cannot be accepted as
providing more than a rough indication of the time-scale, and
for the earliest times even this can hardly be claimed. At Ọyọ,
for example, it is said that Alafin Abipa was born twenty years

after the fall of Ọyọ ile, that Ọrompọtọ ruled for twenty years, and that the return to Ọyọ from Igboho was accomplished in the twentieth year of Abipa's reign; each case can be taken as signifying no more than 'rather a long time' or 'towards the end of the reign'.

Another approach consists in establishing an average length of reign for a kingship over as long a period as possible and then multiplying the number of known ọba by the average to obtain an approximation to the date of origin of the dynasty and other events.[9] For Ọyọ, an average of 11·8 years reign can be calculated, taking 1754, established as the probable date of the accession of Alafin Labisi,[10] as the starting-point and ignoring the two interregna which are recollected in order to compensate for the series of extremely short reigns during Gaha's tyranny. This suggests that Ọyọ was founded in the first part of the fifteenth century, that the town was abandoned by Onigbogi in the second quarter of the sixteenth century, that Igboho was founded towards the end of the sixteenth century, and that Ọyọ ile was re-occupied early in the seventeenth century after an exile lasting some three-quarters of a century.[11] But at Ketu, where the list of Alaketu, as recorded by Parrinder, contains forty-nine names, four more than the list of Alafin of Ọyọ, the average length of reign, calculated from that of Oje (c. 1748–60), is 21·5 years and from Adegbede (1853–8) is 18·5 years; the first average would give approximate dates of A.D. 931 for the emigration from Ile Ifẹ and 974 for the foundation of Ketu under Ede, while the second yields 1085 and 1101. This conflicts with the conclusion above that the tradition of the sending forth from Ifẹ of some six or more founding princes at one time, or over a short period, represents an historical event.

Clearly, the averaging method cannot be accepted as giving more than the broadest approximation; experiments carried out with lists of rulers whose completeness is unquestioned, for example, the sovereigns of England, illustrate the range of possible inaccuracy.[12] In the case of Ọyọ, moreover, there seems to have been a change in the method of succession, from primogeniture in early times, which would tend to produce long reigns, to a combination of the hereditary and elective systems, which would produce greater stability but shorter reigns. Again, in the older Yoruba kingships it seems likely that the lists are incomplete. In Ọyọ it is said that the names of many early Alafin who died away from the capital and were not buried in the Bara, or royal mausoleum, were deliberately omitted from any enumeration – as apparently happened with Oluodo, who according to some accounts succeeded Ọbalokun and was drowned in the Niger while being pursued by the Nupe. Indeed, it is claimed at Ọyọ that there have been in all some seventy Alafin, which is twenty-three more than those usually enumerated and would give by averaging a founding date of about 1170. A similar statement about unrecorded ọba is made in connection with the king-lists at Ilẹṣa and Ado Ekiti, and doubtless elsewhere. But the Ketu list seems to have been kept with unusual care and commands more confidence, though the average length of reign seems by comparison with some other African lists to be rather long.[13] Two main possibilities present themselves: first, to accept that Ọyọ is a state of more recent origin than Ketu, which would accord with the description in some versions of the legend of Ọyọ as the junior kingdom (though the reason here is that it was founded by Oduduwa's youngest son or grandson) and that the migration of princes from Ifẹ took place over a period of several centuries, which is inherently improbable and would seriously conflict with tradition about the dispersal; the second approach would be to average the averages and to postulate a founding date of about 1300 for Ọyọ, Ketu, and the other senior kingdoms where the names of thirty-five or more rulers (to follow the criteria suggested above) are recollected. The second alternative seems at present to provide the best working basis for a chronology, and the founding date of c. 1300 is supported by examination of one further king-list, that of neighbouring Benin.

The Benin list is relevant to a discussion of Yoruba chronology, since not only is the dynasty held, in both Benin and Yoruba tradition, to stem from Oduduwa, but there has also been considerable contact between Benin and its Yoruba neighbours and, as has been seen, a number of events in the history of the latter are assigned in Benin to the reigns of particular Oba. Fortunately, the list of Oba of Benin appears to have been preserved with singular care. Unfortunately, on the other hand, the fifteenth-century Portuguese visitors to the capital did not include in their accounts the names of the Oba with whom they dealt, so that the first identifiable name from written record is that of Osifo, the personal name of Obanosa, mentioned by Landolphe, who came to the throne only about 1804.

The list of Oba of Benin, in the versions collected by Roupell (in 1898), Talbot, and Egharevba, has provided the basis for a study of Benin chronology by R. E. Bradbury,[14] who, working backwards and adducing local traditions and some information from non-Benin sources, establishes approximate dating for the Oba back to the late fifteenth century. His conclusion about the earlier period is that if the strong tradition in Benin that Ozolua was ruler at the time of the Portuguese visit in 1485 is correct, and if he is correctly enumerated as the fifteenth Oba, then 'it appears likely that the dynasty began not later than about 1300'; Egharevba's claim that it began about 1200 must on his own evidence 'be regarded as too early. But for this period nothing is certain.'[15] This conclusion is reached without reference to the averaging method, but it is worth noting that taking 1735, the probable date of accession of Oba Eresoyan, as the starting-point, a high average length of reign of 24·7 years is reached; this would give a date of c. 1050 for the beginning of the dynasty and of about 1390 for the accession of Ozolua, both of which seem, in the light of the other evidence, much too early. This discrepancy may be due to the change from brother-to-brother succession to primogeniture in the Benin kingship, which took place possibly as late as 1700. As explained above, primogeniture tends to produce a longer average reign, so that extrapolation backwards can be expected to produce a result which is too early.[16] But Bradbury has also shown that Egharevba's assignment of the Oba from Ewuare to Orhogba to part of the fifteenth and most of the sixteenth centuries is probably accurate, and this in turn enables approximate dates to be affixed to a number of events in Yoruba history.

To sum up, the evidence derived from the king-lists leads to the tentative conclusion that the major kingdoms of the Yoruba, and also the second dynasty of Benin, were founded around the beginning of the fourteenth century, perhaps in the course of a generation or perhaps during a period of sustained political vigour at Ifẹ lasting for a hundred years or more on either side of 1300. Until the eighteenth century no firm dates can be given, but the exile of the Alafin of Ọyọ at Igboho can be provisionally assigned to the sixteenth century and the return to Ọyọ ile, followed by the expansion of the kingdom, to the first part of the seventeenth century. A comparison of the traditions of Benin with those of the Yoruba suggest that at the turn of the fifteenth century Benin was engaged in wars with the eastern Yoruba kingdoms, and also with Ijẹbu, and that from the mid- or late-sixteenth-century Benin was extending her authority in a south-westerly direction along the coast and founded a politically subservient dynasty at Lagos during this period.

VIII · An Ọba and his People[1]

Two closely associated institutions dominated the political life of the Yoruba in pre-colonial times: the king and the town. Nearly all Yoruba were (and are) townspeople in the sense that they belonged to a town, even though they might spend most of the year on farms up to 20 miles distant (and perhaps nearer to another town than to the parent one).[2] This was a feature which, apparently for centuries, distinguished them from most other African peoples. Their towns were many and populous, and at the centre of each (with one or two relatively recent exceptions) dwelt an ọba in his afin or palace, a building of some pretensions with its gabled entrance and external veranda, usually facing on the main market-place.

The settlement of the ọba provides the most probable explanation of this Yoruba propensity for town dwelling and the willingness of many of them to live up to several miles from their farms. The ọba's office and person were sacred; he was the priest and protector of his people, and they naturally wished to live in his shadow. Considerations of defence supplied another motive, for though most Yoruba towns do not seem specifically sited for defensive purposes, all settlements of any importance were walled and surrounded by a protective zone of thick bush. The town was also the centre of commerce, where markets were regularly held, usually every four days,[3] and tolls paid to the ọba. Finally may be cited that intangible but real factor, national character: the Yoruba are a social and gregarious people, and these qualities can best be satisfied in an urban life.

But transcending the town and its ọba was the kingdom or state, and it could be maintained that the most imposing political achievement of the Yoruba in pre-colonial times was in organizing themselves into substantial units of government well adapted in size to their resources. Among these states Ifẹ enjoyed seniority and prestige. Its ruler, the Ọni, commanded respect not so much as the ruler of one of the Yoruba group of kingdoms, since Ifẹ is not remembered as having attained political or military importance, but as the king of a town which was regarded as the cradle of the race and whence the rulers and leading elements in the populations of most of the other kingdoms traced their origins. According to Akinjogbin, the traditions of relationship between the kingdoms and of the seniority of Ifẹ amounted to a system of government to which he gives the Yoruba word for family, ẹbi. He claims that under this ẹbi system the Ọni exercised a constitutional and divinely sanctioned control over the other kingdoms, expressed especially in his influence over the consecration of their rulers. The sending of the sword of state and the divination calabashes (igba iwa) from Ifẹ to a new Alafin provides some support for this in the case of Ọyọ.[4] Nevertheless, the individual traditions and histories of all the kingdoms, and of Ọyọ in particular, refute this theory, and indeed it seems that the Ọni's own state was politically subordinate to its stronger neighbours in at least two periods of its history – to the Ọyọ empire and later to the short-lived Ibadan empire. Under the stable conditions of the colonial regime the Ọni of Ifẹ did attempt to assert a superiority over the other ọba, and on one occasion he was rebuffed, when he told the chiefs of Ekiti on his visit to Ado in 1936, 'I am on the throne as the father and you are on thrones as sons'; to this the Deji of Akure, in the names of his brother ọba, replied that as the Ọni was on the throne of his father, so also were all the Ekiti ọba on the thrones of their own fathers.[5] In like manner the pretensions of the Alafin to seniority were resisted by the other Yoruba kings whenever their political power allowed this independence, and it is remarkable that even where Ọyọ extended military and economic control over adjacent states, this was exercised indirectly through resident officials accredited to the rulers of the respective towns. No case seems to be recollected where an ọba, much less a royal family, was dispossessed by either an Alafin or an Ọni (though on one occasion, as related on page 79 above, an Alafin seems to have intervened to impose a new Awujalẹ at Ijẹbu Ode).

Each of the Yoruba states was thus a sovereign entity, though related by tradition and sentiment to Ifẹ and the other states of the Ifẹ family (much like the ties between the seven Hausa Bakwai of northern Nigeria). The kingdom had a recognized centre in its capital town where the leading ọba resided, surrounded by his chiefs, officials, and priests. This leading ọba was the wearer of a beaded crown, bestowed on his ancestor, according to legend, from Ifẹ, and his town was defined as *ilu alade*, 'crowned town' or capital. Subordinate towns were classified as *ilu ereko* (literally, 'towns on the fringe of the farmland'), which in turn ranged from the *ilu ọlọja* (a market town with an ọba not entitled to a beaded crown) to the *ileto* (village), *abule* (hamlet), and *ago* or *aba* (camp, settlement); village heads were known in Ọyọ as Balẹ, a title which has now spread to most kingdoms. In some cases a kingdom contained more than one crowned ọba and *ilu alade*; as a result of regrouping during the nineteenth-century wars, two towns, Abẹokuta and Ṣagamu, each had a number of crowned ọba reigning in their different quarters. The titles of the ọba usually derived from their towns, as in the case of the Ọlọwọ ('the lord of Ọwọ') and many others. There are some notable exceptions to this, such as the Alafin and the Awujalẹ, where other circumstances explain the title. The practice of forming titles from the name of a town or village has spread in recent years, and former Balẹ, such as the Olubadan of Ibadan and many lesser rulers, have assumed territorial designations.[6]

In addition to its recognized centre, there were also recognized boundaries to the Yoruba kingdom. These were apparently sometimes demarcated by earthworks, of which the

Eredo of Ijẹbu Ode is the most conspicuous, but in any case the allegiance of every town was known, though liable to change with the fortunes of the kingdom, and there were clear, and strongly held, opinions about the extent of its farmland and forest. Certain obligations were laid on the subordinate towns by the government of a kingdom; for example, G. J. A. Ojo has identified the towns within the Owo kingdoms from which service was required in maintaining and repairing the ruler's palace, the Afin Olowo.[7] In size the kingdom varied considerably, from Oyo, covering over 10,000 square miles, to the miniature states of Ekiti, where, for example, the Ẹwi of Ado ruled over only some seventeen small towns or villages. The larger kingdoms were subdivided into provinces. In addition, there were city-states, such as Badagry and the Ẹgbado towns. In Oyo, which seems to have been the most centralized in government as well as the greatest in extent, there were four provinces: the Ẹkun Osi, or 'left-hand district' (that is, east of the Ogun) surrounding the capital; the Ẹkun Otun, the 'right-hand district' (west of the Ogun); Ibolo, and Epo. In each there were a dozen or more lesser ọba ruling over the more important towns with their internally autonomous sub-kingdoms; in the Ẹkun Osi, for example, the leading ọba was the Onikoyi of Ikoyi. These rulers were required to visit the Alafin during the annual Bẹrẹ festival, when they presented him with thatching grass (*bẹrẹ*) for his palace.[8] The large Ijẹbu and Ẹgba kingdoms consisted of distinct but associated sub-kingdoms, among which two of the crowned ọba, the Awujalẹ and the Alake, were respectively pre-eminent. This quasi-federalism seems to reflect the historical development of these two kingdoms, each of which has traditions of several separate migrations into their areas.

The Yoruba ọba is usually described as a sacred or divine king.[9] His coronation and installation were performed with solemn and lengthy rites which set him apart. He lived a life thereafter of ordered ceremonial, secluded in his palace, subject to many ritual restraints and approached only with infinite respect and by designated persons of the Court. He rarely appeared in public, and then always robed and, in the case of the great ọba, wearing a beaded crown whose fringe hid his face. He was not only the head of the town and kingdom but their personification, reincarnating also all his ancestors back to the origin of the dynasty, and he was titular head of all religious cults in the kingdom. This sacred aspect of Yoruba kingship did not lead to the ọba's becoming an autocrat but rather the reverse. Not only was he bound by rules and precedents in his personal life but these also required him to submit all business to councils of chiefs and officers, and only after consultation and deliberation by these bodies could a policy be decided upon and proclaimed in the ọba's name. Every ọba had at least one council of chiefs who formed a powerful, usually hereditary, cabinet, and in most kingdoms there were lesser councils for the regulation of the different aspects of government. Thus the ọba was at least as much fettered by constitutional procedure as a ruler in a modern democracy. Moreover, the chieftancies were hereditary within the 'descent group' or extended families which made up the population of the town. Thus the chiefs were representatives of their family groups as well as being officials of the king and kingdom. It was these restraints which most sharply distinguished the Yoruba kingdom from the authoritarian monarchies of, for example, Benin and Dahomey, and from those based on conquest, like the Fulani emirates of northern Nigeria.

There is a tradition that the kingship at Ọyọ originally descended by primogeniture in the male line, and this may have been the case in other kingdoms of the Yoruba. But at some period, apparently in the seventeenth century, the patrilineal hereditary system was modified at Ọyọ so that the choice of Alafin was exercised by the Ọyọ Mesi among a number of candidates from the royal house. This system was followed in most of the kingdoms and towns, with the notable exceptions of Egba Alake and Oke

Ọna, where all freemen were theoretically qualified to be chosen as ọba by divination.[10] The royal family in most cases divided into two or more branches occupying different compounds in the town (and the usual practice in the present day is for the branches to take turns in presenting candidates to the leading chiefs as king-makers on each vacancy). With one or two exceptions (for example, the reputedly Borgu dynasties of Ṣaki and Kiṣi), the royal lines claim descent from the founders of the town who were of the same Yoruba stock as their followers. There is thus no trace of a ruling caste in these kingships, such as obtains in the Hausa and Nupe states since the establishment of the Fulani dynasties in the nineteenth century. The royal wives were usually chosen from local women, and at Ọyọ new members of the Ọyọ Mesi were required to present a daughter in marriage to the Alafin. Ọyọ tradition, however, records an occasional marriage alliance with a neighbouring dynasty; Ṣango's mother is said to have been given in marriage to Ọranyan by her father, the King of Nupe; Ofinran was the offspring of a Borgu woman, and in 1729 the King of Dahomey bestowed 'one of his Handsomest Daughters' on the Alafin.[11]

Many considerations determined the king-makers' choice of an ọba, but a guiding principle was to select a ruler who would respect and conform to the constitutional conventions of the kingdom. This would usually be a man neither youthful nor elderly, and in certain circumstances the king-makers deliberately avoided a candidate whose presence or personality seemed too commanding; at Ado Ekiti in 1910, for example, a prince was rejected because he was so tall he would have looked down on his subjects.[12] The rules governing the succession varied from kingdom to kingdom. At Ọyọ there was a custom, broken on the death of Atiba in 1859, that the Alafin's eldest son, the Arẹmọ, who was associated with his father in the government, should take his life on his father's death. In Ijẹbu and Ọwọ it was held that no prince was eligible for the throne unless he had been born to a reigning ọba. In early times it was not necessarily a male who was chosen as ruler, and the traditions of Ọyọ, Ṣabe, Ondo, and Ileṣa record the reigns of female ọba.

Despite the limitations on his power, the ọba was no cipher or fainéant. In the first place, the sacredness of his office was neither empty nor nominal: he was really regarded by his people as a divinity with whose well-being their own condition was bound up. Then he was almost always the richest man in the town, since all tolls at gates and markets were paid to him, as well as various other forms of tribute. He was also the source of honour, able to bestow (usually within certain families), and in some cases to withdraw, titles and chieftaincies. With the chiefs he controlled the use of all land belonging to the town. Though legislative and judicial matters were discussed and decided by his councils, all laws were promulgated in his name, and he was the supreme arbiter in appeals. Military power was not in his hands, since the army was controlled by the war chiefs, but he alone could authorize a campaign; he also had at his disposal a personal bodyguard of household officers and slaves. Thus, if relations with other parties in the town or kingdom were strained the ọba had many means of exerting his influence, though intrigue rather than a display of force was his usual weapon. For their part the chiefs could assert themselves against the ọba by boycotting the palace, but an attempt to govern for long without his participation would be considered detrimental to the welfare of the town. In extreme cases of disagreement or the collapse of a policy the chiefs could contrive the deposition of an ọba or even require his suicide. In general, however, 'a delicate balance of power' (in Lloyd's words) was achieved, and all parties in the state were usually at pains to maintain this.

The organization of the Alafin's household as re-created at New Ọyọ by Atiba is described in detail by Johnson.[13] It is clear that the life led by the inhabitants of the palace at Ọyọ was as elaborately ceremonious as that at Versailles or Schön-brunn, and based similarly on a hierarchy of office and honour;

it has been stigmatized by Morton-Williams as 'over-elaborate and anachronistic', and certainly it no longer reflected the true power of the king and his ministers at New Ọyọ. After the long rites of his coronation and installation, the Alafin disappeared into the seclusion of the palace and thereafter appeared in public only on the annual Ifa, Orun, and Bẹrẹ festivals, when, crowned and robed, he took his place in the throne room (*aganju*) or on its gabled veranda (*kọbi aganju*). Apart from this, he rarely left the palace officially, although on moonlight nights he was permitted by custom to take an evening stroll incognito. Within the palace he was attended by numerous, carefully graded officials: his master of the horse, chaplains, musicians, drummers, and others, amounting to several hundreds. In addition, there were two bodies of officials of particular importance. The first were the eunuchs, called *iwefa* or 'lordlings of the palace' in Johnson's agreeable translation. The three principal iwẹfa bore high titles and represented the Alafin in various ways: the first, the Ọna Ẹfa ('eunuch of the centre') personated the Alafin in judicial processes; the second, the Ọtun Ẹfa ('eunuch of the right'), in religious ceremonies, especially the Ṣango rites, and the third, the Osi Ẹfa ('eunuch of the left'), in administrative and military functions. Secondly, a grade lower than the iwẹfa were the sixty-eight tonsured ilari ('scar heads'), royal slaves, each of whom bore a title alluding to some attribute or intention of the ọba (for example, the *ọba ko ṣe tan*, 'the king is not ready'). Members of this corps provided the royal bodyguard, and others journeyed round the kingdom supervising the government. Almost equally powerful were the ladies of the palace, led by the *iya ọba* or official mother of the Alafin (his real mother having been invited to 'go to sleep' and 'decently buried' on her son's accession) and including numerous wives (*ayaba*, 'the queens'), officials, priestesses, and a group of female ilari. Apart from all these palace residents, certain members of the royal family held official positions at court. These included the Arẹmo, the three relatives designated as the 'fathers of the king', and his six 'brothers'.

Though the Court of Ọyọ, the most powerful and highly organized kingdom, was probably the most elaborate, descriptions of the households of other ọba suggest that it was repeated on a smaller scale, and with local differences in titles and duties, in the capitals of the other kingdoms and, on a still diminishing scale, in the subordinate towns everywhere. A visitor to any Yoruba ruler today, even in a small town or village, is at once aware of the courtly and privileged atmosphere which surrounds these kings.

The royal Court formed but one of the three pillars of government at Ọyọ, the two others being the corporation of major chiefs known as the Ọyọ Mesi and the Ogboni society.[14] The Ọyọ Mesi consisted of seven chiefs or councillors, all holding titles hereditary in their families. Of these the leader was the Baṣọrun, whose power and influence, according to Johnson, were 'commonly greater than those of the others put together'. His position derived from his role as principal king-maker and as interpreter through annual divination of the Alafin's personal *orun*, or spirit, as well as from his command of the army of the capital. Johnson writes that, 'There were times in the history of the nation when the Baṣọruns were more powerful than the Alafin himself', and the example of Gaha at once comes to mind. The Ogboni, which was devoted to the cult of the earth, was by no means peculiar to Ọyọ, being prominent in most of the other kingdoms, especially among the Ẹgba, where it constituted the leading civil authority;[15] in Ijẹbu the same society was known as Oṣugbo. In all these places it was charged with both judicial and political functions. At Ọyọ it played a 'mediating role' between the palace officials and the Ọyọ Mesi, and is described by Morton-Williams as second to the Ọyọ Mesi in its 'capacity to sanction the king's rule'. Members of the latter attended its meetings, held within the palace, though they had no priestly office. Its transactions were reported to the

I

Alafin, who took no part in its deliberations or decisions, by a woman member. Its priests played an important part in the installation ceremonies of a new Alafin, ensuring the transmission to him of the powers of his ancestors.[16] In addition to the Ogboni, other cult organizations, usually of lesser importance, existed in all towns and kingdoms; at Oyo the Egungun, a masked association led by the Alapini, a member of the Oyo Mesi, had a share in government by virtue of its function of recalling the ancestors. Overlapping and parallel with all these bodies were associations of chiefs concerned with particular aspects of government and daily life, especially the conduct of war, of trade, and of hunting. Among the Egba the leading chiefs were members of the Ogboni; the Parakoyi were the trade chiefs, while the hunters, who in war acted as scouts for the main army, were grouped together as the Ode. Under Lisabi a fourth order was created in the towns, the Olorogun, leaders of the militia or war chiefs.[17] Biobaku writes that the first three organizations 'corresponded very much to the division of life into youth, middle age and old age'.[18] In the Ijebu kingdom there were three main councils, occasionally overlapping in membership. The highest, the Ilamuren, consisting of the great magnates and officials under the presidency of the Olisa, discharged legislative, executive, and judicial functions relating to the whole kingdom. Next came the Osugbo under the Oliwo, mainly concerned with the maintenance of order and the dispensing of justice, and then the Pampa, composed of the younger men and overseeing administration and warfare. Whereas there was only one Ilamuren, that of the Awujale's capital, Osugbo and Pampa councils on the lines of those in Ijebu Ode existed in all the other major towns.

The government of a Yoruba kingdom and its capital thus presents a complex and somewhat confusing picture, mainly because of the fusion of political, judicial, and religious concepts and the division of responsibilities. Even in so small a kingdom as Ikerre (in Ekiti), for example, the Government exhibited this Byzantine quality; there were two groups of leading chiefs, each divided into three grades, and four main councils: the Iyare Mẹfa, or inner council, meeting daily; the Ajo Iyare, meeting every eight days to discuss town affairs; the Ajagun, or war council, and the Ajo Ilu, or general council of the town, held four times yearly.[19] Yet in practice all seems to have worked smoothly enough in these delicately balanced governments, except when some external pressure or crisis intervened to overthrow the slow and deliberate processes of the constitution. Naturally each kingdom developed different mechanisms for dealing with its individual problems, so that it would be futile to postulate any 'model' constitution for a Yoruba kingdom. On the other hand, with the notable exceptions of the new states of the nineteenth century, the main features of government – the town, the sacred ọba at its centre, the hierarchy of hereditary chiefs and priests with their jealously guarded responsibilities – remained constant.

This form of government was not confined to the capital, but was repeated throughout the kingdom, every town forming a microcosm of the central government. The place of the crowned ọba was taken by a lesser ruler, generally entitled to wear only a simple crown or coronet (called *akoro* in Ọyọ) or a cap of office. Usually these rulers were chosen like the greater ọba by kingmakers from royal houses and presented for approval to the ọba of the kingdom, while in some cases the latter nominated the provincial rulers. In the Ijẹsa kingdom the majority of the provincial rulers were cadets of the royal family of the capital, and an Ọwa of Ilesa was required to have served as a Lọja in the provinces before becoming eligible for his throne. In most kingdoms the leading ọba exercised the right to promote his uncrowned subordinates by conferring simple crowns and other insignia on them and their descendants. Like the office of the ọba, that of village head or balẹ was hereditary, as indeed were nearly all chieftainces in town or country.

Finally, turning from the ọba and his court and nobles, the

ọba's people[20] must be considered. From the sociologist's point of view, the most important feature of Yoruba society was its organization into patrilineal 'descent groups' or 'extended families' of which the royal lineage was one. These consisted of persons who claimed descent from a common ancestor, usually living together in one quarter of a town and often numbering over a thousand. Despite its hierarchical character, Yoruba society was in practice surprisingly democratic. Distinctions of rank and wealth were offset by the obligations and benefits of the family and by common ownership of the land ; opportunities to acquire high office and wealth were many, and no freeman was without a protector among the chiefs of his town. Then, just as all Yoruba were townspeople in the sense of either living in or having close ties with some parent town, so all were farmers, having a share in the family land and taking a part in its cultivation. But for many, farming was only a part-time or seasonal occupation, and a variety of crafts and trades were practised in the towns and countryside. Among the most prominent crafts were weaving and the working of iron, while some important crafts, such as pottery making and cloth dyeing, were reserved for women. The followers of these occupations often came from one family or group of families and compounds, and were bound together in guilds under the protection of their own deities and chiefs. In addition to these guilds, the population was grouped into associations (*egbẹ*) of different kinds; in some places, notably Ekiti, these were 'age-sets', associations of those born within a certain period to whom appropriate duties and public works were assigned by the town authorities, but elsewhere, for example at Ọyọ, the age-set system either never existed or was long ago replaced by associations of a social or professional kind.[21] In this society women played an important role, engaging in trade and crafts and admitted to a share in the conduct of government and religion.

Apart from the free subjects of the ọba, every kingdom contained an unfree population.[22] A distinction must first be made between slavery and the system known as *iwọfa*, which was practised among the Yoruba. In the latter a person could voluntarily pawn either himself or a relative (usually a child) as security for debt or to raise capital for trading or other purposes. This was a temporary measure which was discharged after the agreed services had been rendered to the creditor by the debtor. True slavery also existed, apparently on a large scale. The slaves were usually employed as farm labourers or servants in households and as bodyguards to the chiefs. Though they were liable to be used as sacrifices by their masters, they seem otherwise to have been well treated. They were allowed to own property and to cultivate their own plots of land. The children of slaves remained the property of their parents' master, but the child of a freeman and a slave was free. It was possible for a slave to emancipate himself if he succeeded in accumulating enough property to satisfy his master. The ranks of the slaves were recruited from debtors, criminals, and (probably the major source) prisoners of war. Thus they were of mixed origin, some being native to the kingdom, others Yoruba from elsewhere, and others non-Yoruba. Unfortunately there is little evidence to determine either the proportion of the population which was unfree or the proportion of slaves who were of foreign origin. To Clapperton and the Landers the establishment of the regimes of Afọnja and the Fulani at Ilọrin was repeatedly described as a revolt of the Alafin's Hausa slaves,[23] which suggests that in the Ọyọ kingdom the alien slave population had increased to a dangerous extent.

IX · War

The reviewer of a recent history of Dahomey complained that *l'histoire-bataille* played too large a part in the work.[1] This suggests that the critic had thought little about the nature either of man or of his history. War is the most decisive act of policy undertaken by any nation. Moreover, among the Yoruba kingdoms, and most West African states, campaigns were so frequent as to be a normal, though seasonal, activity. Political and military history are so closely connected in the area and period covered by this book as to be almost synonymous. Wars, campaigns, and battles are of first importance, both in themselves and in their consequences. It is therefore pertinent to consider how they were fought, though until the latter part of the nineteenth century the evidence is fragmentary.[2]

The leadership of the armies of the different states and towns belonged to the chiefs who bore military titles. The Ọyọ system seems to have been the most highly developed, and as well as being reproduced in the provincial towns of that kingdom, it became the pattern for Ibadan and other states in the nine-teenth century. The Alafin, like other ọba, rarely took the field himself, and on Atiba's accession it was decided that in future he should never do so. The commander of the army of the capi-tal, and so the senior general, was the Bashọrun, who was also the Alafin's first minister. The field command was exercised by a series of war chiefs of whom the leader was the Balogun ('war lord' or 'war father'). Separate ranks or titles were con-ferred on the leaders of the vanguard (made up of youthful warriors), the cavalry, and the older chiefs, who accompanied the army as advisers and looked after the camp and baggage. Apart from these officers, there was also the *corps d'élite*, known as the Ẹsọ, a body of seventy noble captains usually resident in the capital, ranking next to the Ọyọ Mesi. In later times one of the Ẹsọ was appointed as Arẹ Ọna Kakamfo (usually abbreviated to Kakamfo or Arẹ) or generalissimo. The Kakamfo was given wide powers to carry out specific military operations. He established an independent base near the frontiers of the kingdom and was not usually allowed to visit the capital.[3] Finally, among the important changes in Yoruba warfare during the nineteenth century was the emergence of a class of professional military leaders or war lords, of whom Ogedengbe of Ilẹsa and the chiefs of Ibadan are examples. Such men owed their positions to their soldierly qualities rather than to birth, and their restless ambition was a contributory factor to the prolongation of the wars.[4]

Military service was theoretically obligatory on all able-bodied freemen. The households of the chiefs, with their numerous slaves and bodyguards, formed the nucleus of the army, and in the nineteenth century, when the new professional warriors maintained large numbers of 'war boys', this element grew in importance, especially in Ibadan, until it resembled a standing army. Apart from these, an army was normally raised on a short-term basis from those who responded to the call to arms for each campaign and enrolled with their weapons in the ranks of the particular chief to whom each owed allegiance. The army of the capital provided the main army of the kingdom, but every town had some sort of force, and contingents from these towns were absorbed into the army of the kingdom where conditions allowed; in the Ibadan empire, and probably in other kingdoms too, quotas of troops, food, and ammunition were required from the provincial towns. The size of the Yoruba armies must have varied considerably according to the resources of the kingdom and the situation. Snelgrave writes of an Ọyọ army sent against Dahomey in the early eighteenth century as consisting of 'many Thousands' of horsemen,[5] and Norris writes:

> The *Dahomans*, to give an idea of the strength of an *Eyoe*
> army, assert, that when they go to war, the general spreads
> the hide of a buffaloe before the door of his tent, and pitches
> a spear in the ground, on each side of it; between which the
> soldiers march, until the multitude, which pass over the hide,
> have worn a hole through it; as soon as this happens, he
> presumes that his forces are numerous enough to take the
> field.[6]

According to Clapperton, in 1826:

> The military force of Ọyọ consists of the caboceers [chiefs]
> and their own immediate retainers, which, allowing one
> hundred and fifty to each, will not give such immense armies
> as we have sometimes heard stated; that of Yoruba is per-
> haps as numerous as any of the kingdoms of Africa.[7]

On the other hand, Jones, the author of a professional report on the Ẹgba army in 1861, emphasized that the chiefs' warrior retainers formed only a small proportion of the Ẹgba forces when that state engaged in full-scale war; the majority were 'Farmers or engaged in peaceful occupation' who either enlisted voluntarily or, in time of crisis, were conscripted. He estimated that in the battle which he witnessed at Ijaye on 23 May 1861 '17,000 men engaged in mortal combat' – of whom 'the killed on both sides, as ascertained by spies were five and the wounded under fifty!'[8]

Bosman writes that the (presumably) Ọyọ army which attacked Allada in 1698 was a wholly cavalry force.[9] Snelgrave and Dalzel[10] confirm that the Ọyọ armies sent to the south-west in the first part of the eighteenth century were cavalry, though the passage quoted above from Norris suggests the occasional inclusion of infantry. It seems reasonable

to conclude that the predominance of Ọyọ over its neighbours, and also the exceptional extent of the kingdom, were
based upon the possession of a skilled cavalry. The capital
and most of the kingdom lay within the savannah, where
cavalry could move with ease and speed. Horses could be better
maintained here than in the tsetse-ridden forests of the south,
and though breeding was unprofitable, because of the combination of the long gestation period of the horse with some danger
even in the savannah from tsetse, remounts of good quality
could be readily obtained from the north and north-east, a
position which was to change in the troubles of the late eighteenth century.

In the other Yoruba kingdoms, situated mainly or wholly
within the forest belt, it is doubtful whether a cavalry arm
was developed to any extent, despite the adoption of cavalry
ranks and titles by the Ibadan and Abẹokutans in the nineteenth century. These armies must therefore have been almost
wholly composed of infantry, though, as nineteenth-century
observers noted, chiefs and their immediate followers (the latter
acting as scouts and messengers) were mounted. The majority
of the horses in the south were small and usually of poor quality,
though Jones observed of the Ẹgba horses that they were
'numerous and hardy'.[11]

Before the general introduction of firearms into Yoruba warfare the primary armament of the soldiers consisted of swords,
throwing spears or lances, javelins, and bows and arrows, including cross-bows, and these all continued to be used as sup-
plementary to firearms up to the end of the nineteenth-century
wars.[12] Infantry and cavalry weapons do not seem to have been
differentiated; the spear and the lance were apparently the
same weapon, and in the eighteenth century the Ọyọ horsemen
were sometimes armed with bows as well as the more usual
swords and lances.[13] Swords were of two main types: the heavier, single-bladed and eccentrically curved *agedengbe*, and the
ida, usually double-bladed and either with an elongated leaf-

shaped blade or approximating to European or Near Eastern types. Other varieties of swords and knives were also used, such as the short *jomo*, the *tanmogayi* (sabre), *ada*, *ogbo* or *ele* (cutlass), and *ọbẹ* (dagger). With the exception of the *ọbẹ*, all these were designed primarily for cutting rather than for thrusting or stabbing. Spears and arrows all carried iron heads, often barbed. In addition to these primary weapons, clubs of different types, in both iron and wood, throwing knives, fighting bracelets, and slings were used as secondary armament, though probably only by foot-soldiers. Apart from that small proportion of the swords and knives which had steel blades, all these weapons were of local manufacture.

Firearms were not brought into general use in the Yoruba armies until around the 1840s, considerably later than in some other Guinea states.[14] Yet the Ekiti had encountered firearms probably as early as the sixteenth century, when Benin soldiers, armed with guns, supported the Ikẹrrẹ in a war against the Ado.[15] Again, in the early eighteenth century an Ọyọ cavalry force lost an engagement to Dahomean infantry armed with guns, the noise of the firing so alarming the Ọyọ horses that their riders could not bring them to charge the enemy.[16] Unlike the older weapons, firearms could not be manufactured locally, but it is surprising that the Ọyọ did not earlier obtain supplies from their non-African partners in the Atlantic slave trade. It is significant that the first use of firearms on any considerable scale by a Yoruba army was in the 1820s, when the Ijẹbu, noted for their trading contacts on the lagoon, equipped their soldiers with guns in the Owu war, while about this time the Ọyọ, according to Lander, were procuring 'Quantities of muskets' from the east, though they were of little use as 'the people . . . do not know how to handle them with effect' and sometimes carried them into battle without powder or ball.[17] As late as the Battle of Osogbo, about 1840, firearms played little part, but by the time of the Ijaye war, opening in 1860, the musket had become the primary weapon of the Yoruba infantry. These muskets were primitive flintlocks firing shot.[18] They were known as Dane guns, from the major source of import. Breech-loading rifles, firing cartridges, were introduced by the Ẹgba during this war, and these modern precision weapons assumed great importance during the Sixteen Years' War.[19]

The dress and accoutrement of the Yoruba warrior can be reconstructed in some detail, at least so far as nineteenth-century use is concerned. Though Jones refers to the Ẹgba foot-soldiers at Ijaye as wearing distinctive striped war jackets,[20] there does not seem to have been any concept of uniform; friend could usually be distinguished from foe at close quarters by his facial marks. Most soldiers doubtless wore the padded jackets, sewn over with cowries and charms, known as *gberi* or *lenku* and still used by hunters, and their leaders would have worn more elaborate versions of these with such additions as the *wabi*, or war-apron. Except for the tradition that Alafin Ofinran's Baṣọrun wore a coat of iron (*ẹwu irin*), and the preservation of a probably imported coat of chain mail in the palace at Ọwọ, there seems no trace of any use of metal armour by the Yoruba. Horse trappings and equipment probably varied according to the status of the rider. Both 'English' and Oriental saddles were in use, the latter with high pommel and cantle. Bits and stirrups were often cast in brass and handsomely decorated with geometrical patterns; surviving metal stirrups are all of the curved Arab type.[21]

Most towns were encircled by 'walls'. These were usually mounds or ramparts of banked-up earth, though occasionally free-standing mud walls were built; exceptionally, low dry-stone walls were constructed in hill country, where this material was abundant.[22] Though these served to mark the boundaries between the town and its outer farmland, they seem to have been primarily designed as fixed defences, and there are several accounts of their construction or repair in time of danger and of fighting along them. Often there was a double circuit of walls, enabling an army to be drawn up in the intervening space of one or two hundred yards, and sometimes – as at Ọyọ ile and Igboho – there were even three walls. The walls were of two main types: a mound up to about twenty feet in height and correspondingly broad, and a low breastwork only about four feet high. Both were provided with outer ditches planted with thorns and converted into a partial moat by the rains, beyond which there was usually a zone of dense bush for further protection. Gates and gatehouses were inserted at intervals; in some cases these were elaborate structures with angled entries and free-standing walls with slits for bowmen. Presumably the tops of the higher walls were flattened to allow movement along them; occasionally the lower walls were protected against erosion by a sloping roof of thatch, and elsewhere were increased in height by the addition of a bamboo palisade. In the nineteenth-century wars the Ẹgba and Ẹgbado erected wooden watch towers along their walls, though more often sentries were posted in high trees at the edge of the town or camp. At Ijaye Jones noted that most of the chiefs used 'reconnoitring glasses or telescopes' for observation of the enemy.[23]

Several European observers of the 'interior wars' of the Yoruba in the nineteenth century have dismissed them as mere slave raids and as conducted in a desultory and haphazard way, without strategy and with little attempt at tactics. But as has been demonstrated elsewhere,[24] the issues of these wars were primarily political, concerning, as in most wars in the world's history, questions of power, and this seems equally to apply to the earlier wars described in the first part of this book. Nor were strategic concepts lacking. The encirclement of the Ọyọ empire by Ojigi's army, for example, was an enterprise on a grand scale (if the tradition is accepted) while the withdrawal of the nineteenth century into the forests and Alafin Atiba's subsequent redisposition of responsibilities to Ibadan and Ijaye suggest an appreciation of the military and political situation at the level of strategy. Yet it is also true that war was often undertaken, at least before the nineteenth century, mainly as an annual or bi-annual exercise. Johnson writes: 'In early times expeditions were sent out every other year by the Alafin of Ọyọ to distant countries chiefly among the Popos. War was then for spoils and to keep their hands in . . .'[25] The dry season was chosen for such campaigns, and Snelgrave was told by the Dahomeans that the Ọyọ were obliged to retire at the beginning of the rains for want of forage (a rather unconvincing story).[26]

Warfare was undertaken by the Yoruba with deliberation. Only after lengthy discussion in the councils of the kingdom, exhortatory speeches to the troops, and sacrifices to the war standard did the army move out to the vicinity of the enemy. The next step was the formation of a camp. In the nineteenth-century wars, which were often prolonged from year to year, these camps were of such extent and elaboration as to resemble small towns. Walls (of the breastwork type) and an outer ditch were built, and within these the living-quarters of the troops were constructed of mud or branches and thatched with grass, and farms were planted with maize, cassava, and other crops.[27] A large part of the military operations in the nineteenth century consisted in skirmishes around these comfortable camps and in the maintenance of sieges, with only occasional clashes in the open and assaults along the walls of a town or camp.

The character of the fighting in the field was largely determined by the contrasting nature of the country. In the open savannah cavalry was predominant,[28] while in the forests of the south – as the Fulani learnt – horses were hindered in their movement and decimated by disease.[29] When battle was joined it usually took the form of isolated skirmishes, tactics being confined after the initial deployment to the use of reserve troops. Commanders were, however, able to exercise some control over their men by beating-out orders and information on their war-drums, which could also be used for deceiving the enemy. The introduction of firearms led to a decrease in close fighting, though it did not otherwise greatly affect methods of warfare. Descriptions of the fighting at Ijaye agree that the respective armies engaged in a series of short advances and retreats, each line of infantry discharging its weapons and then retiring to the rear to reload.[30] No concepts of covering fire or of fire and movement by even the smallest formation seem to have developed. This is understandable when the only firearms in use were the inaccurate and short-range flintlock muskets, but these tactics – if they can be so called – persisted even after rifles had become available from the 1860s onwards. Despite the high price of the rifles, there were considerable numbers in use by both sides in the later stages of the Kiriji war, though they continued to be used by individual marksmen rather than as a mass weapon, and were accordingly less effective than would be expected. In the fighting between the Ibadan and the Ilọrin farther north, firearms played little part, even down to the final skirmishes on the Ọtin in the 1890s. This last phase of the wars, indeed, resembled the sometimes unreal warfare of Rennaissance Italy, and at Ilobu in one of the last actions a battle was opened in Ariosto-style by a single combat between two champion lancers from the respective armies.[31]

Almost all reports about Yoruba warfare concern fighting on land. But naval battles must have occurred on the lagoon, where the Ijẹbu and Lagos peoples, and probably also the Ẹgba and Ẹgbado, maintained fleets of war canoes. There is a glimpse of this form of warfare in the eighteenth century when Dalzel, describing operations against Badagry by the Dahomean army, assisted by Ọyọ and Lagos, writes that the Ọba of Lagos sent thirty-two large canoes up the western lagoon in order to cut Badagry's communications, and took many prisoners in the course of this action.[32] Finally, though West African warfare apparently followed its conservative pattern for many centuries, human ingenuity could always play a part. On one occasion in the early eighteenth century, for example, an Ọyọ cavalry force invading Dahomey was baited with brandy and then attacked while they slept off their drunkenness.[33] Again, in 1825 the Fulani, according to a story told to

Clapperton, mounted an aerial incendiary attack against a group of Yoruba villages near Ọyọ ile. Clapperton writes:

> Algi consists of three walled villages, and before it was burnt down had been of considerable size: they pointed out a rock close to the south side of the town, from whence the Fellatas [Fulani] flew the pigeons to set fire to it. The mode of doing it was, by making combustibles fast to the tails of the birds, which, on being left loose from the hand, immediately flew to the tops of the thatched houses, while the Fellatas kept up a sharp fire of arrows, to prevent the inhabitants extinguishing the flames.[34]

Evidence about the casualties inflicted in Yoruba warfare is contradictory.[35] It seems likely that the scornful references by Burton and Jones to casualties almost derisorily low in comparison with the numbers involved in the nineteenth-century battles cannot be considered as applying to all the major engagements. The reports of missionary observers at Ijaye and Abẹokuta show that on occasion the numbers of killed and wounded were high; this applied particularly to engagements with the fierce Dahomeans. The fate of captives varied according to circumstances: the most unfortunate were executed on the battlefield, the most fortunate were released or redeemed, while the majority were sold into slavery. As to the general effects of the wars, it seems likely that both in the nineteenth century and earlier economic and social dislocation was confined to the towns which were the main protagonists, and that the lives of the country people continued to follow the old patterns. Nevertheless, these wars cannot be dismissed as mere slave raids nor as, in Trevor-Roper's picturesque phrase, 'the unrewarding gyrations of barbarous tribes'. They concerned real issues of politics and power, and in their consequences for the men and women of the Yoruba kingdoms they were momentous.

PART III

PART III

X · The Decline and Fall of Old Ọyọ

On 23 January 1826 Captain Hugh Clapperton, R.N., accompanied by his servant Richard Lander, an English merchant from the Benin River, Mr Houtson, and a small party of Africans, reached Ọyọ ile after travelling for forty-seven days, at first by canoe and then by horse and on foot, from Badagry up the road which was the main artery of the trade of the Ọyọ kingdom.[1] Lander was destined to return down the road to Badagry at the end of 1827 after Clapperton's death, taking only thirty days on this occasion,[2] and then travelled up it again with his brother John in 1830 on the journey from which he returned by sailing down the Niger to the sea, settling the long controversy about the course of the river. Although Clapperton and his companions may not have been the first Europeans to visit Ọyọ, having been preceded, according to Adams,[3] by a French officer from a slave ship, their accounts[4] provide the first known descriptions of the interior of Yorubaland.

Perhaps the most striking aspect of these journeys is the comparative ease and security with which they were accomplished. The diseases prevalent in West Africa took their toll, and before Ọyọ was reached Clapperton's colleagues, Captain Pearce and Dr Morrison, as well as the sailor Dawson, had died, but this was no reflection on political conditions along the road. Everywhere peace and order seemed to prevail. Escorts, carriers, and horses were available throughout without great difficulty, and the travellers and their goods went forward in safety. At 'Jannah' (Ijana in Ẹgbado) Clapperton writes:

133

I cannot omit bearing testimony to the singular and perhaps
unprecedented fact, that we have already travelled sixty
miles in eight days, with a numerous and heavy baggage,
and about ten different relays of carriers, without losing so
much as the value of a shilling public or private; a circumstance evincing not only somewhat more than common
honesty in the inhabitants, but a degree of subordination
and regular government which could not have been supposed to exist amongst a people hitherto considered bar-
barians.[5]

Lander described the road near 'Chaadoo' (about a day's
journey south-west of Ṣaki) as 'not at all inferior to a drive
round a gentleman's park in England'.[6] The towns were busy,
populous, and prosperous: in Ijana, for example, cloth and
earthenware were manufactured and the market was supplied
with many commodities, while the number of inhabitants of the
'large, double-walled town' of Kuṣu was reckoned to be at least
twenty thousand.[7] The farms were planted with many different
crops, and the people owned horses, asses, and mules and 'a
great abundance of sheep and goats'.[8] From Ọyọ down to the
coast the country still seemed firmly under the control of the
Alafin. The kingdom, according to Clapperton, extended in the
south to 'Puka' (Ipokia, a few miles inland from Badagry
across the River Yewa), Lagos, and Whydah, and was bounded
in other directions by Ketu, Borgu, 'Accoura, a province of
Benin' (presumably Akurẹ), and Ijẹbu. But the Alafin's claim
that 'Badagry, Alladah, and Dahomey' belonged to him was a
nostalgic recollection of the past tributary relationships rather
than a description of the contemporary situation, since all
three had by this time escaped from their allegiance to Ọyọ.[9]

The capital of this still large state was built 'on the sloping
side and round the base of a small range of granite hills which,
as it were, forms the citadel of the town', and was of imposing
size.

A belt of thick wood runs round the walls, which are built of clay and about twenty feet high, and surrounded by a dry ditch. There are ten gates in the walls, which are about fifteen miles in circumference, of an oval shape, about four miles in diameter one way, and six miles the other, the south end leaning against the rocky hills, and forming an inaccessible barrier in that quarter.

From the north gate to the palace was an hour's ride, or about five miles, much of the intervening ground being 'open and cultivated'. Within the town seven different markets were held every morning, selling a great variety of foodstuffs, animals, cloth, and apparently also slaves. Of the palace, Clapperton writes that it occupied about a square mile and was built of clay with thatched roofs, 'similar to those nearer the coast', and presumably the other compounds in the town were built in this way. He admired the decoration which he saw applied to the houses: 'The people of Katunga are fond of ornamenting their doors, and the posts which support their verandahs, with carvings; and they also have statues or figures of men and women, standing in their court yards.'[10] Lander was deeply impressed by the principal 'fetish hut' with its many carved figures, and noted that there were fifty other such shrines in the capital.[11] Most of these statues were presumably carved in wood, but these and other passages, together with a small number of objects associated with the town, suggest that there may also have been a tradition at Ọyọ of sculpture in bronze, stone, and terra-cotta, and there was evidently an Ọyọ art as distinct in style as the arts of Ifẹ and other towns of Yorubaland.[12]

But despite all the evidence afforded to Clapperton and the Landers, both on their journey from the coast and in the capital, that the people of Ọyọ enjoyed good 'mild' government and a prosperous economy, there were disquieting reports and signs that all was far from well in the kingdom. In the first place there had occurred the serious 'rebellion of the Hausa slaves against the king of Yarriba', as it was described to Clapperton at Ṣaki,[13] which led to the establishment at Ilọrin, only some twenty miles to the south-east of Ọyọ, of a base for the advance of the Fulani-led jihad of the recently founded empires of Sokoto and Gwandu. But the Fulani did not comprise the only danger with which the Ọyọ – and indeed, the Yoruba as a whole – were now faced. In addition, a number of the rulers of other large towns within the kingdom followed the example of Ilọrin in asserting their independence, and then, after successfully defying the Alafin, fell to quarrelling among themselves. Even more serious, a general state of war involving almost the whole of Yorubaland was approaching, usually referred to, rather misleadingly, as the 'civil' or 'inter-tribal' wars. This was precipitated by a war which broke out in the south between the Owu and a coalition of the Ifẹ and Ijẹbu, but fundamentally it was a consequence of the decline in the power of Ọyọ which, as has been seen, set in towards the end of the reign of Alafin Abiọdun in the late eighteenth century. The security and economy of the kingdom were breaking down; already Borgu bandits and slave-raiders infested the roads of northern Ọyọ,[14] and soon armies were marching and counter-marching about the country, leaving in their wake desolation and confusion.

To explain the collapse of this ancient kingdom, once the most powerful of the Guinea states, requires, as in most problems of this kind, a balancing of internal against external factors and an awareness of the danger of confusing cause and effect. I. A. Akinjogbin has recently suggested that two important internal developments were mainly responsible.[15] The first was a decrease in the efficiency of the army in Abiọdun's time, which he ascribes to its deliberate weakening by the Alafin in order to undermine the power of the military chiefs and their families. But such a course seems inherently unlikely, and there is no evidence for it; as pointed out above (p. 48), it was in fact the support of the army leaders which had enabled the Alafin to overthrow Baṣọrun Gaha. Nevertheless, the effectiveness of the army clearly declined considerably during the eighteenth century; expansionist wars were no longer undertaken and important provinces or tributaries escaped from control. A factor which does seem to have played an important part either in causing this decline or in accelerating it was the difficulty which the Ọyọ must have encountered in obtaining suitable mounts for their famous cavalry after the Nupe had asserted their independence; the best horses were obtained from the north, and breeding was rarely possible south of the Niger. The second main cause suggested by Akinjogbin is the dependence of Ọyọ upon the slave trade, which, he claims, tends to weaken any exporting country, since it drives out other economic activity and saps the productivity of labour. Certainly this trade was attended by grave dangers, arising not so much from the determinist reasons just given (though they may have operated to some extent) as from the rivalry and jealousy which it excited among Ọyọ's neighbours, from the shift of economic interest and wealth from the north of the kingdom to the extreme south-west, remote from the capital, and from difficulties, probably also an actual decline, in the trade after its 'abolition' by the British in 1807. The Ọyọ seem also to have been less successful than their southern neighbours, the Ijẹbu, in obtaining firearms and gunpowder in return for their slaves; having little or no direct contact with the Europeans – since the trade at the coast was dominated by the middlemen there – they possibly failed to realize in time the importance of such weapons when used on a large scale.

To these reasons others may be added. It appears that there had developed a dangerous build-up in the foreign and unfree population of the kingdom, largely from the partly Moslem area to the north; as Clapperton found, the Hausa language was understood throughout his journey from Badagry. To the Alafin and his subjects, events at Ilọrin were explicable initially as a rebellion of the Hausa slaves. Another factor, less tangible but not less important than the rest, was a decline of impetus and morale at the centre of government, remarked upon by Lander on his visit to Ọyọ in 1830. Such a decline is symptomatic of a malaise to which any ancient polity is prone, but was aggravated at Ọyọ by the ambitions and disloyalty of the great men of the kingdom, and it is in this connection that the usurpation of power by Gaha in the mid-eighteenth century may be seen as initiating the decline of Ọyọ. Morton-Williams has suggested, furthermore, that the chiefs of the capital, who should have been the natural upholders of the Alafin's government, resented the methods adopted for the administration of the new territories acquired by Abiọdun for the protection of the south-western trade route. This administration was kept in the hands of the palace officials, upsetting the constitutional balance of power between the king and his magnates and giving rise to internal rivalries. After Abiọdun's reign the Alafin was unable to rely on the loyalty either of his home army or of the armies of his provincial rulers.[16]

In addition to the operation of these internal factors, grave dangers from without were also threatening the Ọyọ and, indeed, the whole Yoruba people. In the latter part of the eighteenth century the successful wars waged by the Borgu, Nupe, and Egba against the Alafin had undermined the empire. Then in the first years of the nineteenth century the reforming movement of the Fulani preacher, Usman dan Fodio, swept through Hausaland, transforming the peaceful Moslem farmers there into a holy army bent on carrying the Koran to the sea. Islam had already penetrated among the Yoruba, and thus the Fulani found co-religionists and sympathizers as they rode south.[17] The subversion and capture of Ilọrin by the jihad threatened to cut off Ọyọ ile, already exposed to attack by the nearby Borgu and Nupe, from the major part of the kingdom, and when the Landers reached the city in 1830 its situation must have resembled that of Byzantium in the fifteenth century. Finally, under Ghezo their warrior king, the Dahomeans not only threw off their allegiance to Ọyọ but also began a determined drive eastwards across southern Yorubaland.

The complex events in the half-century (or perhaps rather less) which elapsed between the death of Abiọdun and the abandonment of Ọyọ ile, covering the reigns of six Alafin and one interregnum in the kingship, are described in detail by Johnson.[18] Yet even for this relatively recent period, much of the history of which has been preserved, there is great difficulty in establishing a clear narrative. Not only are the dates of the main events unknown but even their sequence cannot be determined with confidence.

Abiọdun's successor was Awọle Arogangan, a man whom Johnson describes as 'too weak and mild for the times'. One of his first acts was to order out his army against the town of Apomu in Ife territory in order to satisfy a personal quarrel which he had had with its ruler in the days when, before ascending the throne, he was trading up and down the country. Fearful of the consequences, the Bale of Apomu fled to the court of the Ọni at Ife, where he later took his own life. Awọle now abandoned the chastisement of Apomu and ordered his army to march instead against the strong town of Iwere.[19] But now he was faced by a revolt of his leading chiefs. Akinjogbin's explanation of this revolt is that in threatening war on an Ife town, the Alafin had flouted the constitution of the land and rendered illegitimate not only his own authority but that of his successors.[20] Whether this is so or not – and in the absence of support in tradition it remains no more than a suggestion based on a theory of the relationship between Ife and the other Yoruba states which is not generally accepted – the army leaders, who included the Basọrun and the Owata (a leading Ẹsọ) from the capital and the Onikoyi and the Kakamfo with the troops from the provinces, during the course of a half-hearted siege of Iwere conceived and carried out a plot against their

king. After murdering the palace officials who had accompanied
them the mutineers marched back to Ọyọ. For some weeks they
camped irresolutely outside the walls, until at length they sent
to the Alafin an empty, covered calabash as an indication of his
rejection. Awolẹ pronounced a solemn curse on the traitors,
shooting arrows to the north, south, and west to signify the
directions in which they would be carried into slavery, and then
obeyed custom by taking poison.

The decline of the kingdom now became precipitate. An Ọyọ
song reflects the times:

Laiye Abiọdun l'afi igba wọn 'wo	In Abiodun's day we weighed our money in calabashes,
Laiye Awole l'adi adikale	In Awolẹ's reign we packed up and fled.

As was the practice at Ọyọ, the Baṣọrun took charge of the
affairs of the kingdom on the Alafin's death, and the tradition
has already been cited above (pp. 84–5) that it was during this
short regency of Baṣọrun Aṣamu that the revolt of the Ẹgba
under Liṣabi took place. When Adebọ was eventually chosen as
successor to Awolẹ the new Alafin proved to have little authority, and now even towns within the metropolitan area of Ọyọ
were falling away from their allegiance. The assertion of independence by Afọnja the Kakamfo at Ilọrin was especially
menacing. In the midst of these troubles Adebọ died after a
reign of only a few months, to be followed as Alafin by Maku. A
deputation was sent from the capital to inform the Kakamfo
that 'the New Moon has appeared', meaning that a new king
had ascended the throne; Afọnja replied arrogantly, 'Let that
New Moon speedily set.' After leading a disastrous military
expedition the unhappy Maku was required to take his life
within three months of his accession. There followed an interregnum of unknown length until Majotu, who is usually
identified with the elderly Alafin who entertained Clapperton

at Oyo in 1826 and Lander in 1827 and 1830, was chosen as king.[21]

Afonja, whose actions contributed so largely to the Yoruba catastrophe, was a nephew of Alafin Awole and ruler of Ilorin, which his great-grandfather Laderin had built up into one of the most important towns in the Oyo kingdom;[22] his praise-name, *l'aiya l'oko*, describes him as 'the brave warrior with the spear'. From Awole he obtained the office of Kakamfo, generalissimo of the kingdom and foremost of the Eso. Even before Awole's death he seems to have aspired to the throne itself,[23] despite the fact that he was only connected to the royal house through his mother, and he was a leading member of the conspiracy which led to Awole's enforced suicide. During the brief reign of Adebo, Afonja proclaimed his independence of Oyo, as did the Bale of Gbogun and the rulers of other towns in the north of the kingdom. But he now took steps which were to prove disastrous both to himself and to his country: he enlisted into his army the numerous Hausa slaves who were employed (as 'barbers, rope-makers and cowherds', Johnson says) in the surrounding towns, protecting them against their masters and, according to the account of a contemporary observer in Yorubaland, Ali Eisami of Bornu, who had himself been brought to Oyo as a slave, giving them their freedom.[24] He also invited to Ilorin a Fulani preacher from Sokoto, Sahil, usually called Alimi ('the learned'), whose sons were destined to be leaders in the southward drive of the jihad. With this alien help he succeeded in beating off determined attacks made on him by Ojo Agunbambaru, a son of Gaha, who was acting nominally in the cause of the Alafin. It is significant that Ojo, like Afonja, relied largely on soldiers from outside the kingdom, having recruited his army among the dreaded warriors of Borgu.

'Afonja was now the sole power in the kingdom; the King and the capital were left to manage their own affairs by themselves,' Johnson writes[25] – the king at this time being, presumably, Alafin Majotu. But the disloyal Kakamfo was encompassing his own doom. He had offended by his arrogance, and doubtless alarmed by his ambition, the rulers of the neighbouring towns, and even his friend and ally, Ṣọlagbẹru, a leading Yoruba Moslem, whom he had established with his followers at Oke Suna on the outskirts of Ilọrin. At last, realizing the precariousness of his position, isolated from his natural allies and dependent upon his Hausa troops, the Jama'a ('disciples'), he attempted to reconcile himself with the Onikoyi and other chiefs. Hearing this, the Jama'a rose against him; according to an Ilọrin account their leader was Alimi's eldest son, and successor as Iman of the Moslems there, Abdussalami. He was besieged in his compound and deserted by some of his guards; Ṣọlagbẹru refused his plea for help. But he fought on until 'He fell indeed like a hero. So covered was he with darts that his body was supported in an erect position upon the shafts of spears and arrows showered upon him'.[26]

Ilọrin now passed under the control of the Fulani leaders, and Abdussalami was recognized by the Sultan of Sokoto as an Emir within the Fulani empire (and flattered by his Yoruba subjects as *ọba digi aiye*, 'king, mirror of the world').[27] But the overthrow of Afọnja had at last roused some of the Ọyọ to a sense of their peril. The new Kakamfo, Toyejẹ of Ogbomọṣọ, made a first attempt to dislodge the Fulani from the base which they had acquired through his predecessor's treachery, but was defeated in a bloody engagement at Ogele, where the Fulani cavalry was aided by Ṣọlagbẹru with his Yoruba Moslems. Again the Ọyọ rallied, this time obtaining help from the ruler of the Nupe at Rabba across the Niger, but again they were defeated in the 'locust fruit' (*mugba mugba*) war, when this was the only food to be found by the troops on the now desolate farms. Yet, despite the growing danger, the Ọyọ chiefs, no longer restrained by the power of the Alafin, began again to quarrel among themselves. A coalition was formed against the Onikoyi in which Ṣọlagbẹru joined. The Onikoyi thereupon sent a message to Ilọrin affirming his adherence to the Emir.

Abdussalami, doubtless rejoicing that the Oyo were playing into his hands in this way, sent his army against the allies and routed them at Pamo. Solagberu fled back to Oke Suna, but his turn soon came and, his religion notwithstanding, he met the same fate as Afonja.

Meanwhile a serious war had also broken out in the south of the Yoruba country.[28] It arose out of the kidnapping of Oyo subjects by the Ife for sale at their market in Apomu. The Onikoyi and Toyeje of Ogbomoso, hearing of this and acting probably during the interregnum in the kingship, asked the Olowu, always a loyal upholder of Oyo interests in the south, to take punitive measures against a number of towns in Ife territory. Johnson lists thirteen towns which were chastised by the Owu in obedience to this order, including Apomu, Ikire, and Gbangan. The Oni of Ife in retaliation sent an army against the Owu, but this was routed at Safirin, near the confluence of the Osun and Oba rivers. Soon after this victory the Owu became involved with a more powerful enemy. The new quarrel grew out of a fracas between Owu and Ijebu traders in the market at Apomu, which led the Owu to destroy the town there. The Ijebu now made common cause with the Ife. In the ensuing war the Owu, armed only with their traditional weapons, were unable to check the advance of the Ijebu, who had obtained firearms from the European traders on the coast, with whom their kingdom had long been in contact. A lengthy siege of the town of Owu, with its strong walls, now began, during which the allies were reinforced by some neighbouring Egba and also by refugees from Oyo towns already overrun by the Fulani. The superior arms and numbers of the allies, aided by famine inside the walls, could not prevail against the obstinate Owu until at length the Olowu himself opened one of the gates and made good his escape. His town was entered and completely destroyed by the enemy, who forbade that it should ever be rebuilt – an interdict which was obeyed until recent times.

The collapse of Owu and the ending of the war released into the south of Yorubaland many Ọyọ soldiers. Since their own towns and villages had been conquered or destroyed by the Fulani, these men could no longer return to their farms; thus they came to look on war as their profession and found their reward in captives who could be traded as slaves. A number of these 'war boys' (ọmọ ogun) now moved under Ijẹbu patronage to Ipara, where they were employed in subjugating some of the Rẹmo towns in the name of the Awujalẹ and in raiding the adjacent Ẹgba districts.[29] The situation grew more serious when this army of freebooters, reinforced by some Ifẹ chiefs with their followers, were involved in a dispute between the Ẹgba Oke Ọna and the Ẹgba Gbagura provinces. Taking sides with the former, they overran the northern parts of the Ẹgba forest, burning and laying waste, until finally they settled on the abandoned site of Ibadan. This was one of the few Gbagura towns which had escaped destruction and, as its name implies (ẹba ọdan, 'near the grassland'), it lay just within the sheltering Egba forest. Here a great military camp was formed in which the numerous Ọyọ refugees came together with contingents under Ifẹ, Ijẹbu, and Ẹgba leaders.

While the kingdoms of the south were being plunged by these events into a general state of warfare, Ọyọ was fast breaking up. The rulers of the subordinate towns, their obedience to the Alafin forgotten and the example of Afọnja's fate ignored, quarrelled and leagued among themselves, while the Fulani cavalry scoured the country. One of many similar episodes which must have occurred at this lawless time, and which contrast with Clapperton's experience of peaceful conditions on the Badagry road, was the overrunning in March 1821 of the small town of Oṣogun in Ibarapa (south-western Ọyọ) by a mixed band of Ọyọ Muslims and Fulani. A vivid account of this was given by Samuel Crowther, who, as a boy of about 15, was taken captive there and sold into slavery.[30]

The end of Ọyọ ile was approaching. Johnson describes

Majotu's successor, Alafin Amọdo, as 'virtually King of the capital only',[31] and relates that during his reign the Ilọrin succeeded in entering the town after a siege; however, having plundered its treasures (including some 'Ọyọ beauties') and forced the citizens to profess Islam, they withdrew without taking captives: a rather mysterious episode. But even now the leaders of those Ọyọ towns which maintained their independence of the Fulani were unable to sink their differences and forget their ambitions in the common cause. When at length the Alafin succeeded in raising an army and leading it against Ilọrin any chance of victory was ruined by the treachery of Ẹdun, the ruler of Gbogun, and the Ọyọ were routed at Kanla. The Fulani followed up this success by intervening in the disputed succession to the kingship at Ikoyi, installing their own candidate and bringing the town under their control, and then by making war on the important town of Gbogun, which fell to them after a desperate resistance.

A number of the kingdom's war leaders had meanwhile withdrawn southwards towards the forests under the Kakamfo Ojo Amepo. The wisdom of this move was shown by the defeat of the expedition sent into Ijẹsa territory by the Fulani, whose cavalry found itself unable to operate in the close country there and suffered severe losses in the Polẹ war. For a time the Ilọrin encamped at Agọ Ọja, the town later to be renamed Ọyọ, in order to keep up pressure against these remnants of the Alafin's forces, but eventually the Ọyọ succeeded in disengaging and securing a base at Ijaye, a deserted Gbagura town, where leadership was assumed by Kurunmi, the Balogun of the abandoned town of Ẹsiele.

Ọyọ ile was now isolated, and in the midst of these troubles Alafin Amọdu died, worn out by anxiety. Oluewu, the new ọba, was required by Shitta, who had succeeded his brother Abdussalami as Emir, to visit him in Ilọrin. On this occasion the Alafin was treated with honour, but when he received an invitation to pay a second visit during which he would be asked to profess

Islam by 'tapping the Koran' he declined and preferred to risk calling on the Borgu for help. Ọyọ ile was now besieged by the Ilọrin, who were joined by Lanloke, the renegade ruler of Ogodo, a Yoruba town on the Niger east of Ọyọ ile, where in more prosperous times much trade had been done between the Ọyọ and the Nupe.[32] The highest of the kingdom's officers, the Baṣọrun and the Aṣipa, had already entered into communication with the Fulani, but they were put to death, and the Alafin and his Borgu allies, aided by a providential storm, succeeded in repelling the enemy. Realizing that the capture of Ọyọ, a city of formidable size and strength, still presented many difficulties, Shitta now turned upon Gbodo, probably the last of the towns in the north-east of the kingdom which had not acknowledged Fulani rule.

Once again the Alafin had to rely on his Borgu allies, but on this occasion the forces of the old kingdom secured a real victory in the field against their enemy. The Ilọrin army outside Gbodo had been joined by a number of Ọyọ chiefs, including even Atiba, a son of Alafin Abiọdun – though to his credit (Johnson thinks) his men were only firing blanks! Now the besiegers were attacked from the rear and put to so precipitate a flight that many were driven into the River Ogun and drowned. Though the victory had been achieved with outside help, and has been attributed to the skill in archery of the Borgu,[33] the Battle of Gbodo demonstrated that the forces of the jihad were not invincible, even against a divided foe.

The Borgu leader is known in Yoruba accounts as the Eleduwẹ and seems likely to have been ruler of Nikki or possibly Kaiama.[34] This brave prince now encouraged the Alafin to follow up his success at Gbodo by an attack on Ilọrin itself. Oluewu agreed, and determined to raise as large an army as possible from those parts of the kingdom not yet overrun by the Fulani. A number of leading chiefs, including Atiba from Agọ Ọja, Kurunmi of Ijaye, and the Ọkẹrẹ of Ṣaki, rallied to the camp which Oluewu and the Eleduwẹ formed at Ọtẹfan, about ten miles west of Ogbomǫsǫ. Numbers there grew so large that the Emir of Ilǫrin sent in alarm to Sokoto for help, and was re-inforced by the Nupe of Raba (where the Fulani had by now established their ascendancy). The combined forces of Ilǫrin and the Nupe then attacked the Ǫtęfan camp, but the defend-ers, inspired by the example of the Eleduwę, drove them back. This victory was a costly one, but it nevertheless encouraged Oluyǫle of Ibadan and other Yoruba leaders to join the Alafin.[35] But as the army passed slowly on to Ogbomǫsǫ, and thence, after some indecisions, towards Ilǫrin, the usual rivalries and disaffection broke out, complicated by jealousy of the Borgu, who were contributing so much towards the war, and by fear that if the campaign were successful the Alafin would turn next on his over-mighty subjects. Before Ilǫrin was reached a conspiracy had been made among the chiefs to desert the Alafin and his ally, and a message was sent to tell the enemy of this. Thus, when the army took the field only Oluyǫle, who had not been party to the plot, attacked vigorously, while Atiba and the Timi of Ędę, firing no shot, retired before the enemy and opened a way for them to surround the two kings. The Eleduwę fought desperately, but at last was slain and executed; his defeat was a disaster from which Nikki and Kaiama took many years to recover.[36] The fate of the Alafin Oluewu is less certain; by some he is believed to have fallen in the battle, but according to Johnson, he was taken captive to Ilǫrin and there put to death.[37]

The defeat at Ilǫrin sealed the fate of Ǫyǫ ile. Already the city was being pressed by the rapacious Lanloke of Ogodo, and by this time it is probable that many of the citizens had left their homes to seek greater security in the south; from the time of Awolę they had been 'packing up to flee', and on his visit there in 1830 Lander had remarked on the emptiness and desolation of the streets. Men still remained to hold the walls against Lanloke's attacks, but when news came of the disaster at Ilǫrin all those left in the city decided upon immediate flight.

L

Some escaped to Kiṣi, others to Igboho, some even to Ilọrin, and their descendants may be traced in these and other towns of Yorubaland.[38] But to the Fulani the city was now of little importance and, ironically, it was not they but Lanloke and his marauders who, learning of its abandonment, entered the undefended gates and pillaged what remained of its riches: an epitome of the treachery and tragic opportunism which marked and in large measure accounted for the swift decline and fall of Ọyọ ile, 'Katunga, the great metropolis'.

The narrative above is based on Johnson's *History*. The attempt to construct a chronology of the period which follows is based on indications about dating given by Johnson and on other sources, including a chronology drawn up by I. A. Akinjogbin.[39] The only absolute dates in this account are those of the situation as recorded by Clapperton and Lander in their journeys, though information collected by the Yoruba missionary Crowther at Egga on the Niger in 1841 and the evidence of Ali Eisami of Bornu are also valuable.[40]

Clapperton refers several times to the troubles in the Ọyọ kingdom. At 'Assula', twenty-six days from Badagry, he found that the inhabitants had newly dug a ditch round the town 'on account of the existing war' – almost certainly meaning events at Ilọrin – and three days later he wrote that, 'A war is now carrying on only a few hours' ride from us; not a national but a slaving war.'[41] At Ṣaki and 'Enkoosoo' he learnt that his journey was being interpreted as a mission to make peace between the Alafin and his Hausa slaves. The Hausa

have been in rebellion these two years, and possess a large town only two days' journey from Katunga [Ọyọ], called Lori [Ilọrin]. The Youribanis are evidently afraid of them; they say they have a great number of horses, and have been joined by many Fellatahs [Fulani].[42]

Both from the wording and the context, these remarks seem to
describe the overthrow of Afọnja and the establishment of
Ilọrin as an outpost of the jihad, and the information from
'Enkoosoo' enables this to be dated at about 1824. At Ọyọ the
Alafin 'feelingly deplored the civil war occasioned by his
father's death' and said that he had 'sent to his friend the King
of Benin for troops to assist him'; he reminded Clapperton of
the ruined towns on the Badagry road, all 'destroyed and
burned by my rebellious Hausa slaves, and their friends, the
Fellatahs'.[43] This is best explicable as a reference to the mutiny
of Afọnja and the other leaders at the end of Awolẹ's reign, the
interregnum, and Afọnja's assertion of independence and its
aftermath. Unfortunately, tradition has not recorded Majotu's
parentage; it seems probable that he was a son of Awolẹ,
though in any case he might speak of his predecessor as his
'father'. When Lander was in Ọyọ in 1830 the signs of trouble
had multiplied: '. . . the wandering and ambitious Falatah has
penetrated into the very heart of this country . . . with little, if
any, opposition'. Lander adds that the discontented slaves of
the kingdom had been flocking to 'Alorie [Ilọrin] as far back as
forty years'.[44] Presumably this again refers to Afọnja's rebellion and subsequent defiance of Ọyọ, rather than to the more
recent establishment of Ilọrin as a Fulani base. Even so, this
seems a considerable over-estimate, since according to Ali
Eisami, the period can hardly have exceeded fourteen or fifteen
years.[45] Early in the 1840s Crowther made inquiries about
events in Ọyọ. His most important information, so far as a
chronology is concerned, was that Awolẹ reigned for seven
years and Adebọ and Maku for only about three months each,
and that the interregnum at Ọyọ lasted for five years. He also
implies that the Battle of Gbodo was fought in 1834 and that at
Oṣogbo in 1838/9.[46]

Crowther's statement about the interregnum raises considerable difficulty. A date has been suggested for Abiọdun's death
of c. 1810, yielding a five-year interregnum between c. 1818 and

c. 1823, which would be consistent with the tradition that Majotu ascended the throne as an elderly man and was the Alafin whom Lander names as Mansolah. But Akinjogbin has adduced evidence from which it appears that Abiọdun died as early as 1789.[47] This, taken in conjunction with traditions about the short reigns of his first three successors, leads to the conclusion that either Majotu's reign was of unexpected length or that the interregnum lasted for much longer than five years, perhaps even up to twenty-five years as Akinjogbin suggests.[48] Meanwhile, Crowther's information, combined with Johnson's narrative, places the Battle of Ilọrin and the subsequent abandonment of Ọyọ ile in or about 1835.

As regards the chronology of the war in the south, the difficulties are even greater. The Owu war was fought in two phases: first, the Ifẹ–Owu war, and secondly, after an interval of about five years during which the shattered Ifẹ army took shelter at Adunbieye in Iwo territory, a combined Ijẹbu–Ifẹ attack on Owu, which culminated in the fall of that town after a five-year siege, followed by an extension of the war to the Ẹgba forest.[49] There is evidence that Kesi and Ikereku, both Ẹgba towns, were destroyed in about 1823 and 1826 respectively, apparently in this war, and it therefore appears that the first phase of the war must have opened about 1813 and Owu have fallen about 1823.[50] There are two obstacles to this dating. First, according to Johnson, it was Toyejẹ of Ogbomọṣọ, who, as Kakamfo and acting with the Onikoyi, ordered the Owu to punish the Ifẹ slave-traders.[51] Toyejẹ was Afọnja's successor as Kakamfo, presumably appointed by Alafin Majotu – though a little later the Onikoyi, usurping the Alafin's functions, appointed a rival or anti-Kakamfo, Ẹdun of Gbogun – so that this would seem to place the opening of the war after Afọnja's death in or about 1824, which then throws out the dating of the Ẹgba war. In the absence of other evidence, however, it seems reasonable to suppose that Afọnja's rebellion led the Alafin (or, if it happened during the interregnum, the Ọyọ Mesi) to replace him during his lifetime. Secondly, if the dates suggested above are correct it is somewhat surprising that Clapperton and Lander apparently heard nothing of the southern war and its depredations during their journeys to Ọyọ ile. But sufficient explanation of this may be found, in that their route took them well to the west of the area in which the war was fought and also of the Ẹgba forest in which the subsequent operations were conducted.

Suggested Chronology (*sources in brackets*)

1789	Death of Alafin Abiọdun (Akinjogbin (1965))
c. 1790	Accession of Alafin Awọle
c. 1797	Mutiny of Afọnja and other chiefs at Iwere; Awọle's suicide after reign of seven years (Crowther)
	Ẹgba revolt under Lisabi during short regency of Basọrun Asamu (Bada of Ṣaki)
c. 1798–*c.* 1799	Short reigns of Alafin Adebọ and Maku (with the usual interregnum under the Basọrun's regency)
c. 1800–????	Interregnum (Crowther, five years; Akinjogbin (1966a), up to twenty-five years)
	Accession of elderly Alafin Majotu ('Mansolah'?)
c. 1813	Opening of Owu war, the first phase
c. 1813–*c.* 1818	Ifẹ army at Adunbieye (Johnson)
1816–7	Afọnja asserts independence at Ilọrin and recruits slaves (Ali Eisami)
c. 1818	Opening of second phase of Owu war
c. 1823	Fall of Owu, after a siege of about five years (Johnson)
c. 1824	Hausa–Fulani coup at Ilọrin (Clapperton); Afọnja killed
	Abdussalami becomes Emir of Ilọrin

1826	Clapperton and Lander visit Ọyọ
	Overrunning of Egba Gbagura by Ọyọ free-booters (Irving; Biobaku)
1827	Lander returns through Ọyọ
c. 1829	Foundation of Ibadan
1830	Lander's last visit to Ọyọ
c. 1830	Foundation of Abẹokuta (Biobaku)
	Occupation of Ijaye by Kurunmi
	Amọdo succeeds Majotu as Alafin
	Shitta succeeds Abdussalami as Emir of Ilọrin
c. 1833	Oluewu succeeds Amọdo as Alafin
c. 1834	Battle of Gbodo (Crowther)
c. 1835	Battle of Ilọrin; Oluewu killed (or taken captive and executed in Ilọrin?); Ọyọ ile abandoned
c. 1836	Election of Atiba as Alafin; Ago Ọja renamed Ọyọ
1838/9	Battle of Ọsogbo (Crowther)

The ruin of Ọyọ was of tragic moment for the whole Yoruba country, involving the other kingdoms as well as Ọyọ itself. The sequence of events had been complex. First, the rulers of the populous and prosperous towns of Ọyọ, especially those in the vicinity of the capital, took advantage of the weakening of the Alafin's government to assert their independence, and then fell to prosecuting against their king and among themselves a civil war from which only the enemies of the kingdom could profit. Then the warriors of the Fulani jihad established their strong base at Ilọrin, south of the Niger and in the heart of the kingdom. Finally, the ancient state of Ọyọ had collapsed, ending, it seemed, all possibility of unity among the Yoruba in the face of dangers from without: the Fulani on the north, the Dahomeans on the west, and, as the nineteenth century wore on, the

British on the coast. The history of these years is a terrible one; the tale of the repeated treachery of the Alafin's chiefs is almost beyond bearing, and the breakdown of morale apprehended by Lander on his last visit to the doomed capital was the decisive factor among all those making for the downfall of the kingdom.

The ruin was complete. The empire had long since fallen away; the tributary Nupe and Borgu and the Ẹgba provinces had all thrown off their allegiance to Ọyọ some half-century ago, and by 1826 a town only a few miles from the capital had passed under the control of the ruler of Kaiama.[52] The Dahomeans under their warrior king Ghezo (?1818–58) repudiated the tribute which they had rendered to the Alafin since 1730 (a step which Akinjogbin considers was taken between 1821 and 1825,[53] and which in any case probably preceded the fall of Ọyọ). Now, too, the dependence on Ọyọ of other parts of Yorubaland ceased. Owu, Ọyọ's loyal vassal in the south, had been razed to the ground by the allied Ijẹbu and Ifẹ, while in Ẹgbado, that once-prosperous area through which ran Ọyọ's trade route to the sea, the local rulers rose against each other until their country became a battlefield for Ijẹbu, Ẹgba, and Dahomean invaders. To the north, the Fulani had occupied or overrun most of the Yoruba Proper, and their cavalry continued to raid in all directions. But the forests of the south proved as great an obstacle to their progress as the regrouped remnants of the Yoruba armies. Thus it was southwards, towards these forests, that many of the inhabitants of northern Ọyọ fled for shelter.[54] The towns in this area became *ilu asala*, 'towns of refuge', expanding their sites and their farmlands to accommodate the newcomers. One of these was Oṣogbo in the Ijẹṣa kingdom, where the influence of refugees was so great as to give it the character and allegiance of an Ọyọ town. The site of its rival and neighbour, Ẹdẹ, was moved south across the Oṣun River for greater security. New towns were also founded, of which an interesting example is Modakẹkẹ, established for the Ọyọ by the

Ọni of Ifẹ alongside his own town in order to end the hostility between his own subjects and the refugees. Of these new towns, three were to rank above all others and to emerge as successors to the greatness of Ọyọ, dominating much of Yorubaland within and beyond the old kingdom as well as the refounded capital of the Alafin at New Ọyọ: these were Ibadan, Aboẹkuta, and Ijaye.

XI · The Wars and the New States

The Yoruba country had now been plunged into a state of warfare which lasted almost continuously until the imposition of peace by the British in 1893.[1] But this was a time not merely of conflict but of political, social, and economic change, partly engendered by the wars and partly by the opening of the country to European influence on a large scale and in different forms. New states arose out of the wreckage of Ọyọ, and older states, previously overshadowed by Ọyọ, asserted their independence. Firearms, first the primitive muskets and finally modern rifles, played an increasing part in the wars. Fighting became for many a profession, among both the leaders and their followers the marauding 'war boys', a factor which contributed to the prolongation and spread of the wars. European slave traders, dealing through African middlemen, were gradually replaced by (or transformed into) the buyers of palm oil and other produce of the interior. Christian missionaries blazed a trail inland, establishing themselves first at Badagry and then at Abẹokuta, Lagos, and Ijaye, setting up a chain of stations designed to reach into the Moslem north. The way had been prepared both for their religious doctrines and for the new-style education which they brought, by the Christian recaptives (former slaves liberated by the ships of the British anti-slavery patrol and taken to Freetown) and their descendants, who from 1839 onwards were returning to their homeland.

One result of these changes and in particular of the coming of the Europeans, is the great increase in the amount of material, especially written material, which is available for the writing of history. The missionaries and traders were keen observers of the political and economic scene, and the archives of the missionary societies and trading houses yield much information; the missionaries, indeed, though often identifying themselves too zealously for objectivity with the interests of the town where their station was situated, wrote reports to their superiors which were sometimes almost on the level of diplomatic despatches. With the opening of a British consular post at Lagos in 1851, followed by the Sardinian consulate in 1856, and then in 1861 the establishment of the colonial administration, professional observation began, and statistics of trade, health, and similar matters make their appearance. For the Yoruba themselves, Christianity and literacy went together, and local histories, biographies, and collections of family papers begin to throw light on events. The first newspaper, the fortnightly *Iwe-Irohin* (in Yoruba, but from 1860 with an English supplement) was produced by the C.M.S. in Abẹokuta in 1859, and in 1863 a locally produced newspaper, the *Anglo-African*, appeared in Lagos. The missionaries also led the way in the study of the Yoruba language and its reduction to writing.

Although the activities of the Europeans were to have ever more important consequences, in a history of the Yoruba states in this period the warfare which plagued the country for almost a century demands first attention. Its origins lay in the breakdown of Ọyọ and in the holy war of the Fulani, but these issues were largely settled by 1840, when new political groupings had emerged and the southward thrust from Ilọrin had been held. Why, then, was Yorubaland destined to suffer a further half-century of war? The explanation seems to lie in two main factors, one economic and the other political: the first, the demand for slaves, which could always be met most readily from captives taken in war; the second, and much the more important, the struggle for power among the states, both new and old, which were attempting to fill the vacuum left by the collapse of Ọyọ.

It was a tragic paradox that the success achieved in the first part of the nineteenth century for the Abolitionists' policy of encouraging 'legitimate trade', mainly in the products of the oil-palm which grows wild in southern Nigeria, led to a greatly increased demand for domestic slaves as carriers between the markets and the coast. Burton drew the attention of the 1865 British Parliamentary Select Committee on Africa to this unexpected result of the humanitarian policy,[2] and since then the Yoruba wars of this century have usually been dismissed as slaving expeditions to feed the markets of Lagos and Dahomey.[3] Certainly many, probably a majority, of those taken captive in these wars must have been sent to the slave markets,[4] and a number of the fifty or so 'wars' which Johnson describes in the period were probably little more than slave raids.[5] Nevertheless, there were other, and still more profound, issues in the wars, and slave raiding and trading were as much a consequence as a cause of the long unsettlement.[6]

'Politics cannot be divorced from power,' E. H. Carr has written,[7] and these West African wars illustrate this maxim no less clearly than the fevered interlude in Europe between the two German wars. The issues between the Yoruba states in the nineteenth century were complex and shifting, but all concerned questions about power: first, which among them was to succeed to the hegemony of Ọyọ? Then, when Ibadan had established its ascendancy, though by too narrow a margin for stability, how was the threat to the independence of the rest to be countered? And again, but a question all too often lost to sight among local rivalries, whose was the responsibility of withstanding the triple threat to all from the Fulani at Ilọrin, the Dahomeans on the western borders, and the British at Lagos?

Each of the new states represented in one way or another a break with the traditional Yoruba concepts of government. Thus Ibadan retained throughout the century the characteristics of a military foundation; secure at home on its high ridge of hills, surrounded by forest and ever sending its armies to the field, it was nicknamed *idi ibọn*, 'the butt of a gun'. The Government was vested in separate lines of chiefs, civil and military, whose titles were not hereditary but bestowed for service, generally military service, to the town. The leading chief was known as the Balẹ, the title used by the rulers of the minor towns and villages of the Ọyọ kingdom and illustrating here the nominal subordination of Ibadan to the Alafin. He attained his office by promotion through both the civil and military grades of chieftaincy.[8]

In its earliest days Ibadan had been a composite town, containing Ifẹ, Ijẹbu, and Ẹgba as well as Ọyọ refugees, and leadership devolved at first on Mayẹ, an Ifẹ chief. Within a short time, however, the Ọyọ rose against Mayẹ and drove him and his followers from the town. This led to a series of short, sharp wars, but with the help of their kinsman Kurunmi of Ijaye the Ọyọ succeeded in establishing their supremacy. Under their great leader Oluyọle (who received from the Alafin the high title of Basọrun, which had been held at Ọyọ by Yamba, his grandfather), Ibadan emerged as a leading power in the land.[9] Its military importance soon began to be matched by its rising commercial importance as a market and collecting point for palm oil from the surrounding region.

The foundation of Abẹokuta was made when a group of Ẹgba led by Ṣodẹke of Iporo (known by his military title as the Seriki) left Ibadan, where they had become unwelcome, and joined a small party of Ẹgba hunters whom they found living under an outcrop of rock near the east bank of the Ogun, then on the edge of Ẹgbado country. This took place about 1830, and during the next twenty years there must have been a steady movement into the new settlement of other Ẹgba from towns destroyed or abandoned in all parts of the forest. Unlike Ibadan, Abẹokuta did not grow into a single community but consisted of a federation based on the three former provinces, with the Owu, many of whom were allowed to settle here, as a fourth section. Again in contrast to Ibadan, Abẹokuta had a plenitude of ọba, although, as had been the custom (of all but the Gbagura) in the days when the Ẹgba were scattered through the forest, election was not confined to candidates from specific royal houses. The office of Alake, the leading ọba, had been vacant since the death of Okikilu in the Agbaje war, but in 1854 Townsend, the Anglican missionary in the town, persuaded the chiefs to elect a successor.[10] The move did not have the expected result of strengthening the central government, as the Alake continued to be strictly bound by the constitutional rules of former times, and Burton described Abẹokuta at this time as 'a weak constitutional monarchy, blighted by the checks and limits which were intended to prevent its luxuriance'.[11] The real rulers of the town and its dependencies were the war chiefs, the Ologun, overshadowing the Ogboni, who had been the highest authority in the former provinces.[12] A number of military titles of Ọyọ origin were now adopted among the Ologun. These referred to the Ẹgba as a whole, instead of to the individual component towns of Abẹokuta, and thus to some extent offset the federalism which was a weakness in the new state.

Ijaye, the third in the triumvirate of new states, followed a different pattern of government from either Ibadan or Abẹokuta, yet equally exemplified a departure from Yoruba tradition. Here the warrior Kurunmi, who obtained from the Alafin the title of Arẹ Ọna Kakamfo, established on the site of a former Ẹgba Gbagura town (whose inhabitants were now settled in Abẹokuta) an autocracy in which 'He was king, judge, general, entertainer, sometimes also executioner'.[13] Not only did the town itself grow and prosper but the iron rule of the Arẹ was exercised over a kingdom stretching northwards through the upper Ogun almost to Ṣaki, though it was circumscribed in the south and south-west by Ibadan and Abẹokuta, which were also extending their influence over the surrounding country-side.

The foundation of these three new states preceded by a few years the final abandonment of the old capital of Ọyọ; indeed, the leaders of Ibadan and Ijaye, Oluyọle and Kurunmi, were present on the fatal field of Ilọrin, and their support (in return for the titles of Baṣọrun and Arẹ Ọna Kakamfo respectively) contributed to the choice of Atiba as successor to Alafin Oluewu. Before the coronation members of the Ọyọ Mesi who had taken shelter in the strong northern towns of Kiṣi and Igboho sent messengers to urge the new Alafin to return to Ọyọ ile, but Atiba was determined to establish his capital in his adopted town of Agọ Ọja ('the camp of Ọja', a refugee chief from Ọyọ), in the south of the old kingdom and on the edge of the Ẹgba forest. Here Ọyọ was refounded, and a conscious attempt was made to re-create the glories of the old capital and to preserve the rituals of its kingship. Atiba transported the inhabitants of neighbouring towns and villages to swell the population; he revived the former offices and titles of the Court and Government; a double wall was built around the town, and in the centre, incorporating the palace of Ọja, the former ruler, rose a new Afin, covering a large area and constructed on the plan of the Afin at Ọyọ ile, while the compounds of the Arẹmọ and the great officers of the Ọyọ Mesi radiated round the royal demesne. About a mile from the palace a new Bara, or royal mausoleum, was built between the inner and outer town walls. It is sometimes said that Atiba re-interred here the body of Oluewu, his predecessor, but it is unlikely that this was in fact recovered from the Fulani.[14]

The building of the new capital was accompanied by the enunciation of a new administrative and military policy. Under this the kingdom was formally redivided into two 'provinces', apart from the capital; the first, Ibadan, was charged with the protection of the north and north-east of the kingdom, and whenever possible was to extend its boundaries in the direction of Ijẹṣa and Ekiti, while Ijaye, the second province, was to watch the west and to attempt to reassert the rule of the Ọyọ over Ṣabe and the coast. By this system of palatinates (to use Biobaku's term), the Ibadan would be principally concerned with the threat from the Fulani and the Ijaye with that from Dahomey, while for the future the Alafin was no longer to take the field in war, but should confine himself to religious and political leadership. Ọyọ itself retained under its control a small area between the two provinces, and a number of towns in the north, such as Kiṣi and Igboho, were to be directly subject to the Alafin. These decisions preserved the formal pre-eminence of the Alafin among the Ọyọ, whose territory now extended southwards into the former Gbagura, offsetting to some extent the loss of Ilọrin. At the same time it took account of the reality of the situation by allotting the major respon-sibilities to the new military towns; indeed, Johnson describes the arrangements as 'a compact . . . arrived at between the Alafin and his principal chiefs'.[15]

Already the actions of Gbodo and Ọtẹfan had shown that the warriors of Ilọrin were not invincible. The relief of Oṣogbo and the defeat there of a large army under Ali, the Hausa Balogun, in 1838/9 was an event of even greater importance.[16] It demon-strated the unsuitability to forest warfare of the Fulani cavalry and vindicated the Yoruba withdrawal to the south. The redisposition of the resources of the shattered kingdom by Atiba and his supporters had proved a success, and the Ibadan, triumphantly fulfilling the role assigned to them, emerged as a symbol of hope, offering a prospect of restored security and stability in the land. But this decisive check to the southward drive of the Ilọrin by no means meant the end of the internal wars; indeed, by abating the external pressure from one direc-tion it tended to sharpen local issues, and from now on 'the Fulani were less a common enemy than a convenient ally to one or other side'.[17]

Thus the victory at Oṣogbo was not followed by any

concerted attempt to win back the lost north-eastern lands of
the Ọyọ kingdom. Instead, the Ibadan were drawn by the ambition of their leader, Oluyọle the Basọrun, into the Batedo war
against their co-palatinate Ijaye. This was concluded after two
years by a truce arranged by the Alafin. Then an appeal for
help from the leading Ekiti town of Ọtun (on the former
Benin–Ọyọ border), which was engaged in a feud with Efọn
Alaye, opened up prospects of further expansion for the restless
Ibadan. They responded by sending a large army under
Balogun Ọdẹrinlọ, the victor of Osogbo, while the Alaye sought
help from Ilọrin. In the ensuing battle the Ilọrin not only failed
to raise the Ibadan siege of Ọtun but were again soundly
defeated in the field.[18] The extension of Ibadan influence over
the Ekiti country continued to be contested by the Ilọrin until
in 1854 an Ibadan army under Balogun Ibikunle won a victory
so decisive that the whole of Ekiti soon passed under their
control.[19]

In this way began the building-up of the 'Ibadan empire', a
tract of country which at its greatest extent, after the absorption of a large part of former Ijaye territory, stretched from
Ekiti westwards for some 200 miles, with a north-to-south
depth varying from forty to eighty miles.[20] It consisted of
towns and their districts which were either conquered in the
endemic warfare of these years, like Ilesa and Akoko, or which
voluntarily accepted Ibadan's protection, like Iwo and Ẹdẹ,
thereby virtually recognizing that it was the Ibadan and their
chiefs who were the true successors of Ọyọ ile rather than the
Alafin at New Ọyọ. This empire was loosely administered by a
system of ajẹlẹ based on that of Ọyọ. But whereas the Ọyọ
ajẹlẹ had been supervised by the ilari, those touring representatives of the Alafin of the old kingdom, the subject towns of
Ibadan were instead allotted to the care of one of the chiefs in
the capital (called *babakekere*, 'the little father'), who drew a
revenue in taxes and tolls from his town or group of towns and
represented its interests at Ibadan, while the ajẹlẹ (who was not

necessarily a man of Ibadan or Ọyọ) conversely represented Ibadan in the town.[21]

But though the rapid creation of the Ibadan empire had been achieved in part by the voluntary adhesion of weaker towns and afforded stability and protection to a wide area, it also exacerbated the internal rivalries of the Yoruba. At this time power in the south-west of the country was divided between the new states: Ibadan and Ijaye, the heirs of the military and administrative traditions of the old Ọyọ kingdom, and the re-constituted and concentrated Ẹgba state at Abẹokuta. Despite the careful dispositions of Alafin Atiba, it soon became clear that the situation hardly allowed room for the co-existence of three such close and ambitious neighbours. As early as 1832, the Ẹgba at Abẹokuta had almost suffered extinction when they were attacked by the Ijẹbu in alliance with the Ibadan (who were only able to contribute a small contingent to this campaign). They had been saved by Ọba Adele of Lagos, who had recently regained his throne with Ẹgba help and who now sent firearms and gunpowder up the Ogun River and himself led troops to reinforce the Ẹgba on the banks of the Owiwi. Three years later the Ẹgba inflicted a decisive defeat on the Ibadan (who were allied this time with the Ijaye) in the Arakonga war, and thus established Abẹokuta as a leading power in the land. Yet in the event it was Ijaye which seemed to offer the major obstacle to Ibadan expansion, and this factor underlies the Ijaye war of 1860-5, which dominates the history of this period.[22]

The outbreak of war between Ibadan and Ijaye followed some twenty years of tension between the two towns, and had been preceded by the Batẹdo war. In 1859 occurred the death of Alafin Atiba, 'the revolutionary prince turned conservative king' as Ajayi calls him.[23] In his place his son, the Arẹmọ Adelu, was elected to the throne, a breach with tradition in which all acquiesced except for Kurunmi of Ijaye, who protested that Adelu should have followed his father to the grave. Relations

M

between Kurunmi and the new Alafin worsened when Adelu
tried to reassert Ọyọ rule over the country west of the upper
Ogun which had been annexed by Ijaye, and turned for support
in this to Ibadan. The first phase of the ensuing war in 1860
consisted of a series of engagements in the wooded country
between Ijaye and Ibadan, followed by the almost two-year-
long siege of Ijaye. Soon after the opening of the siege a strong
army was sent from Abẹokuta to aid the hard-pressed Ijaye.
This resulted in the now aged and ailing Arẹ becoming virtually
the prisoner of his allies, and his death in mid-1861 only emphasized the true character of the war as essentially a contest
between the Ibadan and the Ẹgba. Finally, in March 1862,
after many privations had been suffered by its citizens, Ijaye
was abandoned by the Ẹgba army and then by the Ijaye themselves, most of whom succeeded in reaching Abẹokuta. But
this was not the end of the war, and in the next phase the
Ibadan had to face a coalition between their former allies and
trading partners, the Ijẹbu, and the Ẹgba. While the Ibadan
secured their command of the upper Ogun, the allies occupied
bases in the recalcitrant and pro-Ibadan Rẹmo province of
Ijẹbu, and here the last battles of the war were fought. At last
peace was concluded in August 1864 through the mediation of
Alafin Adelu.

The Ijaye war confirmed the position of Ibadan as the leading
power in Yorubaland, and at the same time seemed to demon-
strate that this new power was not only, or even primarily, concerned with the defence of the Ọyọ and other Yoruba against
their external enemies and with weaker towns against the
strong, but was animated by the restless ambition characteristic of a military state. The Ẹgba and Ijẹbu, equally anxious to
profit from the troubled situation, were alerted to the danger,
and Ọyọ, too, strengthened by the addition of former Ijaye territory in the upper Ogun (except for Ibarapa, which Ibadan had
kept), began to draw apart from its over-mighty vassal. Meanwhile, one of the issues which had come to the fore in the war

but had been ignored in the peace settlement assumed first importance for all parties: this was the control of the 'roads' or tracks along which trade flowed in the interior of the country and between the interior and the coast (especially the harbour at Lagos). As states bordering on the lagoon, both the Ijẹbu and the Ẹgba of Abẹokuta occupied key positions, while for the inland states, especially the Ibadan and other Ọyọ Yoruba, free movement on the roads and between the markets was vital, both for the provision of food and for the import of guns, ammunition, and gunpowder (purchased now by the sale of local produce rather than by slaves). So far as war material was concerned, the importance of communications had increased greatly with the use of firearms, which became widespread about 1840; this factor had been demonstrated in the Owiwi war and again, rather ludicrously, on the Arakonga when the Ibadan, running out of gunpowder, were reduced to pelting the Ẹgba with gourds gathered on the battlefield.[24]

The struggle for power between the Yoruba states, together with the ever-present menace of the Fulani at Ilọrin, constituted a situation which was complicated and worsened by the aggression of the western neighbours of the Yoruba, the dreaded Dahomeans under their kings Ghezo (?1818–58) and Glele (1859–89). After their final refusal of the annual tribute to Ọyọ, apparently during the 1820s, the Dahomeans carried out several major expeditions and innumerable raids into the Ẹgba and Ẹgbado countries, and though it was Ijaye which had been designated by Alafin Atiba as guardian of the west, in the event it was Abẹokuta which bore the brunt of the Dahomean attacks and was the involuntary shield of the whole Yoruba against the western danger.

The pursuit of war was one of the principal characteristics of the Dahomey kingdom from its beginnings.[25] Campaigns were undertaken every dry season, a main objective being the taking

of captives, most of whom were then either sold to slave traders
for export, bringing in large revenues for the monarchy, or retained by their captors as domestic slaves. Yet even for the
Dahomeans, warfare cannot be explained as simply undertaken
for the supply of the slave market. It was that and much more.
Having been the essential element in the building-up of this
West African Prussia, warfare remained equally a central factor
in the maintenance of its political structure and its religion. It
provided, for example, the human sacrifices to the ancestors on
which the continuation of the kingdom's prosperity was held to
depend.[26] Expeditions were mounted in all directions from
Abomey, but it was against the Yoruba, and in particular the
Egba, that the two great warrior kings mainly directed their
aggressions. One major reason for this specific hostility between
the Dahomeans and the Egba was their rivalry for control over
the Egbado territory lying between them. Dahomey already
exercised control over the slave trade from Whydah and Porto
Novo, and was always anxious to block the Egba policy of opening a route from Abeokuta via Ado to the coast at Badagry.

The first major clash between the Egba and the Dahomeans
seems to have taken place in 1844. Two years earlier the Egba had
annexed the Awori town of Otta and had then continued their
westward expansion by besieging Ado, inland from Badagry.
During this long siege (1842–53) a Dahomean army led by Ghezo,
and including, it is said, a contingent of women soldiers (the
first record of these redoubtable Amazons[27]), marched to the
help of Ado, a town which they regarded as subject to their ally
the King of Porto Novo. On this occasion they were defeated in
the field by the Egba and driven off with great loss. Ghezo himself had a narrow escape from capture, leaving his state um-
brella, stool, and war charms in the hands of the Egba. Then in
1851, perhaps in revenge for this humiliation, a strong and
determined attack was launched on Abeokuta itself. But after a
fierce battle along the walls (in which the European missionaries in the town played some part), the Dahomeans were forced

to retreat.[28] A few years later they succeeded in bringing about an anti-Egba coalition in which they were joined by Ijaye, Ibadan, Ijebu, and the exiled King Kosoko of Lagos (now installed at Epe in Ijebu territory); this, however, proved abortive, partly as a result of the intervention of Consul Campbell at Lagos, to whom the Egba had sent an urgent appeal. Ghezo died in 1858, but this did not abate the Dahomean threat to the Yoruba. After attacks on Isaga and Ibara in 1862 and 1863 respectively, another large-scale and determined assault was made on Abeokuta in 1864. Again the walls were held and the enemy driven back. On this occasion, unlike that of 1851, the Dahomean army suffered far heavier losses than the Egba and was unable to make an orderly retreat. But the hope that after this failure the Dahomeans would desist from their attacks was unfulfilled and their armies continued to raid westwards up to the end of the century. In 1873 and 1874, for example, they encamped outside Abeokuta, pillaging nearby towns and villages.[29] They also sent expeditions against Okeodan in Egbado and, farther north, against Ketu and Sabe. Ketu was captured in 1883 during the absence on campaign of its army, and was attacked again in 1886. On the second occasion it was destroyed and abandoned, though in 1893 the refugees were able to return to the site and rebuild their town.[30] Thus the Yoruba of the far west passed first under Dahomean and then French rule. Meanwhile the upper Ogun and Ibarapa country continued to undergo Dahomean raids down to the 1890s.

While northern and western Yorubaland contended with the invasions of the Fulani and the Dahomeans, the kingdoms of the east were suffering from a renewal of Benin's westward expansion. This apparently began in the early years of the nineteenth century during the reign of Oba Obanosa. First, part of the Owo kingdom was once again brought under obedience to Benin. Then, in the reign of Oba Osemwede of Benin, Akure was reconquered and Ekiti overrun. The Benin forces for a time established a base at Otun, and a new Deji of Akure was appointed 'to watch over the interests of Benin in the Ekiti country'.[31] About this time the Ado waged an unsuccessful war against the Bini and the Ikerre (the traditional allies of Benin in Ekiti), which resulted in the abandonment for some years of their town and the diminution of the Ewi's territory. Soon after mid-century the brief resurgence of Benin's military power came to a halt, and much of Ekiti was then subjected to Ibadan. Yet, according to Egharevba, the Ekiti paid tribute to Benin up to the British occupation of the area in 1897, while payments from Lagos were maintained until about mid-century. Even after the establishment of the British administration, the authority of Benin was respected in eastern Yorubaland, and as late as the reign at Benin of Eweka II (1914–33) the chiefs of Ondo looked to that Oba for his ruling in land and succession disputes.

The collapse of Oyo ile was followed within twenty years by the establishment of the British consular regime in Lagos, overshadowing the monarchy there, and within a further ten years by the annexation of the town as a crown colony. Already the importance of this island kingdom was becoming apparent. The first half of the nineteenth century had seen the steady growth of its slave market. Captain Adams noted the existence of the trade there at the turn of the century, but it does not seem to have reached large proportions until the decay of Porto Novo, which followed the first Anglo-Portuguese anti-slave-trade treaty of 1810, and the increase in the supply of slaves due to the interior wars. The population was becoming more mixed; apart from the original Awori and the Portuguese and Brazilian slave dealers (white and creole), from the 1830s there had been a flow of immigrants, or 'repatriates', from the former slaves in Sierra Leone, Brazil, and Cuba. The education and background of the Sierra Leonians, or Saro as they were called, and the

Brazilians or Amaro, enabled them to play a prominent part as middlemen between the British administration and the traditional authorities, especially at Lagos and Abẹokuta. Meanwhile, at the head of the town the Ọba of the line established by Benin still ruled. By now there was probably no attempt by Benin to impose its authority in Lagos, even though the traditional tribute continued to be paid. The power of the Ọba may in consequence have somewhat increased, but he was always subject to the constitutional restraints characteristic of the Yoruba kingdoms (and also of Benin), and especially to the influence of the chief known as the Eletu Odibo. During the 1830s troubles broke out over the kingship which led to the deposition and subsequent reinstatement of Ọba Adele and then to a feud between the party supporting first Oba Oluwọle and then his successor Akitoye, to which the Eletu adhered, and that of Akitoye's nephew Kosọkọ, an ambitious young prince and claimant to the throne, who was the son and brother of previous Ọba.[32]

It was this dynastic dispute which provided the occasion for the British intervention in Lagos of 1851. Kosọkọ, after being forced into exile, had engaged in the slave trade at Porto Novo and Whydah, where he gained the support of the Portuguese and Brazilian merchants. In 1845 he was allowed by the mild and kindly Akitoye to return to Lagos, and within a few months he succeeded in replacing his uncle on the throne. Akitoye took refuge at Badagry, where he became the protégé of the missionaries and repatriates in the town. Soon his partisans were urging the British that they should restore Akitoye and thereby wipe out the notorious slave market at Lagos. Samuel Crowther was sent to London to point out also that 'if Lagos were under its lawful chief . . . an immense extent of country, abounding with cotton . . . would be thrown open to commerce'.[33] The British Government hesitated, and the naval commander in West Africa advised caution. But their Consul for the Bights of Benin and Biafra, who had been appointed to this post in 1849 as its first holder, was John Beecroft, determined equally to stamp out the slave trade and to extend British influence in his area,[34] and he did not scruple to commit the home authorities. Kosǫkǫ had already refused to sign an anti-slave-trade treaty with the British, and after a second refusal Beecroft decided on a show of force. In November 1851 the Consul entered Lagos lagoon with a naval escort, but after a sharp exchange of fire the party was repulsed. The attack was renewed in greater force at Christmastide a month later, and on 28 December. Akitoye landed in the town with his British and other supporters and resumed his throne. On New Year's Day 1852 he signed a treaty with the British representatives in which he agreed to abolish the slave trade and expel the slave traders, to trade freely with British subjects, and to protect the missionaries.

The British assertion that they bombarded and brought Lagos under control in 1851 in order to put an end to the slave trade there has in recent years been questioned.[35] Ajayi, for example, has written:

> The anxiety of Britain to intervene in Lagos was not just the philanthropic desire to destroy the slave trading activities of the Portuguese and Brazilians there, but also the economic desire to control the trade of Lagos from which they [sic] had hitherto been excluded and from where they hoped to exploit the resources of the vast country stretching to and beyond the Niger.[36]

Explanation in history is rarely simple, and in this case the interests and ambitions of traders, missionaries, and government agents who were pressing for action against Kosǫkǫ had become inextricably mixed, and after agreeing that selfish motives alternated and mingled with altruistic ones, it seems impossible to determine which were uppermost. The soundness of the doctrine that 'legitimate trade' must be encouraged as a substitute for the export of slaves had been demonstrated on this coast, even though it had unexpectedly increased the domestic demand. Incontestably, an immediate result of the action taken in 1851 was the abatement of the export of slaves. The establishment of the British Consulate was quickly followed by the arrival in the town of the palm-oil factors and the Christian missionaries.[37] The British, in their several manifestations as protagonists of commerce, Christianity, and sound government, had now become a part of Yoruba country, and their presence at Lagos was a portent of even greater moment than that of the Fulani at Ilọrin.

The consular period in Lagos lasted only ten years, and was almost covered by the career there of Consul Benjamin Campbell, who was appointed in 1853 and died at his post in 1859. The policies and preoccupations of the British administration up to 1893 quickly became apparent: the development of legitimate trade, in palm produce above all else, with its consequential emphasis on the opening of the interior and the maintenance of free and secure movement on the roads, aims and interests which, for rather different reasons, were shared by the Ibadan; the ending of the war in the interior, a purpose which for a time in the post-consular period seemed to the British administrators best able to be achieved by supporting the extension of Ibadan's influence, which in turn involved a clash with the missionary party at Abẹokuta; and in general the spread of European ideas of ethics and conduct. But for this programme the consular regime could not provide adequate means. The end of Campbell's life saw the trade routes closing all round as the Ijaye war drew near, and a revival of the slave trade at Porto Novo and Whydah. The trade of Lagos declined sharply, and it was in these circumstances that Palmerston, the British Prime Minister, acceded to the promptings of his Government's agents on the coast and gave permission for the annexation of the town in 1861: an acquisition which was regarded as a 'deadly gift from the Foreign Office' by the officials at the Colonial Office, who rightly anticipated that, like the other West African possessions, it would require the support of a Parliamentary grant-in-aid.[38] In August 1861, under the guns of H.M.S. *Prometheus* anchored in the lagoon, Ọba Dosumu agreed to cede his kingdom to the British. Sir Richard Burton (the recently appointed Consul for the Bights) sardonically described the scene as the Union Jack was hoisted, the guns of the *Prometheus* fired a salute, a choir of missionary boys sang a hymn, and forty-four officials and traders sat down to dine on the quarter-deck of the warship.[39]

The new Governor, Freeman, arrived with instructions from the Colonial Office to restrict his activities to defence of the local inhabitants and to putting down the slave trade. But the colony was from its beginning involved in the politics of the interior, since the only means of defraying the cost of its administration was by the imposition of customs duties, a device with which West Africans were familiar, but which in Lagos proved to require the control of commerce with the hinterland by extending the boundaries east and west along the coast. The full development of the commerce of the colony depended moreover on the opening of the roads through the interior to direct trade, as opposed to that through the markets set up for external trading by the middlemen states of Egba and Ijẹbu; in this, the interests of Lagos were soon seen to coincide with those of Ibadan. Thus, despite attempts to apply the brake by the Colonial Office in London, bewildered by events yet approving the financial principle, Freeman and his successors continued to intervene in the wars of the Yoruba and to enlarge the area subject to their administration.[40]

There now appeared on the scene the eager and evangelical Captain Glover. His first appointment at Lagos was as harbour master, but on two occasions during Freeman's leaves he acted as Governor, and in 1866, when the colony was placed under the Governor of the West African Settlements in Sierra Leone, he became Administrator.[41] He had taken part in the Niger expedition of 1857 and after the wreck of the *Dayspring* near Jebba had made three journeys overland between the Niger and

Lagos, passing through Ilọrin and Abẹokuta. Already he had been fired by his experiences with the ambition to gain control for Britain of both the Niger highway and the port of Lagos, and despite the opposition of Government and public opinion in England – expressed, in particular, by the recommendations of the 1865 Select Committee – he bent all his great energies to realizing these aims. As early as 1863 the area under British control was enlarged by the addition of the old trading settle-ments of Palma and Lekki; these lay on the coast to the east of the colony in territory claimed by the Ijẹbu and were 'ceded' by the now-tamed Kosọkọ, who had been allowed by the Awujalẹ to take refuge nearby at Ẹpẹ as a sort of tenant ruler. Glover now succeeded in checking a threatened expansion by the French from their short-lived protectorate at Porto Novo and signed treaties with local rulers which brought Ado, Ipokia, Okẹodan, and Badagry on the west under Lagos, a move which he followed by a boundary agreement with the French admiral. Meanwhile, towards the end of 1864 when the Ijaye war was in its final stages, the Ẹgba and Ijẹbu blocked the tracks linking Ibadan with Lagos and Ẹgba forces laid siege to Ikorodu in Ijẹbu Rẹmo, the important market town at the northern corner of the lagoon which was allied to Ibadan. Finally repudiating the policy of favouring Abẹokuta, long urged by an influential section of the missionaries, Glover fell on the Ẹgba at Ikorodu in March 1865 with troops from the West India Regiment and his recently formed Hausa Constabulary, firing rockets and shells, and drove them off in disorder.

Thereafter Glover continued to press for the opening of the roads. This was a policy which especially alarmed the Ẹgba, who in 1867, in order to prevent merchants from by-passing their town, set up a customs post at Isẹri on the River Ogun near its exit to the lagoon. Glover, suspicious of this attempt to extend Ẹgba influence almost as far south as the Lagos main-land, established constables at posts on the roads as far as Ọtta and up the Ogun to Isẹri, and he announced that Ebute

Mẹtta was Lagos territory. His action was resented at Abẹokuta and was followed by the rising against Europeans in the town known as *ifọle*, 'housebreaking', and their subsequent expulsion. In 1871 Glover tried to achieve the opening of the roads for direct trade by calling a conference in Lagos to which came representatives from Ọyọ, Ijẹbu, Ibadan, and at a later stage also from Ilaro, Ijo, Ketu, and even Benin. But neither the Ẹgba nor the Ijẹbu (still firmly in alliance) would co-operate, and these efforts came to nothing. From his home government Glover continued to receive little support and frequent opposition, and in 1872, on the reversal of his policies by the Governor-in-Chief, Pope-Hennessy, he was recalled. As a contemporary noted, he had been in advance of his time – but only by a few years, for within two decades his policy was vindicated by the actions taken by his successors at Lagos with the approval of Whitehall.

XII · On the Threshold of Nigeria

The last quarter of the nineteenth century saw the end of the sovereignty of the Yoruba states and the beginning of their elimination as political units. In 1892–3 all were brought under British control as a protectorate administered with the colony of Lagos, with the exception of the Ẹgba at Abẹokuta, who were allowed to maintain an anomalous semi-independence until 1914. In 1906 the colony and protectorate were amalgamated with the Niger Coast (formerly Oil Rivers) Protectorate and in 1914 with the Protectorate of Northern Nigeria. The colonial government, advancing from the system of informal rule typified by the consuls, extended its influence by its apparatus of Travelling Commissioners and later by Residents and District Officers posted to the major towns, a system which to some extent kept alive, and after the introduction of Lugardian indirect rule into Yorubaland from 1914 even strengthened, the identities of the kingdoms. Political independence had been lost, but in the longer term more important than the establishment of this alien rule was the absorption of all the Yoruba, Ọyọ, Ijẹbu, Ẹgba, and the rest into a wider grouping, that of Nigeria.

Before all this was achieved, the last quarter-century of independent Yorubaland witnessed profound changes of many kinds. In politics and warfare Ibadan's predominance, which had offered one solution to the problems posed by the decline of Ọyọ and the external threats, was rejected and its short-lived empire broken up. There was a resurgence of vitality in some of the ancient kingdoms, especially Ijẹbu, and the much-divided Ekiti drew together in a military confederation against Ibadan.

These were variations on old themes, but there were changes, and portents of changes, of a deeper nature. Missionaries of various churches – Anglican, Roman Catholic, and the Protestant sects – and of many lands, European and American, were penetrating the kingdoms and everywhere challenging old ways of life and thought, and wherever the missionaries went, new educational systems were introduced. Traders both followed and preceded the missionaries, and the work and influence of the two were more often complementary than antagonistic. In Lagos a new kind of society was being created, based on the westernized Yoruba and other West Africans, who were emancipated not only from slavery but also from former ties with their towns and families. Against this background took place the political movement of Europe into Africa known as the Partition of Africa – or, when the fifteen years or so of heightened activity after 1884 are considered, as the Scramble – momentous not so much because of the establishment of the colonial regimes, which nearly all proved to be ephemeral, as for the new nation states which were created after the European pattern.[1]

It is possible that the comparative richness and accessibility of the archives of the missionary societies has led to some exaggeration of the role which they played in the life of Yorubaland during this period. Their direct influence on events was often less than they realized or hoped; at Abẹokuta, for example, Townsend, the Anglican agent, was constantly disappointed in his ambitions to convert the town into a peace-loving, Christian polity. Nevertheless, the missionaries were the most powerful vehicles of change, first, because they were identified in the minds of the Yoruba with the material power of the British settlement at Lagos, and secondly, because of the educational and economic programme which they were determined to implement as the pre-condition, according to their theory, of the Christianization of the land and which met with a growing and enthusiastic response from those they taught. Unlike the leaders of the Moslem jihad, they could not – or would not – compromise with existing conditions and institutions. Wherever they went, a pro-missionary party sprang up around them, dedicated not so much to their dogmatic and moral teaching – the Ẹgba, for example, remained keen slave traders almost to the end of the century, despite their numerous Christians – as to exploiting their political and economic support. This in turn was usually soon followed by the development of a party hostile to the missionaries, equally animated by political and economic motives. To a great extent, support for the missions was based on the early Western-educated Africans, the Saro or repatriates from Sierra Leone living in Lagos, Abẹokuta, and (in much smaller numbers) elsewhere, but such men were also found in the ranks of the anti-missionaries. Among the latter a prominent example was G. W. Johnson, the Secretary of the Ẹgba United Board of Management which was established as the government at Abẹokuta during the regency following the death of Alake Okukenu.

The relations of the missionaries with the British administration varied. All missionaries continued to demand that British protection should be extended to them wherever they went, and in order to further their aims – religious, educational, and political – welcomed and encouraged the establishment of British rule. Thus in many ways they prepared the way for the extension of the protectorate over the whole of the Yoruba country; one writer has contended that the work of the missionaries was the primary factor in bringing about this extension by peaceful and gradual means.[2] There were many occasions when the missionaries strongly disapproved of the actions of the British administrators at Lagos, and especially of the restless and ambitious Governor Glover. Nevertheless, the interdependence of missionaries and officials was so strong, and so clear to all concerned, that it could not be broken by such disagreements. During the major and protracted war which broke out in 1877 it was to the missionaries, and to the British power behind them, that many among the distracted Yoruba looked for intervention and help amid their intractable rivalries.

The Sixteen Years' War (1877–93) between Ibadan and a grand coalition of other Yoruba states, allied from 1879 with the Ilọrin, was on a larger scale than any of the previous wars and lasted for a longer time.[3] Essentially it arose from the widespread hostility engendered by the Ibadan, who had not only succeeded to much of the central and southern territories of the old Ọyọ kingdom, including a large part of the former territory of Kurunmi of Ijaye, but had also brought the Ekiti and Ijẹṣa under their rule. More immediately, it concerned the issue of the freedom of the roads along which food and other supplies moved to the towns and Ibadan's need for access to the coast, where guns and powder could be obtained. The outbreak of war in 1877 was occasioned by the Ẹgba, who, resentful of an Ibadan expedition through their country to collect a consignment of gunpowder bought by the Alafin from Porto Novo, barred the roads to Ibadan traders. The Ibadan opened hostilities in a desultory manner by raids on Ẹgba farms, but the war was soon extended as the Ijẹbu joined in a coalition with the Ẹgba. Next, the Ekiti and their northern neighbours, the Ila, rose in revolt, murdering the Ibadan ajẹlẹ in their towns, a move which brought the Ilọrin, always interested in this eastern area of Yorubaland, to join in the war against Ibadan.

The extension of the war to the north-east was in part a consequence of the development of an eastern route from the coast to Ibadan which had been advocated by Governor Glover in 1872 in order to avoid Ẹgba and Ijẹbu territory. This route had two southern termini: the western one at Atijere at the eastern end of the lagoon, and the other at Aboto on the creeks in Mahin country. From these it ran northwards to Ondo, whence it was known as the Ondo Road and where at Glover's suggestion the Church Missionary Society established a mission station in 1875. From Ondo the road continued to the Ifẹ town of Oke Igbo, where it divided, one branch running westwards to Ibadan and the other north to Ilẹṣa.[4] The road at first served its purpose in enabling military and other supplies to reach Ibadan without interference from the Ẹgba and the Ijẹbu, but it soon became a focus of dissension. In particular, the Ijẹṣa at its northern end, who had been brought back to obedience by Ibadan after a rebellion in 1870 under their war leader, Ogedengbe, were determined to regain their independence. A group of educated repatriates formed an Ijẹṣa Association which, though it began in 1876 as a Christian prayer group, was soon directing its activities to stirring up resistance to Ibadan, both in their own state and among the neighbouring Ekiti. They strongly supported the maintenance of the Ondo Road, since it linked them with Lagos and allowed them to import firearms and ammunition into their area. This was of special importance at this time when the southern Yoruba were replacing their muzzle-loading muskets by modern breech-loading rifles and securing thereby a marked superiority in armament over the Ibadan.[5]

The first major engagement of the war took place in 1878 at Ikirun, north of Ilẹṣa, where the Ibadan attacked and drove off in disorder strong armies from Ilọrin, Ekiti, Ila, and Ijẹṣa encamped north of the town.[6] But Ibadan's victory in this action – known as the Jalumi or 'rush into the water' war from the drowning of many of the fleeing Ilọrin in the nearby River Ọtin – was singularly indecisive. The Ijẹbu declined Ibadan's offer of alliance with them, and the Ẹgba continued to bar the roads through their territory to the coast, while the Ekiti and Ijẹṣa strengthened their alliance, the former grouping themselves into the military confederation called the Ekiti Parapọ, whose armies were placed under the command of Ogedengbe of Ilẹṣa. Soon the Ibadan were fighting on three main fronts: around their own town and to the south and west against the

N

Ẹgba and the Ijẹbu; in the north against the Ilọrin, who were besieging their allies the Ọffa, and in the north-east against the Ekiti and Ijẹṣa on the battlefield among the hills and rocks near Oke Mẹsi (north of Ilẹsa) known as Kiriji (a word derived onomatopaeically from the report of the firearms).

Fighting continued at Kiriji for over a decade. Meanwhile, in or about 1882, a new front against Ibadan was opened up by Ifẹ. Relations between the Ifẹ and the Ọyọ refugees resettled at the contiguous town of Mọdakẹkẹ had never been easy, and at some period, probably about 1850, had degenerated into active hostilities during the course of which Ifẹ had been abandoned by its inhabitants. About 1854, however, the Ibadan persuaded the Ifẹ to return to their former homes.[7] It seems that from this time until the 1880s the ancient town and kingdom of Ifẹ were within the Ibadan empire, though apparently no ajẹlẹ was posted to the capital, probably from deference to its prestige and since in any case there was one resident in nearby Mọdakẹkẹ.[8] During the Sixteen Years' War the Ifẹ were required to contribute a contingent of troops to the Ibadan forces at Kiriji. But they grew ever more restive under Ibadan rule, and were especially resentful of the imposition on them through Ibadan influence of an unpopular Ọni. In 1882 these troubles came to a head, and again the Ifẹ expressed their hostility to the Ibadan and other Ọyọ Yoruba by attacking their neighbours at Mọdakẹkẹ, and again Ile Ifẹ was destroyed. But now the Ijẹṣa and Ijẹbu sent troops to their aid, while their own soldiers under the war chiefs decamped from Kiriji and returned to help in the siege of Mọdakẹkẹ. Johnson writes: 'Thus stood the Ibadan lion at bay facing five fronts, with ammunition spent, yet flinching from none, at Ọfa, at Kiriji, at Mọdakẹkẹ, and against the Ẹgbas as well as the Ijẹbus at home.'[9]

Despite Ibadan's difficulties, the war was now approaching stalemate, and war-weariness was widespread. Many Yoruba, and especially the educated, looked to British intervention to bring the fighting to an end. But at this time vigorous action could hardly be expected from the Lagos administration. Between 1874 and 1886 the Government of the colony was incorporated with that of the Gold Coast, an arrangement which inhibited a forward policy; Lagos, moreover, was only just beginning to pay its way and to justify its maintenance.[10] Not until pressure was applied by trading interests, for example, did the local Administrator take steps to foil the cession of Mahin beach to the Germans in 1885 by the Amapetu. In this situation it fell to the missionaries to explore the prospects for peace, a task to which they were suited, since not only did they themselves regard a settlement as a matter of urgency in the interests of Christianity but also their reputation stood high with the chiefs and people of the country. A series of meetings was held in Lagos at the end of 1882, apparently on the initiative of the veteran Anglican missionary at Ibadan, David Hinderer, to which came representatives from the main kingdoms. This led to the sending of a Lagos mission to Ijẹbu Ode, where it was found that though Awujalẹ Fidipotẹ wished to continue the war against Ibadan, a strong party in the kingdom was in favour of peace and the resumption of trade. The upshot was the deposition of the Awujalẹ and the gradual return of peace and trade between Ijẹbu and Ibadan, the latter being now enabled to obtain from the Ijẹbu, at high prices, enough new rifles and cartridges to hold their positions at Kiriji.

These efforts for peace brought about what Johnson calls a 'rift in the clouds', but on the main fronts fighting continued. In January 1884 the Reverend J. B. Wood, an influential missionary at Abẹokuta, succeeded in visiting the opposing camps at Kiriji, but he failed to persuade the combatants to accept terms. Hostilities dragged on there, as also at Mọdakẹkẹ and Ọffa. Then, in January 1886, the Colony of Lagos was detached from the Gold Coast and again became self-administering. Almost at once Governor Moloney dispatched two delegations

into the interior to reopen peace negotiations. Both delegations were headed by Yoruba clergymen of the Church Missionary Society, the first, to the Ibadan camp, being led by the
Reverend Samuel Johnson, the historian, and the second, to
the Ekiti and their allies, by the Reverend Charles Phillips of
Ondo (later Assistant Bishop of Western Equatorial Africa).
A cease-fire was arranged by the delegates, first at Kiriji
and then at Mọdakẹkẹ, and a peace treaty was signed at Lagos
in June 1886. By this treaty Ibadan recognized the independence of the members of the Ekiti Parapọ, and it was provided
that the Ọyọ town of Mọdakẹkẹ, whose contiguity to Ifẹ had
long been a source of trouble, should be broken up and rebuilt
on Ibadan territory between the Oṣun and Ọba rivers; by
implication the treaty also severed the formal dependence of
Ibadan on Ọyọ.[11] Special Commissioners were named, this time
two officials of the Lagos administration, who proceeded to
Kiriji and supervised the firing and evacuation of the war
camps there at the end of September. They went next to the
Mọdakẹkẹ battlefield. Here, although the cease-fire was in
operation, they failed to persuade either the Mọdakẹkẹ to
comply with the Lagos treaty by quitting their homes or the
Ifẹ to leave their camp and return to their town. Nevertheless,
fighting was not resumed there.

The wars in Yorubaland had now been brought to an end and
peace restored, even though precariously, with an important
exception: the contest between Ibadan and Ilọrin still continued, centring on the siege by the Ilọrin of Ọffa, once their
vassal town and now Ibadan's ally in the north. The Ilọrin,
commanded by Karara, the fierce and intransigent Balogun
of the Gambari (general of the Hausa population of Ilọrin),
had rejected the peace proposals brought to them by Phillips
and had no part in the Lagos treaty, though they did agree
to carry on negotiations with the Ibadan. But during the next
year (1887) the latter, wearied of hostilities and nervous about
the isolated position of their army at Ọffa, withdrew from the

besieged town, after rescuing its ruler, the Ọlọffa, and returned
to their base at Ikirun. Karara now entered Ọffa, which for
so long and so obstinately had resisted him. Its remaining
chiefs came at his summons to do homage, and while they lay
prostrate before him at the palace gate he gave the order for
them all to be slaughtered on the spot. Yet the fall of Ọffa did
not end the war, and desultory fighting continued between the
Ibadan at Ikirun and the Ilọrin encamped at Yanayo for a
further six years.

Ibadan's attempt to assume the mantle of Ọyọ had now
decisively failed. This was mainly due, Mrs Awẹ has written,
to its lack of a 'traditional heritage' and its consequent in-
ability to command the loyalty of the former Ọyọ towns,[12] but
it was bound up too with the difficulties arising from the control
of the roads by its enemies, and especially in obtaining the
newer types of firearms. Meanwhile the Ẹgba, who since
1879 had taken little part in the war, were split by a religious
dissension reminiscent of the Franza–Ingleza troubles in
Uganda. One party, which included most of the chiefs, supported the extension of French influence in the town, for which
the way had been prepared by the Roman Catholic missionaries who had been working in Abẹokuta since 1880, while a
'Protestant' party, led by Wood, the Anglican missionary,[13]
looked to Lagos for protection. In 1888 a young French trader
named Viard, who claimed to represent the French Government, obtained a treaty from the chiefs of Ilaro, the leading
Ẹgbado town, and then moved on to Abẹokuta, where again he
persuaded the chiefs to enter into a treaty; under this, Abẹokuta was to become a French protectorate, and in return the
French would build a railway from Porto Novo via Ilaro and
would recognize domestic slavery. Wood and his party immediately raised the alarm. The Colonial Office in London
realized that this French penetration threatened the main
source of Lagos trade, and the issue was taken up with the
French Government through diplomatic channels. In 1889 the

British and French Governments signed a treaty settling what was to be Nigeria's western frontier on a line well to the west of Abẹokuta and Ilaro. Against the background of these events Governor Moloney hastily concluded a treaty (in July 1888) with Ọyọ by which the Alafin agreed to cede no territory without the consent of the Lagos Government,[14] and he made renewed attempts to bring the Ilọrin war to an end. After Moloney's departure in 1891 the Acting Governor, Denton, hoisted the British flag in Ilaro and other parts of Ẹgbadoland. His object was to divert the Ẹgbado trade towards Lagos and away from Porto Novo, but the annexation incurred the indignation of the Ẹgba, who retaliated as usual by closing the roads and the River Ogun.

The Anglo-French clash of interests in Abẹokuta was one facet of the Scramble for Africa. The Berlin Conference of 1884–5 is conveniently, but rather misleadingly, held to have partitioned Africa; in fact, the famous provision in its Final Act that international recognition of territorial acquisitions in Africa must be preceded by an effective occupation of the area concerned was specifically confined in its application to the coastal districts, most of which had already been brought under control by the European powers, and left the boundaries between the spheres of influence of the powers in the interior undefined. Thus it was fortunate for the British, and in the long run for the Yoruba, that Viard's treaty with Abẹokuta in 1888 so stirred the Protestant party there that, as a result of their pressure, the British Government exerted themselves in time to secure an agreement with the French under which most of the Yoruba country fell to the east of the demarcation line – though the Ketu, Ṣabe, and other western Yoruba were left to be incorporated eventually into the French colony of Dahomey, and are still separated by an international frontier from the Yoruba in Nigeria. But the treaty had done nothing to clarify the position in the area east of the line and within the British sphere. Only in 1891, when the scholarly Moloney was replaced as Governor at Lagos by Carter, was a vigorous forward policy undertaken, and it was not until Chamberlain came to the Colonial Office in 1895 that the old informal system of rule was abandoned.

When Carter arrived in Lagos in September 1891 three major obstacles remained to the extension of British rule within the limits determined by agreement among the European powers: the Ilọrin–Ibadan war in the north and the recalcitrance of the Ẹgba and the Ijẹbu in the south, which all hindered free movement and the flow of trade between Lagos and the interior. Carter dealt first with the problem presented by the determinedly independent Ijẹbu. Denton had already visited the Awujalẹ and had been ill received. Carter now demanded an apology for the insult to the Acting Governor, and at a meeting in Lagos towards the end of 1891 he secured both this and a 'treaty' under which the Ijẹbu promised to open the roads through their country to all. The validity of this treaty was somewhat doubtful, since the members of the Awujalẹ's delegation, pleading illiteracy, refused to sign it, though they allowed its signature on their behalf by two Ijẹbu residents of Lagos. In any case, its terms were soon broken when the Awujalẹ picked a quarrel with Ibadan, demanding the execution of two missionaries there (one a Yoruba and the other English) whom he accused of having brought Europeans and their goods into his territory without permission, and threatening to close the roads. Carter now received permission by telegraph from the Colonial Secretary to take coercive action, and in May 1892 he sent a military expedition against the Ijẹbu. The force was under the command of Colonel Scott of the Gold Coast Constabulary and consisted of some 450 men from the West India Regiment, the Lagos and Gold Coast Hausa, and a contingent of Ibadan warriors, with eleven British Officers. They sailed down the lagoon in a small flotilla and landed at Ẹpẹ, whence after two days' preparation they marched on Ijẹbu Ode. The Ijẹbu, who had expected the landing at Itoiki nearer their capital, were taken by surprise, but they resisted the advance with determination in the thick forest through which the Lagos force was making its way. A particularly fierce engagement was fought at the crossing of the Yemọji River, but after two and a half hours' fighting there the invaders, with their rockets, Maxim gun, and three seven-pounders, prevailed over the Ijẹbu with their Sniders, and seven days after setting out from Lagos they entered the Ijẹbu capital. After a further ten days the main force withdrew, leaving behind a detachment of the Lagos Constabulary under a British officer.

Carter's decision to attack the Ijẹbu rather than the Egba, who had caused the greater inconvenience in closing the interior roads, has been attributed in a recent study to the influence of the Anglican and Protestant missionaries, who had met with continuous rebuffs in their attempts to extend their missions to Ijẹbu from the Awujalẹ and his chiefs, strong conservatives intent on maintaining the traditional isolation of their state.[15] The missionaries were right in their assessment of the potential importance of Ijẹbu to their cause. After 1892, as Ayandele shows, Ijẹbu supplanted Abeokuta as the leading centre of missionary activity among the Yoruba.[16]

Politically and economically, the Ijẹbu expedition transformed the whole situation in the interior. Not only was the northern shore of the lagoon now brought under British control but, as Johnson writes, 'a shock of surprise and alarm' was felt throughout the land.[17] The Egba (unaware that the Colonial Office in London were demurring at proposals from the War Office that operations should next be mounted against them) reopened the Ogun to the traders' canoes and barges and invited the Governor to visit Abẹokuta. Encouraged by these developments, Carter set out at the beginning of 1893 on his trek through Yorubaland, accompanied by a posse of local soldiers.[18] He went first to Abẹokuta, where he signed a treaty of trade and friendship with the Egba. But the chiefs there successfully resisted proposals for posting a Resident to their town and for cessions of land for a railway linking Lagos with Ibadan, and also obtained the inclusion in the treaty of a clause guaranteeing their independence. From Abẹokuta Carter continued to Ọyọ, where he again made a treaty, here less favourable to the local authorities, and thence to Ilọrin, where he interviewed the Emir. Turning south, the Governor had a series of meetings near the Ọtin River with the leaders of the opposing war camps of the Ilọrin and the Ibadan, at which he succeeded in obtaining their recognition of the Awẹrẹ stream (near Ẹrin, between Ikirun and Ọffa) as the boundary between the territories of the two towns and their agreement to the breaking-up of the camps. By the end of March the Ibadan army had returned to its town. Carter followed in its wake to Ibadan, where he was disappointed in his hopes of obtaining a treaty providing for the posting there of a Resident. He then returned to Lagos, to receive the plaudits of the merchants for his successful pacification of so wide an area. A few months later, in August 1893, the Ibadan chiefs reopened negotiations with the Governor and, after assurances that no interference with their government was intended, agreed to a treaty with the British. Under this their town was recognized as the administrative centre of the larger part of the old Ọyọ kingdom and the chiefs now agreed to provide land for the construction of a railway and to accept a British Resident.[19]

Thus ended the Sixteen Years' War, and also the history of the Yoruba states as independent political units. There remained the two problems of Ilọrin and of French infiltration into an area which, although still undemarcated, clearly belonged under the Anglo-French agreements to the Lagos hinterland. Despite Carter's visit and the Emir's protestations of friendship, the Ilọrin continued to harass the countryside, and in 1894 Captain Bower, the Travelling Commissioner (and later Resident) at Ibadan, established a camp on the River Ọtin a little north of Ikirun in order to protect the area and to demarcate the boundary between Ilọrin and Ibadan. But still the Ilọrin were hostile, treating Bower roughly on a visit he paid to their town and launching attacks during his absence in 1896 on the camp at Odo Ọtin. Ilọrin now fell within the territory of the Royal Niger Company, the chartered trading company which preceded the establishment of the Protectorate of Northern Nigeria. Carter sent many protests to London about the Company's supine attitude over the Ilọrin situation, but until they were pressed by the Colonial Office to take action the Company showed little interest in asserting its rule in this part of the huge area assigned to them. At last, in January 1897, Goldie, the Governor of the Company, led out his troops from Lokoja. Having first conquered Bida, the Nupe capital, he continued to Ilọrin. After overcoming a brief resistance the troops entered the ruins of the city, which they had shelled and set on fire. The Emir signed a treaty, agreeing to accept a frontier with Lagos 'as the Company shall decide'. Even now the Company did not have the resources to bring about proper control of the area, but for the future the Lagos Government was able to complain about the behaviour of the Ilọrin not to the Company alone but more effectively to the West African Frontier Force. This had been established in 1897 under Lugard in order to check the French, one of whose expeditions from Dahomey in January 1897 had for a time even occupied Kiṣi in the extreme north of Yorubaland.[20]

The settling of the Ilọrin–Lagos boundary resulted in a large number of Yoruba in the north-east corner of the old Ọyọ kingdom and also most of the Igbomina and Kabba peoples to the north of the Ijẹṣa and Ekiti coming under the rule of the Royal Niger Company and being included, from 1900, in the Protectorate of Northern Nigeria. In independent Nigeria they constituted a sort of irredenta in the Northern Region (at least from the point of view of the Western Region), but since the administrative rearrangements of May 1967 they have belonged to the West Central State with its capital at Ilọrin.

In 1893 the inhabitants of the Yoruba states stood on the threshold of a wider polity and wider loyalties were offered them. Though the ending of the Sixteen Years' War, in shattering Ibadan's attempt to impose its own form of unity on the country, had restored for a few years the independence of the eastern kingdoms, this independence lost its meaning in the new situation created by the peace which British rule brought about. Shielded by foreign arms and power from the incursions of the Dahomeans (whose capital was occupied by the French in this same year) and the Fulani, and forbidden to engage in their own internecine wars, the Yoruba were free to discover their cultural unity within the new political unity imposed upon them, and in a few years were invited to share in an even wider identification as Nigerians fellow-citizens, with the Hausa, Kanuri, Ibo, Ijo, Edo, and the rest of Nigeria's many different peoples. Within a half-century this was to engender among the educated a sense of belonging to a nation, the most populous and one of the most important in Africa. It also led to the assertion, within this wider context, of the linguistic, cultural, and political ties which give unity to the Yoruba of the different kingdoms, the diverse 'children of Oduduwa'. Time must show which of these concepts, the national and the tribal, unhappily often in rivalry, will prevail.

The British peace was paid for by a loss of political independence which lasted for sixty-four years. But in the history of the Yoruba kingdoms the colonial period, and the longer period covered by European penetration, are but a fraction, though an important one. The dangers and uncertainties of the present can be explained only by a study of the past which both takes account of the rapid changes of the last hundred years and goes beyond them to the earlier centuries when these kingdoms flourished as the political framework within which the ancestors of the Western Nigerians of today lived their lives from generation to generation.

Notes

CHAPTER I

1. P. 65.
2. WRIGLEY (1960), p. 199. Thurston Shaw's recent discovery of a Stone Age habitation site near Akurẹ has established the antiquity of settlement in the Yoruba forest.
3. OLIVER and FAGE, p. 109. In the West Sudan, according to E. W. Bovill (p. 127, n. 1), cowries 'have been in continuous use as a currency . . . since the eleventh century, and probably much longer'.
4. See the discussion in OMER-COOPER (1964), especially pp. 105–8.
5. BOVILL, p. 119. John II of Portugal was allowed by the Pope in 1481 to style himself 'Lord of Guinea'.
6. Information from Denis Williams.
7. P. 110.
8. KẸNYO, Chapters 1–3.
9. For an introduction to the oral history of the Yoruba and its problems, see BIOBAKU (1956).
10. This version of the myth may well qualify as the type of 'Authorized Version' whose very coherence and wide acceptance are somewhat suspect; see p. xi above.
11. These legends are given, according to an Ọyọ version, in Johnson, Chapters I and II. But the Ifẹ account of the Creation is that a 'priest' named Ojuma threw down earth which was spread by a fowl (ADERẸMI, p. 3; ADEMAKINWA, p. 14), while IDOWU (p. 19) records a tradition that it was Orisha-nla who wrought the earth.
12. Such views were first propagated by Leo Frobenius, who early in the twentieth century drew attention to the art of Ifẹ.
13. For example, by OMER-COOPER (1964), p. 104.
14. Johnson briefly discusses the possibility of an Egyptian origin (pp. 6–7), but it is most fully developed and argued by J. Olumide Lucas (1948).
15. R. W. WESTCOTT, review of Lucas in *JAH*, II, 2 (1961), pp. 311–15, and also 'Did the Yoruba Come from Egypt', *Odu*, 4

(n.d.); THURSTAN SHAW, *Archaeology and Nigeria* (1964), pp. 20, 23–4.

16. For example by Thurstan Shaw and G. Connah.

17. Blood-group maps of Africa are given, with important reservations, by J. P. GARLICK (1962), pp. 297–300.

18. Pp. 269–70.

19. LEWIS (1966), pp. 402–5.

CHAPTER II

1. The words *Ile Ife* have been translated as 'the spreading (of earth.' But IDOWU (p. 20) writes that Ife means 'that which is wide' and the prefix Ile (or suffix, as in Oyo ile and many other place-names) signifies 'original home'. Both versions could refer here to the creation of the world at Ife.

2. For exceptions to this, especially the interesting case of Oba, a small town near Akure, see H. BEIER in *Odu*, 3 (n.d.) and IDOWU, 15–17.

3. For example, see BURNS, p. 25. R. E. DENNETT, in *Nigerian Studies* (London, 1910), p. 19, describes the Oni as being 'in much the same position as the Archbishop of Canterbury in England'.

4. AKINJOGBIN (1965), p. 32. For a discussion of this view, see pp. 110–11 below.

5. Editor, *JRAS*, 2 (1902–03), pp. 312–15. See also the Appendix below. According to a chief at Ijebu Ode in February 1968 it is unthinkable that the Awujale should have left his palace for this reason.

6. See especially the article by the present (1967) Oni of Ife, Sir Adesoji Aderemi, and also J. A. ADEMAKINWA, *passim.* IDOWU (pp. 23–7) gives an account of these myths which differs in several respects. For example, he writes that Oduduwa was preceded from heaven by Oreluere, whom he later found living in Ife as leader of 'a community of aboriginal people'.

7. ADEMAKINWA, Part II, p. 34. WILLETT (1967), pp. 210–11, n. 114, even suggests that the Ibo, who are sometimes called Igbo, 'retain the name of the original population of Southern Nigeria'.

8. BEIER (1956b); Stevens.

9. The present Oni (ADEREMI, 1937) writes that the first Oba of Benin from the Ife dynasty was Eweka, son of Oranyan and grandson of Oduduwa. This agrees with Benin tradition as related by Egharevba, pp. 6–9. Johnson (p. 7), however, describes

this first Oba as the third son of Oduduwa, without giving his name.

10. WALSH.

11. BEIER, *Odu*, 3; AKINJOGBIN (1967).

12. JOHNSON, pp. 11, 24–5. This is supported by similar traditions in Ketu (Parrinder (1956), p. 12, quoting Crowther) and Ijẹbu Ode (ǪLǪTUFǪRẸ, February 1968).

13. KẸNYO, p. 9.

14. Personal communication from Mr J. A. Ademakinwa, March 1967. See also AKINJOGBIN (1967).

15. *Esmeraldo de Situ Orbis*, quoted by HODGKIN, p. 94.

16. Quoted by HODGKIN, p. 96.

17. Pp. 25–8. Ryder mentions that 'west' and 'east' to the Bini meant respectively 'seaward' – where the sun sets – and 'inland'. But it is unlikely that De Barros would use 'east' in this way.

18. ABIMBOLA, p. 21; GEORGE, p. 28; RYDER, pp. 36–7.

19. WILLETT (1967), p. 103.

20. WILLETT (1960), p. 244; WILLETT (1967), p. 108.

21. G. J. A. OFO (1966b), pp. 61, 90, 91.

22. ADERẸMI, p. 4.

23. There is a mystery about this head, since in 1950 it was discovered to be a copy made by modern methods. WILLETT (1960b) asserts (p. 238, n. 34) that the substitution must have taken place between 1910 and 1934 when the head was brought into the palace.

24. WILLETT (1967), *passim*.

25. WILLETT (1960b). An interesting comparison is made by John Crook in 'Ifẹ Portraits and Roman Portraits', *Ibadan*, 17 (1963).

26. WILLETT (1958), p. 33.

27. FAGG and WILLETT (1960), p. 21. When Oliver Myers of the University of Ifẹ excavated the Ọbameri shrine in the town in 1965 he found a number of terra-cottas of the classical period which had apparently been buried on this site only some hundred years previously.

29. WILLETT (1960b), p. 233; RYDER, p. 30.

30. WILLETT (1967), pp. 22–3, 28–9, Plates 32, 33.

31. WILLETT (1967), pp. 64–6; WILLETT (1960b), pp. 239–40.

32. See WILLETT (1967), Chapters XIII and XIV, and WILLIAMS (1965).

33. WILLETT (1967), Plate 8 and pp. 51, 169, 172.

34. WILLETT (1967), pp. 154–5. WILLIAMS (1967b), pp. 27–8. The Ifẹ casters prepared their cores and moulds with an admixture of

charcoal, whereas the Benin and also other non-Ifẹ Yoruba casters added dung.

35. WILLETT (1967), pp. 20–1, 26–8, and Plate 2; also see WILLETT (1966).
36. WILLETT (1967), pp. 50, 58, 68–9.
37. WILLETT (1967), pp. 130–1.
38. WILLETT (1967), pp. 132, 149–51.
39. WILLIAMS (1967), pp. 11–13.

CHAPTER III

1. For the traditions and history of Ọyọ, see Johnson, passim. The name 'Katunga' possibly derives from the Hausa *katanga* for a compound wall or the Nupe *tanga* for a hamlet. For a recent visit to the site of Ọyọ ile and a summary of information about it, see Robert Smith and Denis Williams (1966). Frank Willet (1960) has described his archaeological investigations there in 1956–7. He concludes that the site traditionally known as Ọyọ ile is the same as the Ọyọ visited by Clapperton and the Landers in the first part of the nineteenth century, despite a slip in Clapperton's account of its longitude.
2. P. 60.
3. Letter XX, pp. 397–8.
4. See the discussion of chronology in Chapter 7 below.
5. For this period, see ROBERT SMITH (1965), pp. 57–77.
6. Ibid. p. 62.
7. Loc. cit. where it is suggested that Gbere should be identified with Gbereburu, a remote hamlet twelve miles to the north of the Mọsi.
8. Notes in the files of the Yoruba Historical Research Scheme (Ọyọ/1).
9. R. and J. LANDER, pp. 78–9. The American Baptist missionary W. H. Clarke gives an interesting account of his visit to Igboho in 1855 in his *Travels and Explorations*.
10. EGHAREVBA, p. 32; WEIR, *Akure Intelligence Report* (1934); BRADBURY, p. 276.
11. JOHNSON, p. 168, assigns the appointment of this official, called the Onisarẹ, to the reign of Ọbalokun, which immediately followed that of Abipa who brought back the Ọyọ from Igboho. MORTON-WILLIAMS (1964a), p. 38, places it much later, in the reign of Abiọdun in the late eighteenth century.

12. JOHNSON, p. 169.
13. AKINJOGBIN (1966), p. 451, citing BOSMAN, p. 396 and BARBOT, p. 352.
14. NEWBURY, pp. 3–6; BERTHO, pp. 121–32. For the history of Dahomey, see ARGYLE, chapters I–III.
15. DALZEL, p. 59; AKINJOGBIN (1963), pp. 562–3.
16. PARRINDER (1956), p. 28; ARGYLE, p. 25; NORRIS, quoted by HODGKIN, p. 169.
17. P. 174.
18. JOHNSON, p. 173 and, for Awolẹ's suicide, p. 192. See also DALZEL, pp. 12–13, and NORRIS, quoted by HODGKIN, p. 167.
19. JOHNSON, p. 174.
20. MORTON-WILLIAMS (1964a), pp. 29, 40.
21. Ibid., pp. 30–31.
22. Pp. 38–9, and see note 11 above.
23. JOHNSON, p. 168. See also Clapperton's description, pp. 135–8, of the market at 'Koolfo'.
24. ADAMS, pp. 221–2.
25. P. 178 and pp. 178–85 for the whole career of Gaha. Akinjogbin (1966b), p. 454, n. 4, adduces documentary evidence for dating Gaha's advent to power as 1754.
26. AKINJOGBIN (1966), pp. 453–5.
27. WILLIAM MUTTER to African Committee, 27 May 1764 (T 70/31), quoted by AKINJOGBIN (1966), p. 455.
28. Quoted by HODGKIN, p. 167.
29. DALZEL, p. 157; AKINJOGBIN (1966), 455.
30. 'Ajasẹ' is the Yoruba and Adja name for Porto Novo, and if Ọyabi was stationed here his task was presumably to protect the coastal interests of the kingdom. R. C. C. Law suggests, however, that the Kakamfo was more likely to have been at Ajasẹ in the Igbomina district, south-east of Ilọrin.
31. The second version is quoted by AKINJOGBIN (1966) from A. L. HETHERSETT, *Iwe Kika Ekẹrin*, pp. 63–4. The date of the overthrow of Gaha by Abiọdun is established from Dalzel (quoted by HODGKIN, p. 170), who refers to Gaha as 'Ochenoo, the prime minister' (a garbled form of Oṣọrun, an alternative title for Baṣọrun).
32. P. 183.
33. DALZEL, p. 196.
34. AKINJOGBIN (1966), p. 458.
35. AKINJOGBIN (1965), p. 30.
36. DALZEL, p. 229.

CHAPTER IV

1. FORDE, pp. 34–7.
2. Pp. 20–2.
3. KẸNYO, Chapter 5; JOHNSON, pp. 23–4; OLAJUBU.
4. KẸNYO, pp. 74–5; other accounts name Ibokun as the first settlement.
5. KẸNYO, p. 74 lists thirty-seven previous Ọwa; an anonymous article in the *Daily Times* (Lagos) listed thirty-nine, but maintained that the present Ọwa was the forty-eighth to occupy the throne.
6. P. 21.
7. KẸNYO, pp. 38, 65.
8. JOHNSON, p. 156, places the founding both of Ẹdẹ and Oṣogbo in the reign of Alafin Kori, one of the pre-Igboho rulers. The present Timi of Ẹdẹ is accounted the twenty-sixth on the throne, whereas only fifteen rulers are recollected as having reigned at Oṣogbo, though six predecessors of Olarooye, the founder, are said to have reigned at Ipole. See OLUGUNNA, pp. 12–21, and BEIR (1960).
9. P. 25.
10. P. 168.
11. KẸNYO, pp. 77–82; EGHAREVBA, p. 33.
12. P. 38.
13. JOHNSON, p. 23; OJO (*Culture*), pp. 125 (map), 126–9.
14. Pp. 14, 180. The kingship of Ado is examined also by Lloyd (1960).
15. BRADBURY. Egharevba does not mention Ado under this reign, but writes that Ewuare 'fought against and captured 201 towns and villages in Ekiti, Ikare, Kukuruku, Eka and the Ibo country on this side of the river Niger' (p. 14).
16. In his article in *Odu* (n.d.) the Ogoga writes, 'Ikẹrrẹ was the only town in Ekiti Division which conquered almost every town, village and hamlet in Ekiti, and itself was never conquered.' It sold its captives as slaves and did not trouble to make territorial annexations. Its successes were due to the weapons which were provided by Benin.
17. The following account of Akurẹ is based on Arifalo, supplemented by Egharevba and Oguntuyi. The name 'Akurẹ' has been said to signify 'the land of two rivers', although there is only one river which encircles the town. Another explanation is that it refers to the breaking (*re*) of the beads (*akum*) worn by the founding ọba,

O

Asodeboyede, as he made his way through the bush. This illustrates the difficulties which arise in the interpretation of Yoruba place-names. A reliable and systematic study of the subject is much needed.

18. Chapters III and IV.

19. EGHAREVBA, p. 33, asserts that the Deji's title means 'the leopard killer'. JOHNSON, p. 22, lists the Akurẹ title as Ajan-panda.

20. ARIFALO, p. 22.

21. EGHAREVBA, p. 16.

22. EGHAREVBA, p. 32.

23. EGHAREVBA, p. 45–7.

24. D. WILLIAMS (1967a), p. 15.

25. For the history of Idanre, see Akindoju and Ọlagundoye, also BRIDGES and the anonymous article in *Nigeria Magazine*, 46.

26. P. 60.

27. OJO (1966b), pp. 23–4, 64–6.

28. In addition, see the article on the Igogo festival in *Nigeria Magazine*, 77 (1963); this is based on information from the Olowo and a manuscript by Chief J. D. Akeredolu.

29. P. 15.

30. P. 24.

31. EGHAREVBA, pp. 33–4; ASARA, p. 10.

32. WILLETT (1967), pp. 180–1.

33. P. 37.

34. P. 25.

35. BEIR (1956), *passim*.

36. KẸNYO, p. 49.

CHAPTER V

1. PARRINDER (1947), p. 122; FORDE, pp. 42–7 and map.

2. PARRINDER (1947), pp. 125–6; FORDE, pp. 42–4; CORNEVIN, p. 56. In addition to the town of the Ijẹsa, there is at least one other Ilesa in Yorubaland, that lying on the Dahomean frontier north of Ṣaki.

3. NEWBURY, pp. 7–10; PARRINDER (1947), p. 124.

4. CORNEVIN, pp. 48–9, 89.

5. PARRINDER (1956), p. 12 and *passim*. Parrinder makes much use of the work of Dunglas and Moulero.

6. PARRINDER (1956) spells this name 'Sho-ipashan' (see his discussion on page 11).

7. PARRINDER (1956) writes that Ṣopasan was buried at Oke Ọyan (which he spells 'Oke-Awyan') and Owe at Aro in the Ogun shrine there.

8. PARRINDER (1956), pp. 16–17.

9. See PARRINDER (1956), pp. 21–2, 76–7, and AJAYI and SMITH, p. 27 and Plan 1.

10. OJO (1966a), p. 53.

11. ARGYLE, Chapter II, especially p. 24; PARRINDER (1956), pp. 31–5.

12. PARRINDER (1956), p. 12.

13. MOULERO, *passim*, CORNEVIN, pp. 51–6, based on Couchard, Dunglas, and Moulero; also see J. O. GEORGE, pp. 23–4.

14. PARRINDER (1947), p. 126: FORDE, p. 42 and map; CORNEVIN, pp. 156–8, based on Palau-Marti.

CHAPTER VI

1. P. 59.

2. *Esmeraldo de Situ Orbis*, quoted by HODGKIN, p. 92.

3. Quoted by HODGKIN, p. 173.

4. Described by LLOYD (1961).

5. Pp. 171–2.

6. LLOYD (1959), p. 20, and LLOYD (1961), p. 7.

7. OGUNBA (1965).

8. OGUNKOYA, p. 54.

9. OGUNBA (1964).

10. See LLOYD (1957).

11. Recorded by the Bada of Ṣaki in an account of Ọyọ history in the files of the Yoruba Historical Research Scheme.

12. Pp. 174, 179.

13. P. 24.

14. P. 311.

15. LLOYD (1960b), p. 60. This is presumably based on Snelgrave's reference (pp. 148–9) to an attack by the Dahomeans on the 'Yahoo', who lived 'far inland' and retreated 'among their mountains and woods'. It is conceivable that the 'Yahoo' were Ijẹbu, but Dalzel (pp. xvii, 59) thought that they were the people of Mahin.

16. P. 136. Kulfo is forty miles south-west of Kontagora.

17. Pp. 18–19.

18. AJIṢAFẸ, Chapter 6; Biobaku, Chapter I and map, p. 129.

19. P. 3.

20. Pp. 17–18.
21. PARRINDER (1956), p. 12.
22. P. 8.
23. AJIṢAFẸ, p. 14.
24. BIOBAKU, p. 9; AKINJOGBIN (1966), p. 458.
25. *Short History of Ilorin*, p. 13. For the evidence on which 1796 is preferred to the Bada's dating of Liṣabi's revolt to 1810, see Chapter 10.
26. P. 10.
27. AJIṢAFẸ, pp. 45–9.
28. P. 206.
29. This section is partly based on Z. A. Egbeola's unpublished MS.
30. MORTON-WILLIAMS (1964a), pp. 30–1, 40–2.
31. JOHNSON, pp. 226–7; LANDER (1832), p. 62.
32. P. 226.
33. NEWBURY, pp. 30–2 and Figure 2.
34. See VERGER (1959) for examples of the use of the name.
35. HODGKIN, p. 93.
36. HODGKIN, p. 173.
37. Quoted by VERGER (1959), p. 346.
38. BURNS, pp. 33–4, mainly based on J. B. Wood; Losi.
39. P. 30.
40. Pp. 25–6.
41. P. 46.
42. EGHAREVBA, pp. 30–1; BRADBURY, p. 285.
43. See MORTON-WILLIAMS (1964a), p. 30.
44. EGHAREVBA, p. 34. I have not been able to find the River Aghan, where the Oba met his death, on any map.
45. EGHAREVBA, pp. 47–8; BURNS, pp. 35, 38. TALBOT (Vol. I, p. 68) claims that tribute was paid to Benin until Lagos became a British colony in 1861.
46. The estimate was made by Freeman, the Wesleyan missionary, about 1844 and is quoted by NEWBURY, p. 56, n. 1.

CHAPTER VII

1. For the origin of the Yoruba, see, for example, BIOBAKU (1955); for speculation about the aborigines, see BEIER (*Odu*, 3).
2. References to settlers who had preceded the emigrants from Ifẹ may be found in the descriptions of the legends of foundation at Ado, Ekiti, Akurẹ, Ijẹbu, Ileṣa, Ketu, Ondo, Ọwọ, Ọyọ, and

Ṣabe; there is also the account at Ifẹ of the Igbo whom Oduduwa found living there.

3. The word 'lineage' is not used here in the technical sense of anthropology.

4. LLOYD (1960).

5. For example, WILLETT (1967), p. 125.

6. BIOBAKU (1957), p. 2.

7. WILLETT (1960).

8. The Esekhurhe had the tasks of memorizing the dynastic list and of performing sacrifices to every previous Oba during the annual Ugigun rites; see BRADBURY (1959), p.p. 267–8.

9. For general observations on the use of king-lists for the measurement of time, see MCCALL, Chapter 8.

10. AKINJOGBIN (1966), p. 454.

11. It has been suggested (for example, by CROWDER, pp. 60–1) that the conquest of Ọyọ by the Nupe was achieved during the time of Tsoede, the semi-legendary founder of the Nupe kingdom, which now has its capital at Bida. Tsoede is usually held to have flourished during the middle or latter part of the sixteenth century, so that this affords some support for the dating of the abandonment of Ọyọ ile by Onigbogi. See ROBERT SMITH (1965), p. 74, n. 50.

12. Taking the accessions of James I (1603), George III (1760), and William IV (1830) as starting-points and the accession of H. M. Queen Elizabeth II (1952) as terminal point, average lengths of reign of 21·8, 24, and 20·3 years are obtained, giving dates for the establishment of the Norman kings in England (1066) of 1102, 1016, and 1161.

13. Average lengths of reign for the Nupe, Zamfara, and Bakuba work out at 13, 12·3, and 15·6 respectively.

14. BRADBURY (1959) also obtained his own version of the list from the current holder of the office of Esekhurhe.

15. BRADBURY, p. 285.

16. These difficulties in the averaging method were pointed out by R. C. C. Law in a private communication.

CHAPTER VIII

1. The institutions of the Yoruba kingdoms are described in this chapter in the past tense, since this is an historical work, and the traditional system of government has in any case been largely

superseded. Nevertheless, much survives, though in attenuated form.

2. GODDARD, *passim*.

3. HILL, p. 302.

4. The term *ẹbi* refers to the living family, excluding ancestors. For the 'system', see Akinjogbin (1966b), p. 451. Akinjogbin (1965) describes the sending of the sword from Ifẹ as 'The most important ceremony at the coronation of any Alafin', a view which is not held at Ọyọ. Other ọba, for example the Awujalẹ of Ijẹbu, have state 'swords of justice', but none of these swords seem to have any connection with Ifẹ.

5. OGUNTUYI, p. 118.

6. See Ojo (1966a), pp. 126–9. The word 'Balẹ' (*ọba ilẹ*, 'head of the land') must be distinguished from 'bale' (ọba ile, 'head of the house').

7. OJO (1966b), pp. 63–6.

8. JOHNSON, pp. 68, 75–7; MORTON-WILLIAMS (1967), p. 40.

9. Much of this section derives from LLOYD (1960a).

10. AJIṢAFẸ, pp. 103–4. There is a royal family of Egba Gbagura.

11. JOHNSON, pp. 149, 159; SNELGRAVE, p. 135.

12. OGUNTUYI, p. 91.

13. Pp. 40–69; MORTON-WILLIAMS (1967), *passim*.

14. JOHNSON, pp. 70–72. See also MORTON-WILLIAMS (1960) and (1964b).

15. AJIṢAFẸ, pp. 27–8; BIOBAKU (1956b).

16. MORTON-WILLIAMS (1964b), p. 253; MORTON-WILLIAMS (1967), pp. 42, 53.

17. AJIṢAFẸ, pp. 27, 29–30.

18. BIOBAKU (1957), p. 6.

19. ADEGORIỌLA, *passim*.

20. The word 'people' in Yoruba presents some difficulty. In the sense of 'all men' it is *ọmọ araiye*, 'children of the world'. The word 'Yoruba' for the whole linguistic group has been in use for only about a century and is still not always understood in that sense; historically it only applies to the inhabitants of the Ọyọ kingdom. In the cases of the people of a kingdom and sub-kingdom (for example, Ẹgba, Rẹmo), the names connote the inhabitants as well as the political and physical division. The name of a town is also applied to its people, though they are more usually described as its 'children' or 'relatives'; for example, *ọmọ Ọyọ*, a man belonging to and born in Ọyọ, and *ara Ọyọ*, a man of Ọyọ though not necessarily born there – the distinction between

these is not, however, strictly observed. (Based on information from Mr Wande Abimbọla.)

21. FORDE, pp. 10–27.
22. Little attention has been paid to this aspect of Yoruba society, but see FORDE, pp. 26–7.
23. CLAPPERTON, pp. 25, 28, 39; LANDER (1832), pp. 91–2.

CHAPTER IX

1. Review by Béatrice Olympio of CORNEVIN's *Histoire de Dahomey* in *Études Dahoméenes*, No. 2, June 1964.
2. Johnson deals with warfare at pp. 131–7; his account seems to derive mainly from the Ibadan army in the nineteenth-century rather than from Ọyọ in its heyday. See also AJAYI and SMITH, *passim*, for the nineteenth-century evidence.
3. See JOHNSON, pp. 73–5, 131–7, 169. Johnson (p. 75) lists Afọnja of Ilọrin as the sixth Kakamfo, yet ascribes the appointment of the first to the reign of Alafin Ajagbo (pp. 74, 169); this implies that the office was not in continuous existence, appointments being made only in times of emergency. Morton-Williams (1967), p. 57, suggests that the office was created only in the early eighteenth century. The etymology of the title is obscure.
4. AJAYI and SMITH, p. 65; AJAYI (1965b), passim.
5. P. 56.
6. Pp. 11–16 (HODGKIN, p. 167).
7. P. 57.
8. AJAYI and SMITH, pp. 133, 139.
9. Pp. 397–8.
10. SNELGRAVE, p. 56; DALZEL, pp. 12 f.
11. CLAPPERTON, p. 34; AJAYI and SMITH, pp. 15–16, 134–5.
12. See ROBERT SMITH (1967), *passim*.
13. SNELGRAVE, p. 56; LANDER, p. 80.
14. For example, the Ashanti and the Dahomeans were using guns probably before the end of the seventeenth century, and the latter even acquired a few cannon in the eighteenth century.
15. OGUNTUYI, pp. 27–8.
16. SNELGRAVE, p. 56.
17. LANDER (1830), ii, p. 222; JOHNSON, p. 208.
18. AJAYI and SMITH, pp. 17–21.
19. JOHNSON, pp. 357, 415.
20. AJAYI and SMITH, p. 134.

21. CLAPPERTON, p. 2; LANDER, p. 69: JOHNSON, p. 160; ROBERT SMITH, (1967), pp. 100–3.

22. For example, at Ẹrin, near Iseyin (see SMITH (1964), p. 25) and Oke Amo (see OJO (1966a), pp. 149–50). As regards the building of these walls, Clapperton's description of the work which he saw going forward on the walls of Bussa in Borgu would probably apply to Yoruba practice. He writes (p. 98): 'Bands of male and female slaves, accompanied by drums and flutes and singing in chorus, were passing to and from the river with water, to mix the clay they were building with. Each great man has his part of the wall to build, like the Jews when they built the walls of Jerusalem, everyone opposite his own house.'

23. AJAYI and SMITH, pp. 23–8.

24. AJAYI and SMITH, *passim.*

25. P. 131.

26. Pp. 121–2.

27. AJAYI and SMITH, pp. 27–8, 136–7. In the Kiriji war the quarters in the Ibadan camp had mud walls and thatch roofs, whereas the Ekiti Parapọ at Oke Mẹsi constructed their quarters of bamboo and leaves; see JOHNSON, p. 552. For the Dahomean camps, with their thatched quarters 'resembling bee-hives', see SNELGRAVE, pp. 28–9.

28. SNELGRAVE, pp. 56, 121–2; JOHNSON, p. 263.

29. JOHNSON, p. 222; AJAYI and SMITH, pp. 33–6.

30. AJAYI and SMITH, pp. 138–9; STONE, Chapter XVIII.

31. JOHNSON, p. 604.

32. DALZEL, pp. 183–4. For the Ijebu war canoes, see Osifekunde in CURTIN (1967), p. 287. CLAPPERTON (p. 2) notes that the Yoruba mounted cannon in the prows of their canoes, as did the warriors of the creeks farther east (thus taking advantage of an excellent natural means of absorbing the recoil).

33. SNELGRAVE, pp. 57–8.

34. P. 62.

35. This paragraph is based on AJAYI and SMITH, pp. 50–3, 127–8.

CHAPTER X

1. See ALLISON (*Odu*, 4), BASCOM (1960), and MORTON-WILLIAMS (1964a).

2. Clapperton was told at 'Puka' (Ipokia, near Badagry) that Ọyọ was thirty days' journey from there (p. 4), information which proved to be entirely reliable.

3. Quoted by HODGKIN, pp. 171–2. This report has never been confirmed.

4. CLAPPERTON (1829); LANDER (1832).

5. CLAPPERTON, p. 13; HODGKIN, p. 223.

6. LANDER (1832), p. 76. 'Chaadoo' is unidentified and presumably one of the numerous towns and villages which were abandoned in the wars. It was about a day's journey south-west of Ṣaki.

7. CLAPPERTON, pp. 13–14, 26–7 (HODGKIN, p. 223); for Kuṣu see also R. SMITH (1965), p. 65.

8. LANDER (1832), pp. 61, 71.

9. CLAPPERTON, pp. 4, 39, 56.

10. CLAPPERTON, pp. 35–6, 48, 58–9.

11. LANDER (1830), pp. 197–9.

12. See R. SMITH and D. WILLIAMS (1966), p. 60, n. 1 and also D. WILLIAMS (1966); for Ọyọ pottery, see WILLETT (1960a). It has been suggested that the numerous stone figures at Esie, near Ilọrin, were brought from Ọyọ ile.

13. CLAPPERTON, pp. 24–5.

14. CLAPPERTON, p. 31; LANDER (1832), p. 80.

15. AKINJOGBIN (1965), pp. 27–9; (1966), p. 458.

16. MORTON-WILLIAMS (1967), pp. 36, 43.

17. BIOBAKU (1957), p. 13. Islam seems to have been introduced into Yorubaland in the eighteenth century.

18. JOHNSON, pp. 188–268.

19. This is probably the village of Iwere about ten miles west of Oke Iho in the hill-country of the upper Ogun.

20. AKINJOGBIN (1965), pp. 34–5.

21. The identification is made in JOHNSON (p. 210). Lander confirms that the same man was Alafin in 1830 as in 1826 and 1827 (p. 92). AKINJOGBIN (1966) writes (p. 82) that 'there is no basis at all yet known, either in linguistics or in tradition, for equating Majotu with "Manshola"' – the latter being the name given to the ruler of Ọyọ by Lander, though he spells it 'Mansolah'. Yet Akinjogbin's chronology, following these remarks, supports the identification, which does seem to fit best with other known facts. Chief Ojo, Bada of Ṣaki, has suggested, however, that it was either Amọdo, Majotu's successor, or Oluewu who was on the throne when Clapperton visited Ọyọ (*Iwe Itan Ọyọ*, pp. 77–8; *Short History of Ilọrin*, p. 297). CLAPPERTON (p. 49) writes that Majotu's predecessor had been 'murdered by one of his own sons: not the present king'. Johnson suggests (p. 87) that Abiọdun was poisoned by his Arẹmo, and it would be possible for Majotu to

have been a younger son and successor of Abiọdun were it not
for the intervening reign of Awolẹ who seems more likely to have
been Majotu's father. Majotu, according to JOHNSON (p. 216),
was remarkable for having died a natural death, as the result of
an influenza-type epidemic, which seems to rule out the identification of Amọdo as 'Mansolah'.

22. JOHNSON, pp. 199–200.
23. CROWTHER (1852), pp. iv-vii.
24. CURTIN (1967), p. 212.
25. JOHNSON, p. 197.
26. JOHNSON, p. 199. MARTIN, pp. 20–27.
27. It is uncertain when and how the official recognition of the
    Emirate took place – whether the flag, the symbol of recognition,
    was bestowed first on Alimi or on Abdussalami, whether this was
    bestowed by the ruler of Sokoto or of Gwandu, and in what year
    this took place. But it is clear that Ilọrin belonged to the Gwandu,
    or western, side of the Fulani empire. See HOGBEN and KIRK-
    GREENE, pp. 122, 292, 294.
28. JOHNSON, pp. 206–12.
29. JOHNSON, p. 223: BIOBAKU (1957), pp. 13–14. See also the
    narrative of the former slave Joseph Wright in CURTIN (1967),
    pp. 317–33.
30. For Crowther's narrative, see CURTIN (1967), pp. 289–316.
31. JOHNSON, p. 217.
32. It is probable that it was from a horse-fair in this town that the
    Ọyọ cavalry obtained their mounts; see R. SMITH (1967), p. 90,
    n. 13. The village marked on maps as 'Ogudu' on the Niger twenty
    miles below Jebba may well be the same place.
33. JOHNSON, pp. 260–1. But the BADA OF ṢAKI, pp. 22–3, ascribes
    the victory to the warriors of Ṣaki in combination with the
    Borgu.
34. The term may possibly be a Yoruba word for 'king'; cf. 'Elewe'.
    The Borgu ruler who welcomed the exiled Alafin Onigbogi into his
    country is also described as 'Eleduwe' (p. 41 above). For the con-
    nection with Nikki, see HOGBEN and KIRK-GREENE, pp. 290, 580.
35. JOHNSON, 262–3.
36. HOGBEN and KIRK-GREENE, p. 580.
37. JOHNSON, p. 287.
38. See R. SMITH (1965), pp. 64, n. 23 and 72.
39. See AKINJOGBIN (1966a), p. 86, for his chronology. A seminar on
    Yoruba chronology in this period was held at the University of
    Ibadan in 1965.

40. SCHÖN and CROWTHER (1842), pp. 317–18; CROWTHER (1852), Introductory Remarks.

41. CLAPPERTON, pp. 20–1.

42. CLAPPERTON, pp. 24–5, 28.

43. CLAPPERTON, pp. 39, 41.

44. LANDER (1832), pp. 87, 91–2.

45. LANDER (1832), p. 79, makes a much greater error in writing that 'Bohoo' (Igboho) ceased to be capital of Ọyọ only 'about half a century ago', whereas the Alafin had returned from there two centuries or more before 1830.

46. SCHÖN and CROWTHER (1842), pp. 317–18; CROWTHER (1852), pp. v, vi.

47. Akinjogbin's dating of Abiọdun's death as 1789 (AKINJOGBIN (1963a), p. 257, and AKINJOGBIN (1965), p. 30) is based on a reference in a French officer's letter to the death of the 'Roy des Ailliots'. MORTON-WILLIAMS (1967), p. 66, adheres to 1810 as the approximate date of the Alafin's death and suggests that the 1789 reference may be to Abiọdun's Bẹbẹ or jubilee celebration.

48. AKINJOGBIN (1966a), p. 82.

49. JOHNSON, pp. 207, 209.

50. The date of the fall of Kesi derives from Thomas King, an Egba member of the Church Missionary Society, and that of Ikereku from the journal of the missionary Irving, in the *Church Missionary Intelligencer*, ii, (1856), p. 70. Irving's informant was a 'Mr Barber, native cate chist at Ibadan'. Barber had taken part in the siege of Ikereku and remembered it as having occurred in the year before he was liberated from slavery at Sierra Leone, which he knew to be 1827.

51. P. 206.

52. CLAPPERTON, pp. 61–2.

53. AKINJOGBIN (1966a), p. 84. See also ARGYLE, p. 38.

54. See LLOYD (1960c), p. 26. The main influx from the northern Ọyọ was to a belt on the edge of the rain forest, lying between Ogbomọṣọ to the north and Ibadan to the south.

CHAPTER XI

1. See AJAYI and SMITH (1964), *passim*.

2. PP., 1865, QQ 2165–6.

3. For example, see BURNS, p. 27.

4. AJAYI and SMITH, pp. 51–2.

5. For examples, see JOHNSON, pp. 321–4, and BIOBAKU (1957), p. 34.
6. The reaction against this explanation seems to be first found in BIOBAKU (1957), pp. 94, 96.
7. *The Twenty Years' Crisis 1919–1939*, London, 1958, p. 97.
8. For the government of Ibadan, see JOHNSON, pp. 94, 636–67. For the history of Ibadan, see AKINYELE, ELGEE, and AWE (1964, 1965).
9. JOHNSON, pp. 305–07; for Oluwọle, see BIOBAKU in DIKÉ (ed.).
10. AJIṢAFẸ, pp. 48–9, 102; BIOBAKU (1957), p. 52.
11. BURTON (1863), pp. 275–8 (HODGKIN, p. 278).
12. BIOBAKU (1957), pp. 5–6, 21–2.
13. AJAYI and SMITH, p. 67. For Ijaye, see also STONE, BOWEN, and SMITH (1962).
14. JOHNSON, pp. 279–83; SMITH (1965); pp. 415–16 and 416, n. 3; OJO (1966b); MORTON-WILLIAMS (1967), p. 45.
15. P. 282.
16. There is a graphic description of the battle in JOHNSON, pp. 285–9. See also AJAYI and SMITH, Part I, Chapter 5.
17. AJAYI and SMITH, p. 55.
18. JOHNSON, pp. 294–6.
19. JOHNSON, pp. 317–21; AWE (1964), pp. 48–50.
20. Compare maps 2 and 3.
21. AWE (1964), *passim*. See also D. J. MAY. For the Ekiti ajẹlẹ, see OGUNTUYI, pp. 46, 61.
22. For this war, see JOHNSON, pp. 331–54: BIOBAKU (1957), Chapter 6. AJAYI and SMITH, Part I, Chapter 8, and Part II, *passim*.
23. AJAYI and SMITH, p. 76.
24. JOHNSON, p. 252.
25. ARGYLE, *passim*, and especially Chapter 5.
26. ARGYLE, p. 82.
27. AJIṢAFẸ, p. 82, though ARGYLE (p. 87) quotes Foa's suggestion that women were first used as soldiers only in 1851.
28. AJIṢAFẸ, pp. 96–7; AJAYI and SMITH, Part I, Chapter 6.
29. JOHNSON, pp. 362–3; AJIṢAFẸ, pp. 133–4.
30. JOHNSON, p. 455; PARRINDER (1956), chapters 8 and 9.
31. EGHAREVBA, pp. 44–7; OGUNTUYI, pp. 36–41.
32. For KOSỌKỌ, see BIOBAKU in DIKÉ (ed.), also the genealogical table of the Lagos kings in BURNS, p. 301.
33. AJAYI (1961); see also BURNS and NEWBURY for the British in Lagos.

34. See DIKÉ (1956) for an account of Beecroft.
35. For references to earlier views and a re-examination, see AJAYI (1961).
36. AJAYI (1961), p. 97.
37. NEWBURY, Chapters III and IV.
38. ROBINSON and GALLAGHER, p. 36.
39. BURTON (1863b), pp. 212–13 and 216–17 (HODGKIN, p. 281). Burton was appointed to his post in March 1861, but did not sail to take up appointment until the following August, so he was not an eye-witness of this ceremony.
40. HARGREAVES (1963), pp. 58–61.
41. For Glover, see BIOBAKU (1957), Chapter 7, and MCINTYRE, *passim*.

CHAPTER XII

1. For the missionary role in the creation of Nigeria, see COLEMAN (1958), Chapter 4, and AJAYI (1965) and AYANDELE (1966), *passim*. For the partition of West Africa, see ROBINSON and GALLAGHER (1961), especially Chapter XIII, and HARGREAVES (1963). The latter includes the part played by the European and other traders, which has otherwise been somewhat neglected.
2. AYANDELE, p. 29.
3. For this war, see the detailed account in JOHNSON, Chapters XXIII–XXXIV, and also AWE (1965), *passim*, and AYANDELE, Chapter, 2.
4. Governor Glover's sketch map of the trade routes to the interior from Lagos is reproduced in BIOBAKU (1957) as map 4. For the Ondo Road, also see AYANDELE, pp. 33–5. The southern end of the road was the scene of fierce fighting with the 'Biafrans' in August 1967.
5. JOHNSON, pp. 415–16.
6. JOHNSON, pp. 427–36; AJAYI and SMITH, Part I, Chapter 8.
7. JOHNSON, pp. 232–3.
8. Personal communication from MRS B. AWE.
9. P. 478.
10. ROBINSON and GALLAGHER, p. 387, n. 2.
11. For the text of the treaty, see JOHNSON, pp. 527–32.
12. AWE (1965), p. 230.
13. The use of the term 'Protestant' to include Anglicans seems regrettably unavoidable in this context.

14. For the text of this treaty, see JOHNSON, pp. 574–6. Johnson was himself a witness to both this and the 1886 peace treaty.

15. AYANDELE, pp. 54–68.

16. Pp. 68–9.

17. P. 623.

18. The Lagos Constabulary, often called the 'Lagos Hausas', who provided this escort, descended from the force raised in 1863 by Glover from the runaway slaves who had sought his protection in Sierra Leone in 1858 and later that year accompanied him on his return march from Lagos to Jebba. Probably not all those with Glover were Hausa and of the forty 'Hausa' Constables who accompanied Lugard in 1894–95, ten were in fact Yoruba (*Diaries*, ed. PERHAM and BULL, Vol. 4, p. 96).

19. For the texts of these 1893 treaties with Abẹokuta, Ọyọ, and Ibadan, see JOHNSON, Appendix A.

20. For the subjugation of Ilọrin and the aftermath, see FLINT, Chapters 10, 11, and 13. The West African Frontier Force was composed of units from Britain's four West African colonies.

Appendix · Crowned Ọba

The Ọni of Ifẹ visited Lagos in 1903 at the invitation of the Governor, Sir William MacGregor, to give his ruling to the Governor and the members of his Central Native Council (a body mainly representative of Lagos and the Colony) on the complaint of the Akarigbo of Ijẹbu Remọ against the wearing of a crown by the Ẹlẹpẹ, another ruler in Ijẹbu Remo. Sitting with his back to the Council, the Ọni stated that only the following ọba were entitled to the crowns with beaded fringes which were conferred by his predecessors at Ifẹ and which usually denote membership of the house of Oduduwa):

1. Alake of Abẹokuta
2. Olowu of Owu (Abẹokuta)
3. Alafin of Ọyọ
4. Ọba of Ado (Benin?)
5. Oṣemawe of Ondo
6. Awujalẹ of Ijẹbu Ode
7. Alara of Ara (Ekiti)
8. Ajero of Ijero (Ekiti)
9. Orangun of Ila
10. Owa of Ileṣa
11. Alaye of Ẹfọn (Ekiti)
12. Olojudo of Iddo (Ekiti)
13. Olosi of Osi (Ekiti)
14. Ọre of Ọtun (Ekiti)
15. Akarigbo of Ijẹbu Rẹmo
16. Alaketu of Ketu
17. Ẹlẹkọle of Ikọle (Ekiti)
18. Ọlọwọ of Ọwọ
19. Ewi of Ado (Ekiti)
20. Oloko (or Oṣile) of Oko (Abẹokuta)
21. Alagura (or Agura) of Gbagura (Abẹokuta)

The total of twenty-one titles in this list of 1903 compares with the forty-one claimants to Ifẹ crowns in 1966, recorded on the map of *ilu alade* in G. J. A. Ojo's *Yoruba Culture*,[1] which omits no. 4, the 'Ọba of Ado'. It is not clear which Ado was meant by the Ọni as the Ewi of Ado Ekiti is listed as no. 19, but probably he was referring to Benin. A notable omission is that of the Oniṣabe of Ṣabe, perhaps because this kingdom was believed to be extinct. The order in the list follows that given in the report of the meeting of the Council.[2]

1. P. 125.
2. Editor, *JRAS*, Vol. 2, No. VII (1903).

Sources and Bibliography

A. BOOKS

ADAMS, CAPTAIN J. (1823). *Remarks on the Country Extending from Cape Palmas to the River Congo.* London.

AJAYI, J. F. A. (1965a). *Christian Missions in Nigeria, 1814–1891.* London.

AJAYI, J. F. A. and SMITH, R. S. (1964). *Yoruba Warfare in the Nineteenth Century.* Cambridge.

ADEMAKINWA, J. A. (1958). *Ifẹ, Cradle of the Yoruba,* Lagos.

AJIṢAFẸ, A. K. (alias E. O. MOORE) (1924). *A History of Abẹokuta.* London.

AKINDOJU, S. A. and OLAGUNDOYE (1962). *History of Idanre.* Ibadan.

AKINYELE, I. B. (1950). *Iwe Itan Ibadan.* Exeter.

ARGYLE, W. J. (1966). *The Fon of Dahomey.* Oxford.

ASHARA, CHIEF M. B. (1951). *The History of Ọwọ.*

AYANDELE, E. A. (1966). *The Missionary Impact on Modern Nigeria.* London.

BARBOT, J. (1732). *A Description of the Coasts of North and South Guinea.* London.

BEIER, U. (1959). *A Year of Sacred Festivals in One Yoruba Town.* Lagos.

BIOBAKU, S. O. (1957). *The Ẹgba and their Neighbours, 1842–1872.* Oxford.

BOSMAN, W. (1705). *A New and Accurate Description of the Coast of Guinea.* London.

BOVILL, E. W. (1958). *The Golden Trade of the Moors.* Oxford.

BOWEN, T. J. (1857). *Adventures and Missionary Labours in Several Countries in the Interior of Africa from 1849 to 1856.* Charleston.

BUCHANAN, K. M. and PUGH, J. C. (1955). *Land and People in Nigeria.* London.

BURNS, SIR A. (1947). *A History of Nigeria.* London.

BURTON, SIR R. F. (1863a). *Abẹokuta and the Camaroons Mountain.* London.

BURTON, SIR R. F. (1863b). *Wanderings in West Africa*. London.

BURTON, SIR R. F. (1864). *A Mission to Gelele, King of Dahomey*. London.

CLAPPERTON, H. (1829). *Journal of a Second Expedition into the Interior of Africa from the Bight of Benin to Soccattoo*. London.

COLEMAN, J. S. (1958). *Nigeria: Background to Nationalism*. California.

CORNEVIN, R. (1962). *Histoire de Dahomey*. Paris.

CROWDER, M. (1966 revision). *The Story of Nigeria*. London.

CROWTHER, S. A. (1852). *A Grammar and Vocabulary of the Yoruba Language*. London.

CURTIN, P. D. (ed.) (1967). *Africa Remembered*. Wisconsin and Ibadan.

DALZEL, A. (1793). *The History of Dahomey an Inland Kingdom of Africa*. London.

DAPPER, O. (1686). *Description de l'Afrique*. Amsterdam.

DIKÉ, K. O. (ed.) (1960). *Eminent Nigerians of the Nineteenth Century*. Cambridge.

EGHAREVBA, J. U. (3rd edn., 1960). *A Short History of Benin*. Ibadan.

ELLIS, A. B. (1894). *The Yoruba-speaking Peoples of the Slave Coast of West Africa*. London.

ELGEE, C. H. (1914). *The Evolution of Ibadan*. Lagos.

FAGG, W. (1963). *Nigerian Images*. London.

FLINT, J. E. (1960). *Sir George Goldie and the Making of Nigeria*. Oxford.

FORDE, D. (1951). *The Yoruba-speaking Peoples of South-Western Nigeria*. London.

FORDE, D. and KABERRY, P. M. (1967). *West African Kingdoms in the Nineteenth Century* (also cited as MORTON-WILLIAMS (1967)).

GEARY, W. N. M. (1927). *Nigeria under British Rule*. London.

GEORGE, J. O. (1895?). *Historical Notes on the Yoruba Country and its Tribes*. Lagos.

HARGREAVES, J. D. (1963). *Prelude to the Partition of West Africa*. London.

HERMAN-HODGE, H. B. (1929). *Gazeteer of Ilọrin Province*. London.

HINDERER, ANNA (1872). *Seventeen Years in the Yoruba Country*. London.

HOGBEN, S. J. and KIRK-GREENE, A. H. M., *The Emirates of Northern Nigeria*. Oxford.

HODGKIN, T. (1960). *Nigerian Perspectives*. Oxford.

SOURCES AND BIBLIOGRAPHY 213

IDOWU, E. B. (1962). *Olodumare – God in Yoruba Belief*. London.

JOHNSON, S. (1921). *The History of the Yorubas*. Lagos.

KƐNYO, E. A. (1964). *Yoruba Natural Rulers and their Origin*. Ibadan.

LANDER, R. L. (1830). *Records of Captain Clapperton's last expedition to Africa*. 2 volumes. London.

LANDER, R. L. and J. (1832). *Journal of an Expedition to Explore the Course and Termination of the Niger*. London. References are to the edited and abridged edition by R. HALLETT (1965), London.

LOSI, J. B. (1914). *History of Lagos*. Lagos.

LUCAS, J. O. (1948). *The Religion of the Yorubas*. Lagos.

LUGARD, LORD (ed. PERHAM, M. and BULL, M.) (1963). *The Diaries*. Vol. 4.

MCCALL, D. F. (1964). *Africa in Time-perspective*. Boston, U.S.A.

MORTON-WILLIAMS, P. (1967). 'The Yoruba Kingdom of Ọyọ', in Forde and Kaberry.

NEWBURY, C. W. (1961). *The Western Slave Coast and its Rulers*. Oxford.

NIGERIAN MUSEUM (1955). *The Art of Ifẹ*. Lagos.

NORRIS, R. (1789). *Memoirs of the Reign of Bossa Ahadee King of Dahomey*. London.

OGUNTUYI, A. (1957). *A Short History of Ado-Ekiti*. Akure.

OJO, G. J. A. (1966a). *Yoruba Culture*. London.

OJO, G. J. A. (1966b). *Yoruba Palaces*. London.

OJO, O. S. (n.d., a). *Short History of Ilọrin*. Ọyọ.

OJO, O. S. (n.d., b). *Iwe Itan Ọyọ*. Ọyọ.

OJO, O. S. (n.d., c). *Iwe Itan Ṣaki*. Ọyọ.

OLIVER and FAGE (1962). *A Short History of Africa*. London.

OLUGUNNA, D. (1959). *Oshogbo*. Oṣogbo.

PARRINDER, G. (1953). *Religion in an African City*. Oxford.

PARRINDER, G. (1956). *The Story of Ketu*. Ibadan.

PEREIRA, DUARTE PACHECO (ed. R. MAUNY, 1956). *Esmeraldo de Situ Orbis*. Bissau.

ROBINSON, R. and GALLAGHER, J. (1961). *Africa and the Victorians*. London.

SCHÖN, J. F. and CROWTHER, S. A. (1842). *Journals*. London.

SHAW, T. (1964). *Archaeology and Nigeria*. Ibadan.

SNELGRAVE, W. (1734). *A New Account of Some Parts of Guinea and the Slave Trade*. London.

S. O. A. AUTHORITY (1958). *The Happy City, Aiyetoro*. Lagos.

STONE, R. H. (1900). *In Afric's Forest and Jungle or Six Years among the Yorubas*. Edinburgh.

TALBOT, P. A. (1926). *The Peoples of Southern Nigeria*. London.

THORP, ELLEN (1950). *The Swelling of Jordan*. London.

THORP, ELLEN (1956). *Ladder of Bones*. London.

WILLETT, F. (1967). *Ifẹ in the History of West African Sculpture*. London.

WILLIAMS, D. (forthcoming). *Icon and Image*.

B. ARTICLES

ABIMBOLA, W. (1967). 'Ifa Divination Poems as Sources for Historical Evidence', Lagos Notes and Records, I, 1.

ADEGORIQLA I, OGOGA OF IKERRE (n.d.). 'A Note on the Administration of Ikẹrre before the Advent of the British', *Odu*, 3.

ADERẸMI, QNI OF IFẸ (1937). 'Notes on the City of Ifẹ', *Nigeria Magazine*, no. 12.

ADERIBIGBE, A. B. (1962). 'The Ijẹbu Expedition 1892: An Episode in the British Penetration of Nigeria Reconsidered', *Proceedings of the Leverholme Inter-Collegiate History Conference, 1960*.

AJAYI, J. F. A. (1960). 'How Yoruba Was Reduced to Writing', *Odu*, 8.

AJAYI, J. F. A. (1961a). 'The British Occupation of Lagos', *Nigeria Magazine*, 69.

AJAYI, J. F. A. (1961b). 'Nineteenth Century Origins of Nigerian Nationalism', *J.H.S.N.*, II, 2.

AJAYI, J. F. A. (1964). 'Samuel Johnson, Historian of the Yoruba', *The Historia*, I, 1.

AJAYI, J. F. A. (1965b). 'Professional Warriors in Nineteenth Century Yoruba Politics', *Tarikh*, I, 1.

AKINJOGBIN, I. A. (1963b). 'Agaja and the Conquest of the Coastal Aja States, 1724–30', *J.H.S.N.*, II, 4.

AKINJOGBIN, I. A. (1965). 'The Prelude to the Yoruba Civil Wars of the Nineteenth Century', Odu (n.s.), I, 2.

AKINJOGBIN, I. A. (1966a). 'A Chronology of Yoruba History', *Odu* (n.s.), II, 2.

AKINJOGBIN, I. A. (1966b). 'The Qyọ Empire in the Eighteenth Century', *J.H.S.N.*, III, 3.

AKINJOGBIN, I. A. (1967). 'Ifẹ: The Home of a New University,' *Nigeria Magazine*, 92.

* Abbreviations used throughout:

J.A.H.   Journal of African History.

J.H.S.N.   Journal of the Historical Society of Nigeria.

J.R.A.S.   Journal of the Royal African Society.

ALLISON, P. (n.d.). 'The Last Days of Old Qyq', *Odu*, 4.

ANENE, J. C. (1963). 'The Nigeria–Dahomey Boundary', *J.H.S.N.*, II, 4.

ANON. (1955). 'Idanre', *Nigeria Magazine*, 46.

ANON. (1963). 'Igogo Festival', *Nigeria Magazine*, 77.

AWẸ, B. (1964). 'The Ajele System: A Study of Ibadan Imperialism in the Nineteenth Century', *J.H.S.N.*, III, 1.

AWẸ, B. (1965). 'The End of an Experiment: The Collapse of the Ibadan Empire, 1877–1893', *J.H.S.N.*, III, 2.

BASCOM, W. (1960). 'Lander's Routes through Yoruba Country', *Nigerian Field*, XXV, 1.

BEIER, H. U. (n.d.) 'Before Oduduwa', *Odu*, 3.

BEIER, H. U. (1956a). 'The Qba's Festival, Ondo', *Nigeria Magazine*, 50.

BEIER, H. U. (1956b). 'Qbatala Festival', *Nigeria Magazine*, 52.

BEIER, H. U. (1960). 'Oshcgbo, Portrait of Yoruba Town', *Nigeria Magazine*, Independence issue.

BERTHO, J. (1949). 'La Parenté des Yoruba aux Peuplades de Dahomey et Togo', *Africa*, XIX, 2.

BIOBAKU, S. O. (1956a). 'The Problem of Traditional History with Special Reference to Yoruba Traditions', *J.H.S.N.*, I, 1.

BIOBAKU, S. O. (1956b). 'Ogboni, the Ẹgba Senate', 3rd International West African Conference, 1949, Lagos.

BRADBURY, R. E. (1959). 'Chronological Problems in Benin History', *J.H.S.N.*, I, 4.

BRIDGES, A. F. B. (1936). 'Idanre', *Nigerian Field*, V, 4.

DIKÉ, K. O. (1956). 'John Beecroft, 1790–1824', *J.H.S.N.*, I, 1.

DUCKWORTH, E. H. (1952). 'Badagry – its Place in the Pages of History', *Nigeria Magazine*, 38.

EDITOR, *Journal of the Royal African Society* (1902–3). 'Native Crowns.'

FAGG, W. and WILLETT, F. (1960). 'Ancient Ifẹ, An Ethnographical Survey', *Odu*, 8.

GARLICK, J. P. (1962). 'Blood Group Maps of Africa', *J.A.H.*, III, 2.

GODDARD, S. (1965). 'Town–Farm Relationships in Yorubaland: a Case-study from Qyq', *Africa*, XXXV, 1.

HILL, P. (1966). 'Notes on Traditional Market Authority and Market Periodicity in West Africa', *J.A.H.*, VII, 2.

LEWIS, H. S. (1966). 'The Origins of African Kingdoms', *Cahiers d'Études Africaines*, VI, 3.

LLOYD, P. C. (1959). 'Sungbo's Eredo', *Odu*, 7.

LLOYD, P. C. (1960a). 'Sacred Kingship and Government among the Yoruba', *Africa*, XXX, 3.

LLOYD, P. C. (1960b). 'Osifakorede of Ijẹbu', *Odu*, 8.

LLOYD, P. C. (1960c). 'Yoruba Towns', *Ibadan*, 9.

LLOYD, P. C. (1961). 'Installing the Awujalẹ', *Ibadan*, 12.

MARTIN, B. G. (1965). 'A New Arabic History of Ilọrin'. *Research Bulletin*, Centre of Arabic Documentation, University of Ibadan, I, 2.

MAY, D. J. (1860). 'Journey in the Yoruba and Nupe Countries in 1859', *Journal of the Royal Geographical Society*, XXX.

MAUNY, R. (1962). 'A Possible Source of Copper for the Oldest Brass Heads of Ifẹ', *J.H.S.N.*, II, 3.

MCINTYRE, W. D. (1963). 'Commander Glover and the Colony of Lagos, 1861–73', *J.A.H.*, IV, 1.

MORTON-WILLIAMS, P. (1960). 'The Yoruba Ogboni Cult in Ọyọ', *Africa*, XXX, 4.

MORTON-WILLIAMS, P. (1964a). 'The Ọyọ Yoruba and the Atlantic Trade, 1670–1830', *J.H.S.N.*, III, 1.

MORTON-WILLIAMS, P. (1964b). 'An Outline of the Cosmology and Cult Organization of the Ọyọ Yoruba', *Africa*, XXXIV, 3.

MOULERO, R. P. (1964). 'Histoire et legende de Chabe (Save)', *Études Dahoméenes*.

OGUNBA, O. (1964). 'Crowns and *Okutẹ* at Idowa', *Nigeria Magazine*, 83.

OGUNBA, O. (1965). 'The Agẹmo Cult in Ijebuland', *Nigeria Magazine*, 86.

OGUNKỌYA, T. (1956). 'The Early History of Ijebu', *J.H.S.N.*, I, 1.

OLAJUBU, O. (1964). 'Obokun', *The African Historian*, I, 2.

OMER-COOPER, J. D. (1964). 'The Question of Unity in African History', *J.H.S.N.*, III, 1.

PARRINDER, G. (1947). 'Yoruba-speaking Peoples in Dahomey', *Africa*, XVII, 2.

RYDER, A. F. C. (1965). 'A Reconsideration of the Ifẹ–Benin Relationship', *J.A.H.*, VI, 1.

SMITH, R. S. (1963). 'Ijaiye, the Western Palatinate of the Yoruba', *J.H.S.N.*, II, 3.

SMITH, R. S. (1964). 'Erin and Iwawun, Forgotten Towns of the Oke Ogun', *Odu* (n.s.), I, 1.

SMITH, R. S. (1965a). 'The Alafin in Exile', *J.A.H.*, VI, 1.

SMITH, R. S. (1965b). 'The Bara, or Royal Mausoleum, at New Ọyọ', *J.H.S.N.*, III, 2.

SMITH, R. S. (1967). 'Yoruba Armament', *J.A.H.*, VIII, 1.

SMITH, R. S. and WILLIAMS, D. (1966). 'A Reconnaissance Visit to Old Ọyọ', *Odu* (n.s.), III, 1.

STEVENS, P. (1966). 'Orisha-Nla Festival', *Nigeria Magazine*, 90.

VERGER, P. (1959). 'Notes on Some Documents in which Lagos is Referred to by the Name "Onim" . . .', *J.H.S.N.*, I, 4.

WALSH, M. J. (1948). 'The Edi Festival at Ile-Ife', *African Affairs*, 47.

WESCOTT, R. W. (n.d.). 'Did the Yorubas Come from Egypt?', *Odu*, 4.

WILLETT, F. (1958). 'The Discovery of New Brass Figures at Ife', *Odu*, 6.

WILLETT, F. (1960a). 'Investigations at Old Oyo, 1956–57: an Interim Report', *J.H.S.N.*, II, 1.

WILLETT, F. (1960b). 'Ife and its Archaeology', *J.A.H.*, I, 2.

WILLETT, F. (1960c). 'Discoveries in Ilesha', *Odu*, 8.

WILLETT, F. (1966). 'On the Funeral Effigies of Owo and Benin and an Interpretation of the Life-size Bronze Heads from Ife, Nigeria', *Man* (n.s.), 1, 1.

WILLIAMS, D. (1964). 'The Iconology of the Yoruba *Edan Ogboni*', *Africa*, XXXIV, 2.

WILLIAMS, D. (1965). 'Lost Wax Brass-casting in Ibadan', *Nigerian Magazine*, 85.

WILLIAMS, D. (1967a). 'Iron and the Gods: a Study of the Sacred Iron Figurines of the Yoruba', seminar paper, University of Lagos.

WILLIAMS, D. (1967b). 'Bronze Casting Moulds, Cores and the Study of Classical Techniques', *Lagos Notes and Records*, 1, 1.

WRIGLEY, C. (1960). 'Speculations on the Economic Pre-history of Africa', *J.A.H.*, I, 2.

C. UNPUBLISHED MATERIAL

AKINJOGBIN, I. A. (1963a), *Dahomey and its Neighbours, 1708–1818*. Ph.D. thesis, University of London.

AYANTUGA, O. O. (1965). *Ijebu and its Neighbours, 1851–1941*. Ph.D. thesis, University of London.

ARIFALO, S. O. 'An Analysis and Comparison of the Legends of Origin of Akure.' University of Ife, Original Essay, B.A. Special Honours in History, 1966.

CLARKE, W. H. 'Travels and Explorations, 1854–58.' Nashville, Tenn., S.B.C. typescript.

EGBEOLA, Z. A. 'Egbado history.' University of Ife, Original Essay, B.A. Special Honours in History, 1966.

Index

DATE DUE